MW00604841

THOMAS AQUINAS

Selected Commentaries on the Old Testament

THOMAS AQUINAS

Selected Commentaries on the Old Testament

EDITED WITH REVISED TRANSLATIONS,
AN INTRODUCTION, AND NOTES BY

JASON C. PAONE

Published by Word on Fire Academic, an imprint of
Word on Fire, Elk Grove Village, IL 60007

Printed in the United States of America

Design and layout by Cassie Bielak, Rozann Lee, and Clark Kenyon.

Translations of all biblical commentaries by Thomas Aquinas are from the Latin/English Edition of the Works of St. Thomas Aquinas, reproduced by permission of the Aquinas Institute, revised and edited by Jason C. Paone.

All biblical quotations in bold, italic font are from the Douay-Rheims translation. With occasional exception, all biblical quotations in non-bold, italic font are from the Revised Standard Version, Second Catholic Edition (San Francisco: Ignatius, 2002).

ISBN: 978-1-68578-108-8

Library of Congress Control Number: 2023946610

To my children: Julie, Lewis, and Leo

Before there was anything else, there was a father's eternal love for his child.

CONTENTS

ACKNOWLEDGMENTS

This book owes its existence to many collaborators and supporters. First among them is Brandon Vogt, the senior director of Word on Fire Publishing, without whose support the project would have remained in the realm of ideas. I also thank Michael Hahn of Emmaus Academic and John Mortensen of the Aquinas Institute, who permitted me to use their translations of the commentaries collected in this volume.

David Augustine, the associate editor of Word on Fire Academic, provided valuable assistance and feedback on many elements of this volume. Likewise, Matthew Levering read an advance version of the introduction and offered helpful feedback. James O'Neil's contribution as the copyeditor of this uniquely complex manuscript was invaluable. He also wrote the indices at the back of the book. Carolyn Paluch contributed a superb proofread and prevented countless errors and irregularities from making it into print. Daniel Seseske managed the copyediting and proofreading, contributing his editorial expertise at several points. Claire Kalan reviewed all biblical quotations and compared each new version of the typeset manuscript with the last to ensure that all revisions were implemented correctly. Last but not least, I owe many thanks to Rozann Lee, Cassie Bielak, and Clark Kenyon, whose art, skill, and professionalism are on display in the design and layout of this beautiful and functional book.

INTRODUCTION

THE AIMS AND ORGANIZATION OF THIS COLLECTION

Saint Thomas's Old Testament commentaries remain some of his most neglected writings. Historically, this has been due, in part, to their inaccessibility and widely varying quality. Some of the commentaries have only recently become available in English, and often, the translations retain the terseness, clutter, and opacity of the original Latin manuscripts. Again, some of the commentaries, especially those on Jeremiah and Lamentations, are written in the cursory style of a medieval bachelor and thus make for unprofitable reading, offering little more than summary descriptions of a biblical text. Moreover, the extant commentaries on the Song of Songs that have been attributed to him are spurious.[1]

Notwithstanding these obstacles to finding and accessing them, many of his Old Testament lectures merit more attention than they have received from students and scholars of Thomas Aquinas. Indeed, many of his lectures on the Psalms and Job, in particular, must be counted among Thomas's finest biblical commentaries. They contain discussions and emphases, moreover, that cannot be found elsewhere in his work.

This volume aims to promote appreciation for Thomas's Old Testament exegesis by making his best commentaries more accessible. To this end, it offers a topically organized selection of the most theologically profound lectures from his premier Old Testament commentaries—those on the Psalms, Job, and Isaiah. Moreover, the translations used in this collection have undergone extensive editing and revision to enhance their accuracy, elegance, clarity, stylistic consistency, and overall readability. Lastly, hundreds of explanatory footnotes have been added to facilitate study, along with two indices and a bibliography.

1. For a list and description of Thomas's authentic biblical commentaries, see James A. Weisheipl, *Friar Thomas D'Aquino: His Life, Thought, and Works* (Washington DC: The Catholic University of America Press, 1974) 368–74; and, more recently, Jean-Pierre Torrell, *Saint Thomas Aquinas*, vol. 1, *The Person and His Work*, trans. Robert Royal, rev. ed. (Washington, DC: The Catholic University of America Press, 2005), 337–41. William of Tocco claimed that Thomas wrote a Song of Songs commentary on his deathbed, but many have doubted the truth of this claim. For a speculative study exploring the place of the Song of Songs in Thomas's thought and the possible content of a Song of Songs commentary, had Thomas written one, see Daria Spezzano, "'Its Lamps Are Lamps of Fire and Flames': Thomas Aquinas on the Song of Songs," in *Thomas Aquinas: Biblical Theologian*, ed. Roger Nutt and Michael Dauphinais (Steubenville, OH: Emmaus Academic, 2021), 107–32. See also Serge-Thomas Bonino, *Reading the Song of Songs with St. Thomas Aquinas*, trans. Andrew Levering (Washington, DC: The Catholic University of America Press, 2023).

Where possible, the Revised Standard Version, Second Catholic Edition, of the Bible has been used in place of the Douay-Rheims translation for biblical quotations appearing in non-bold italic font. For the primary biblical texts of the commentaries in this collection, the Douay-Rheims translation has been retained as the version that most closely follows the Vulgate editions that Thomas himself used and referenced. Together with its companion volume, *Thomas Aquinas: Selected Commentaries on the New Testament*, this collection offers a curated introduction to Thomas's biblical commentaries, suitable for newcomers, students, and scholars alike.

The topical organization of this collection broadly mirrors the fourfold order of God's agency in the world that Thomas identifies in the prologue to his commentary on the Psalms: creation, governance, restoration, and glorification.[2]

Chapter 1 thus focuses on creation and the ordering of the cosmos, with particular attention to the place of humankind within the created order. The overarching purpose of Thomas's cosmology is to inspire wonder at the glory of God and to dispel any doubts about the reality and goodness of divine providence.

Chapter 2 studies the predicament of human existence, confronting the specters of human frailty, suffering, sin, death, and the injustice we observe in human fortunes on earth. In this chapter, we encounter Thomas's argument that death cannot be absolute, given the unavailability of ultimate happiness in this life.

Chapter 3 explores the closely related topics of divine revelation and prophecy and the role of angelic mediation in both. In this chapter, Thomas also discusses natural revelation and the question of whether and what we can know about God apart from what he has disclosed through the words and deeds of his self-revelation in Christ.

Chapter 4 is dedicated to the problem of sin and its solution in Christ. Here, Thomas studies the nature of sin and Christ's remedying self-sacrifice, the spiritual benefits of which are conveyed to the world through the Church and its sacraments, especially the Eucharist.

Chapter 5 addresses the last things: death, the end of the world, the immortality of the soul, the resurrection, and the life to come.

In the following sections of this introduction, I explore Thomas's conception of literal signification and his conviction that Christ features often as a

2. Thomas Aquinas, "The Prologue of Saint Thomas to the Psalms" (1). All parenthetical numbers included in citations of Thomas's Old Testament commentaries refer to page numbers in this volume.

referent of Old Testament writings in their literal meaning. Then, I provide summary overviews of Thomas's commentaries on the Psalms, Job, and Isaiah.

CHRIST AND THE LITERAL MEANING OF THE OLD TESTAMENT

By a purely historical kind of description, the Old Testament is a collection of ancient books chronicling the history, culture, and god of ancient Hebrew peoples. In the Christian perspective, this ancient anthology is accounted Sacred Scripture and inseparably part of the self-revelation of God that reaches its culmination in the event and person of Christ. Nevertheless, Christians have conceived the interrelationship between Christ and the Old Testament in different ways, and some have imagined a closer and more immediate relationship than others. At a minimum, Christians usually relate these Hebrew Scriptures to Christ, the Hebrew messiah, in terms of a backstory—a historical and cultural record providing the deep context for Christ's person, life, and work.

That the Old Testament represents the historical and cultural context of Jesus Christ is, of course, undeniable. Nevertheless, the earliest Christians—including those who lived when the Old Testament contained all of the Sacred Scriptures Christians recognized—saw a more direct relationship between the Old Testament and Christ than that of a mere backstory. In their estimation, the Old Testament was fundamentally *about* Christ. He was the obvious referent of so many of its oracles and the antitype of so many of its characters. These early Christian readers were, of course, conscious of the immediate historical and cultural circumstances, for instance, out of which its messianic hopes and imagination emerged. For them, however, a certain plurality of reference was the special characteristic of Old Testament Scripture, such that a passage could speak simultaneously about its own contemporary circumstances and also about matters in the distant future. One example of this polyvalence can be found in the book of Joel, whose apocalyptic descriptions equally describe the end of the world and a recent locust infestation that had devastated the region of Judah at the time of the book's composition.

That Christ is referenced *in* and *with* the pre-Christian events and figures of the Old Testament is a fundamental tenet of ancient Christian exegesis. The same presupposition defines Thomas's approach to the Old Testament. Indeed, this collection is designed to highlight his conviction that Christ is its overarching theme. However, what is particularly striking about Thomas's approach is his conviction that Christ *can be* and frequently *is* the referent of the Old Testament not only in figurative, spiritual, or symbolic senses but in its literal meaning.[3] To understand what this means and how Thomas can assert it, however, we must consider how he defines literal signification.

Thomas has two ways of defining literal signification. In one way, following Augustine, he says that the literal sense of an expression is the meaning of its *words* as opposed to the further meaning of the *things* that they signify. The things to which the words literally refer, themselves, can have a further meaning, which Thomas, with much of the Christian tradition, calls the "spiritual" or "mystical" meaning. The word 'lion,' for instance, might signify a particular large cat (or its kind), but the cat itself can, in turn, signify Christ, for example.[4]

In Thomas's second way of defining literal signification, it is the meaning an author or speaker intends in using an expression. But, of course, the meaning an author intends may not be the same as what his expression itself denotes. This is to say that an author's or speaker's intended meaning need not always be the one we—or that Thomas himself, for that matter—would ordinarily call the literal one. Hence, in some cases, this second definition of the literal sense cuts against the first, as Thomas himself indicates when he says, "In metaphorical speech, *the literal sense is not what is signified by the words* but what the speaker means to signify by them."[5]

It is clear, then, that Thomas means something rather different and more expansive by *literal meaning* than what we might expect.[6] The literal meaning of a metaphor, as the previous quotation indicates, might, in fact, be a metaphorical meaning and not the one we would customarily identify as literal. This point is crucial for anyone approaching Thomas's Old Testament commentaries, as their emphasis on the literal sense can sometimes give a misleadingly narrow impression of his intent. Indeed, Thomas's expansive conception of the literal meaning allows him to treat as literal what other medieval authors might have classified as spiritual meanings. Thomas's focus on the literal meaning of the Old Testament, at any rate, does not preclude explicitly Christian interpretations. To the contrary, Thomas follows the Second Council of Constantinople (553) and its condemnation of Theodore of Mopsuestia, which grounds his

3. In connection with this point, see Matthew Levering, "Mystagogy and Aquinas's *Commentary on Isaiah*: Initiating God's People into Christ," in *Initiation and Mystagogy in Thomas Aquinas: Scriptural, Systematic, Sacramental and Moral, and Pastoral Perspectives*, ed. Henk Schoot, Jacco Verburgt, and Jörgen Vijgen (Leuven, BE: Peeters, 2019), 17–40.

4. For Thomas's discussion of the lion metaphor in Scripture, see *Super sent.* 1 prologue 5.

5. Thomas Aquinas, *On Isaiah* 6.1.206 (84) (emphasis added).

6. For more on Thomas's peculiar conception of the literal sense, see Piotr Roszak, "Exegesis and Contemplation: The Literal and Spiritual Sense of Scripture in Aquinas' Biblical Commentaries," *Espiritu* 65 (2016): 481–504; and Mary Healy, "Aquinas's Use of the Old Testament in His Commentary on Romans," in *Reading Romans with St. Thomas Aquinas*, ed. Matthew Levering and Michael Dauphinais (Washington, DC: The Catholic University of America Press, 2012), 183–95.

assertion that Christ is a possible literal referent of Old Testament Scripture.[7] Thus, he identifies Christ as the literal referent of many characterizations of David and Solomon that exceed what can be truly said of them. In fact, Christ is the overarching theme of the Old Testament, in Thomas's interpretation, even in its literal sense.[8] For instance, the prophecies of Isaiah speak so clearly of Christ that, in concert with Jerome, Thomas remarks, "He seems to compose not a prophecy but a gospel."[9] Likewise, of the Psalms, he says, "All the things that pertain to faith in the Incarnation are related so plainly in this work that it seems to be a gospel rather than a prophecy."[10]

Another striking example of Thomas's Christocentric literal interpretation of the Old Testament is found in his commentary on Psalm 21 [22]. Here, Thomas argues that David's descriptions of suffering and dereliction in the Psalm refer literally to Christ's Passion and only figuratively to David and his tribulations.[11] In his interpretation, this Psalm is emblematic of Old Testament passages that seem to reference contemporary historical events and persons but say more than could be true of them alone. When any such passage is more applicable to Christ, the Church, or the life to come, Thomas's rule of thumb is to regard these as its primary and literal referents, and the contemporary Old Testament ones as its figurative meaning.

This picture would be rather implausible if we had to suppose that, for any passage to have a Christian literal meaning, its human author must consciously intend this meaning. Given how Thomas defines the literal sense, we would indeed have to suppose just this if the human author were the only—or even the most important—one to be considered. However, Thomas holds that God is the primary author of Sacred Scripture and, thus, that it is God's authorial intention that defines its literal sense first and foremost. "The author of Holy Scripture is the Holy Spirit," Thomas declares.[12] Thus, the intention of the human authors of Scripture can be quite secondary for Thomas, who says, "In Sacred Scripture, the human tongue is like the tongue of a child saying the words another provides."[13]

7. "Prologue of Saint Thomas to the Psalms" (5); *On Psalms* 21.176 (123).

8. For a study of the place of Christ in Thomas's commentary on Job, see Franklin T. Harkins, "Christ and the Eternal Extent of Divine Providence in the *Expositio super Iob ad Litteram* of Thomas Aquinas," in *A Companion to Job in the Middle Ages*, ed. Franklin T. Harkins and Aaron Canty (Leiden, BE: Brill, 2015), 161–200.

9. See Thomas Aquinas, "The Prologue of Saint Thomas to Isaiah" 2 (11).

10. "Prologue of Saint Thomas to the Psalms" (1).

11. *On Psalms* 21.176 (123).

12. "Prologue of Saint Thomas to Isaiah" 1 (1).

13. "Prologue of Saint Thomas to the Psalms" (3).

Even when Thomas considers a human author of Scripture to have possessed some kind of prophetic foreknowledge or to have spoken prophetically in the person of Christ—as he takes David to have done in Psalm 21—it is the divine agency in and behind the human that makes this kind of prophetic knowledge and speech possible. Thomas's robust sense of the divine agency behind Scripture makes the scope of possibility for its literal sense rather vast—so vast, in fact, that he seems to have less need to speak of spiritual senses at all. The literal meaning can be metaphorical and allegorical if and where God intends to speak in these ways through the authors he employs and inspires, even if they themselves have no such intention.

The prominence of the Spirit's agency in the Old Testament's authorship implies a fundamental unity both among its constituent books and together with the New Testament. For Thomas, both testaments are united in their divine authorship and in their author's intention of revealing himself. Moreover, Christ is the person in whom God has most fully revealed himself and whom the whole arc of the Old Testament anticipates. Thus, Thomas sees Christ as the primary subject of the Old Testament as well as the New—and not merely by a kind of retrospective, Christian interpretation that we would have to conceive in terms of a spiritual meaning but even in its literal sense.

POSTILLA SUPER PSALMOS

The *postilla*[14] on the Psalms is a *reportatio* of lectures that Thomas likely gave at the end of his career during his teaching tenure at the Dominican *studium* at Naples in 1272–73 and while he was composing the *Tertia Pars* of his famous *Summa theologiae*.[15] It thus reflects Thomas's mature thought on a wide range of theological topics, including Christ, prayer, grace, divine revelation, and the moral life. The work, in fact, may represent the final university course of

14. The term *postilla* derives from the Latin phrase *post illa verba textus*, which means 'following those words from the text.' *Postilla* became the generic term for a style of biblical commentary that originally took the form of marginalia or comments appearing in the margins of a manuscript explaining certain of its terms and phrases. In time, however, the term *postilla* came to indicate an intended use within a liturgical context and finally became synonymous with homiletic exposition. An intended liturgical use is suggested by the description given to the commentary by Bartholomew of Capua, one of Thomas's biographers, who labeled the commentary "Lectura super quatuor nocturnos psalterii," indicating their connection to the nocturnal office of Matins. To the contrary, Weisheipl suggests the description of the commentary as a *postilla* is somewhat misleading. Moreover, he points out that the commentary "exclusively follows the order of the Vulgate and not that of the Divine Office," which seems to suggest that its intended use was more academic than liturgical (*Friar Thomas D'Aquino*, 303).

15. However, Weisheipl describes the commentary on the Psalms as "the only academic work that can be attributed to this period [the academic year of 1272–73] with certainty" (*Friar Thomas D'Aquino*, 302).

his teaching career.[16] It ends abruptly after the commentary on Psalm 54, and its incompleteness reflects the abrupt cessation of his scholarly activities on December 6, 1273, the date of a mystical experience after which he came to regard his whole literary corpus as "straw."[17]

The goal of the Psalms, as Thomas explains, is to elevate the mind to God in prayer and praise.[18] In his commentary, he pursues this same goal in several ways while shedding light on the nature of these acts of worship. He magnifies the Psalms' exaltation with lengthy meditations on the glory and greatness of God in his fourfold work of creation, governance, restoration, and glorification.[19] In his elaboration of the meaning of the Psalmist's praise, Thomas's discussions roam widely into topical spaces that one might not expect a biblical commentary to enter, including astronomy, biology, etymology, mythology, metaphysics, and epistemology, to name just a few of the disciplines he brings into the discussion.[20] This kind of topical breadth is perhaps to be expected of a commentary on a book that touches the whole scope of God's work in his created order. On this count, he declares, the book of Psalms "contains the whole of Scripture."[21]

Thomas also emphasizes the glory of God by comparison with the glory of human beings. God is exceedingly greater than we are, and this says a great deal, given Thomas's exalted anthropology. Human beings are rational beings, possessed of an immortal soul and the capacity to know and love God.[22] This makes us "close" to the angels in dignity and as fellow bearers of God's image.[23] We are elevated as "king" of all material creatures below us.[24] Most of all,

16. This is the view of Pierre Mandonnet in "Chronologie des écrits scripturaires de saint Thomas d'Aquin," *Revue Thomiste* 34, no. 55 (1929): 489–519. See also Torrell's discussion of the dating of the lecture series in *Saint Thomas Aquinas* 1:258–59.

17. Bartholomew of Capua, "From the First Canonisation Enquiry" 79, in *The Life of Saint Thomas Aquinas: Biographical Documents* (London: Longmans & Green, 1959), 82–126, at 109. For secondary studies of Thomas's commentary on the Psalms, see Thomas F. Ryan, *Thomas Aquinas as Reader of the Psalms* (Notre Dame, IN: University of Notre Dame Press, 2000); James R. Ginther, "The Scholastic Psalms' Commentary as a Textbook for Theology: The Case of Thomas Aquinas," in *Omnia disce: Medieval Studies in Memory of Leonard Boyle*, ed. A.J. Duggan, J. Greatrex, and B. Bolton (Aldershot: Ashgate, 2005), 211–29.

18. "Prologue of Saint Thomas to the Psalms" (2).

19. "Prologue of Saint Thomas to the Psalms" (1).

20. Indicating the sophistication of the book's many philosophical excurses, the Italian philosopher Carmelo Pandolfi has described Thomas's commentary on the Psalms as "the most philosophical text" and "the existential book par excellence." *San Tommaso filosofo nel "Commento ai Salmi": Interpretazione dell'essere nel modo 'esistenziale' dell'invocazione* (Rome: Studio Domenicano, 1993), 29.

21. "Prologue of Saint Thomas to the Psalms" (1).

22. *On Psalms* 8.55 (26).

23. *On Psalms* 8.56 (26–27).

24. *On Psalms* 8.56 (27).

however, our dignity lies in the honor the Son bestowed when he became one of us in the Incarnation—an honor not even the angels can boast.[25]

We are also gifted with a natural knowledge of God, as Thomas explains in his commentary on Psalm 13:1 (DRB): "The fool hath said in his heart: 'There is no God.'" However, this knowledge is a natural gift that we can refuse in a way that enfeebles our minds and corrupts our hearts.[26] "A certain knowledge of God is naturally implanted in human persons, but they forget the Lord through sin."[27]

Thomas's commentary, like the book of Psalms itself, deals extensively with the problem of sin and the way to redemption. For Thomas, sin is, "first of all, an offense against God," with the character of a "stain" embedded in the soul of the sinner, who, therefore, lives in a state of vulnerability to the kind of punishing effects inseparable from sin.[28] Redemption from sin is God's work, but it requires human cooperation in the form of sincere repentance, which, in turn, demands a certain degree of self-knowledge and finds expression in the act of confession and in the sinner's prayer to God for deliverance.[29] These acts of conversion are prerequisites for salvation, but even they are only possible by God's intervention and gifts—gifts that, first, create a repentant disposition in the sinner and, then, move him to act in accord with it.[30]

God's work of salvation is accomplished for us through Christ's Passion and death, which "washes away all filth and all sins" and gives meaning and sacramental efficacy to the Eucharist.[31] The Psalms manifest God's glory, perhaps most magnificently, for Thomas, in their exquisite descriptions of Christ's salvific Passion, the most explicit and exemplary of which are found in Psalm 21 (page 120 below), which Thomas explores in detail. This and other persecution Psalms are primarily and literally about the Passion of Christ and only figuratively about David and the persecution he faced at the hands of Saul and Absalom.

In his suffering, Christ not only wins salvation for his human brethren but also enters into a greater solidarity with them. In his expressions of anguish and dereliction, Thomas says Christ speaks "in the person of the sinner or of

---

25. *On Psalms* 8.56 (28).

26. *On Psalms* 13.96 (76–78).

27. *On Psalms* 21.198 (142).

28. *On Psalms* 31.295 (113).

29. See *On Psalms* 31.297 (115–16).

30. *On Psalms* 31.301 (117–18).

31. *On Psalms* 21.186 (134). For Thomas's discussion of the Eucharist in its connection to the Passion, see *On Psalms* 21.196–97 (140–42).

the Church."[32] In his Passion, the mystical union of Christ and the Church thus becomes most manifest, in which "Christ transforms himself into the Church, and the Church is transformed into Christ."[33]

The effects of Christ's Passion—and indeed, the effects of the Eucharist—extend beyond the Church. Among these, Thomas lists knowledge of God and conversion. Both are effects of the Passion, and both effects are produced by the instrumentation of the Eucharist, which serves as its memorial.[34]

These salvific effects redound to the greatness of God, but none are more impressively evident than those that occur in the Church and, indeed, constitutively so. "The greatness of his works is evident in all of his creations, but it is especially apparent in the gifts of grace by which the Church has been established."[35] The Church is founded on Christ analogous to the way Jerusalem was built on Mount Zion.[36] It has received attestation and accolades from many of the greatest "kings of the earth" (Ps. 47:5 DRB).[37] This is not to say that the story of the Church has been one of pure triumph and grace. Nevertheless, in Psalm 47:14's injunction, "Set your hearts on her strength and distribute her houses," Thomas finds an admonition not to let the corruption of certain members lead us "to condemn the whole Church" or overlook the magnificence that God has imparted to it in his grace and for his glory.[38]

EXPOSITIO SUPER IOB AD LITTERAM

As an *expositio*, Thomas's commentary on Job represents a much more polished and editorialized presentation of material that he originally gave in lectures delivered at the Dominican priory of San Domenico in Orvieto from 1261 to 1265, near the middle of his career as a master of the sacred page.[39] Thomas

32. *On Psalms* 21.176 (125).

33. *On Psalms* 21.176 (125).

34. *On Psalms* 21.198 (142).

35. *On Psalms* 47.474 (147).

36. *On Psalms* 47.475 (147).

37. *On Psalms* 47.476 (148–49)

38. *On Psalms* 47.479 (153).

39. See Weisheipl, *Friar Thomas D'Aquino*, 153; Torrell, *Saint Thomas Aquinas*, 1:120–22. For more secondary literature on Thomas's commentary on Job, see the essays in *Reading Job with St. Thomas Aquinas*, ed. Matthew Levering, Piotr Roszak, and Jörgen Vijgen (Washington, DC: The Catholic University of America Press, 2020); and Martin D. Yaffe's "Interpretive Essay," in *Thomas Aquinas: The Literal Exposition on Job; A Scriptural Commentary Concerning Providence*, trans. Anthony Damico (Atlanta, GA: Scholars, 1989), 1–65. See also Mauricio R. Naváez's study of Thomas's expository methodology in his "Intention, *Probabiles Rationes* and Truth: The Exegetical Practice in Thomas Aquinas; The Case of *Expositio Super Iob ad Litteram*," in *Reading Sacred Scripture with Thomas Aquinas: Hermeneutical Tools, Theological Questions, and New Perspectives*, 141–69.

identifies the literal meaning of Job as the subject of his commentary, in contrast to Gregory the Great's famous sixth-century spiritual commentary on Job, whose clarity and eloquence, Thomas declares, left nothing further to be said about the book's spiritual sense.[40]

In Thomas's interpretation, Job represents the authoritative disputation on divine providence, composed and included in Scripture by divine providence for human instruction.[41] He makes clear that he imagines the dialogue between Job and his counselors in terms of a *disputatio* or debate of the sort that were standard educational programming in the universities of Thomas's time.[42] Thomas sees a *disputatio* structure in the dialoguing speeches that constitute most of the book and in God's concluding statement in Job's favor, which he interprets in terms of the decision of a presiding judge.[43]

Thomas reasons that Job must reflect real history, given the way other Scriptures reference it, but he admits that questions of historicity and authorship are irrelevant to the work's pedagogical intention, which is "to show that human affairs are ruled by divine providence."[44] The central problem of Job's narrative is the fact that a person's earthly fortune does not always correspond to the moral character of his life. For most interpreters, the primary question at stake is what this lack of correspondence implies about God's providence and justice. For some, it indicates the absence of any divine providence—that either God does not exist or, if he does, he has not given or maintained a just moral order in his creation. Supporting this kind of nihilism, Thomas observes, were the pre-Socratic materialists, who "attributed everything to luck and chance."[45] Thomas, of course, rejects this view, which, he notes, "causes a great deal of harm to humanity, for if divine providence is denied, there will remain no reverence or true fear of God among people."[46] And yet, he must reckon with the fact that "good and evil befall both the good and the wicked indiffer-

---

40. See Thomas Aquinas, "The Prologue of Saint Thomas to Job" 6 (9).

41. See "Prologue of Saint Thomas to Job" 3 (8–9).

42. See "Prologue of Saint Thomas to the Psalms" (2), where he identifies disputation as the genre of the book of Job. For more on the disputation format in terms of which Thomas interprets the dialog of Job, see John F. Boyle, "St. Thomas, Job, and the University Master," in *Reading Job with St. Thomas Aquinas*, ed. Matthew Levering, Piotr Roszak, and Jörgen Vijgen (Washington, DC: The Catholic University of America Press, 2020), 21–41. Ruth Meyer credits Thomas's teacher, Albert the Great, as the first to explicitly interpret the book of Job as a Scholastic disputation in "A Passionate Dispute over Divine Providence: Albert the Great's Commentary on the Book of Job," in *A Companion to Job in the Middle Ages*, 201–24.

43. *On Job* 38.1.491–92 (16).

44. "Prologue of Saint Thomas to Job" 3 (9).

45. "Prologue of Saint Thomas to Job" 1 (8).

46. "Prologue of Saint Thomas to Job" 3 (8).

ently."[47] This is a problem for Thomas no less than for Job and his counselors, who all presuppose the same retributive model of justice according to which good things, if they come to anyone, should come to those who do good, and correspondingly, if anyone has to suffer bad things, bad people should. "The work of justice," Thomas asserts, "is to give each his due."[48]

All the characters of Job agree that, somehow, God does maintain a just moral order in his creation in which people receive what they deserve for the conduct and moral character of their lives. What distinguishes Job's position from that of his counselors, according to Thomas, is the view that human beings do not receive full and final retribution in this life. There are always things in store for people that they do not receive in the here and now. If this weren't so, we would have to say that people can and do achieve the ultimate human end in this life—namely, perfect happiness. Now, for Thomas, it is clear that they cannot and do not.[49] This ultimate, beatific end—which Thomas understands to consist of intimate and immediate communion with God—is also the ultimate reward that one can receive, and to forego it is the greatest deprivation. Job's counselors, because they deny life after death, are forced to deny that human fates in this life ever fall short of perfect justice and insist that any apparent inequity must be illusory. Consequently, Job's suffering, for them, must be deserved and must indicate sin in his life.

By contrast, in Thomas's interpretation, Job solves the problem of his apparently unjust earthly fate by positing a life to come in which God will finally resolve all injustices by rendering to each person the rewards and punishments that were merited but not fully discharged in this life. In Job's lamentations, Thomas thus finds an argument for life after death that reasons *ad absurdum* from the structural injustice of human fate that he finds to be inextricable in the picture where death is absolute.

The life to come is, thus, the solution, for Thomas, both to the puzzle of Job's particular fate and to the general problem of unjust human suffering and flourishing in this life—or at least, it is a large part of the story. It explains why we do not always see people getting all they deserve, whether in terms of rewards or punishments. It does less, however, to explain why they often seem to get positively *more* or *other* than what they deserve. Beyond the explanation of why Job did not get all the happiness that befit his virtue, the story of Job forces us to ask how it does not impugn God's providence that Job was gravely

47. "Prologue of Saint Thomas to Job" 2 (8).

48. *On Job* 4.3.87 (97).

49. *On Job* 7.1.122 (60).

afflicted by God instead—that, instead of happiness, he experienced excruciating affliction, deprivation, and pain.

In Thomas's understanding, the suffering of good people is, perhaps, finally inexplicable for us since "human wisdom is not sufficient to understand the truth of divine providence."[50] In this light, perhaps Job's mournful exclamations and exquisitely rhetorical expressions of aporia represent the most pious and human way of approaching the problem of suffering, oriented, as they seem to be, more to expressing lament and asking questions than answering them.

For Thomas's part, the fact that God allows the innocent to suffer is not simply inscrutable, however. On the contrary, he sees it as divinely ordained for pedagogical reasons. Suffering serves as a test that reveals the moral substance of the just, not to God, but to the just themselves: "God is said to test a person not so that he may learn what kind of person he is but so to inform others and so that the one tested might know himself."[51] Additionally, Thomas seems to view adversity as an inescapable feature of human life. Adversity is thematic in each of the metaphors he uses to describe it—for instance, in terms of a journey, a military campaign, and employment.[52]

In Thomas's interpretation of the book, Job shows himself to be an exemplar of wisdom and virtue. Indeed, although Thomas faults him for the hyperbole of his lamentation and the scandal it causes in the minds of his interlocutors,[53] he presents Job as otherwise a model of pious virtue, wisdom, and innocence. Indeed, although initially he speaks under the influence of his sadness, like a true sage, he rationally contains this sorrow and does not let himself be governed by it.[54] In the end, he succeeds not only in being mostly innocent in how he faces his horrific afflictions but also in being correct, as Thomas argues, in his understanding of divine providence and in deducing a human life after death. In the end, Job finds vindication in God's declaration to Job's critic Eliphaz: "You have not spoken of me what is right, as my servant Job has" (Job 42:8 RSV).

EXPOSITIO SUPER ISAIAM AD LITTERAM

The dating of Thomas's commentary on Isaiah remains a matter of scholarly dispute. However, most scholars consider it—or at least much of it—to be an early work, produced before Thomas became a master of the sacred page.

50. *On Job* 38.1.491 (16).

51. *On Job* 7.4.136 (65).

52. *On Job* 17.1.202, 7.1.122 (60).

53. See *On Job* 38.1.491 (16) and 39.1.524 (not included in this volume).

54. See *On Job* 1.4.32–33 (56)

The commentaries on chapters 12–66, as James Weisheipl observes, have "the form and style of a literal gloss with no theological developments or discussion."[55] This cursory style is characteristic of a medieval bachelor and, thus, represents one compelling reason to ascribe an early date, possibly during the period from 1251 to 1252, while Thomas was a student at Cologne. This, indeed, is the date given by many leading Thomist scholars, including Jean-Pierre Torrell.[56] Nevertheless, the quality of the lectures on Isaiah 1–11, which Weisheipl describes as having "the form and style of a university master," suggests that the commentary, in some way, reflects a transition in Thomas's development as a scholar. [57] It reflects such a transition at least insofar as it represents "Aquinas's first substantial theological work," as Joseph Wawrykow and others have noted.[58]

The commentary on Isaiah is undoubtedly richer than those on Jeremiah and Lamentations—Thomas's two other early commentaries, which are written, unambiguously, in the cursory style of a bachelor. "By contrast" to these, Torrell remarks, "the exposition of Isaiah . . . possesses great riches on certain points."[59] With a similar recognition of its unique status among Thomas's early commentaries "on certain points," this collection features the commentary's prologue along with what are arguably its two most elaborate and emblematic lectures: the commentaries on the temple vision of Isaiah 6:1–7 and the Emmanuel sign in 7:10–25. These lectures arguably reflect a rigor and depth of thought on par with any of his magisterial biblical commentaries. Indeed, they are among the most rigorous of Thomas's Old Testament commentaries in terms of their attention to historical detail and the Jewish interpretive tradition.

The nature of prophecy and revelation are leading topics of the book, the most profound discussion of which appears in Thomas's commentary on the temple vision of Isaiah 6. There, Thomas argues that Isaiah's epiphany, although truly a revelation of God, could not have been a direct vision of God. Following Pseudo-Dionysius, he establishes the law-like necessity of mediation for any divine revelation: "No mere human being—none among the fathers either of the New or Old Testament—received any revelation from God except by the mediation of angels."[60] This thesis establishes the need for the Incarnation, which, Thomas says, represents "the primary subject matter"

55. Weisheipl, *Friar Thomas D'Aquino*, 369.

56. See Torrell, *Saint Thomas Aquinas*, 1:28.

57. Weisheipl, *Friar Thomas D'Aquino*, 369.

58. Joseph Wawrykow, introduction to *St. Thomas Aquinas: Commentary on Isaiah* (Steubenville, OH: Emmaus Academic, 2021), 3.

59. Torrell, *Thomas Aquinas*, 1:27.

60. *On Isaiah* 6.1.215 (86–87).

of Isaiah.[61] Thus, the virgin-birth prophecy of Isaiah 7:14 is the pivotal passage of the book in its unambiguous and literal identification of Christ as the subject of the many messianic oracles that follow. Christ is Emmanuel—God with us. Thomas works to show that Christ is the undeniable referent of the prophecy by methodically examining and refuting alternate interpretations.

In the lecture on the Emmanuel sign, Thomas also outlines his high Christology and notably argues that Christ was developmentally and psychologically complete from the moment of his conception. Even in his infancy, "he has perfect knowledge of everything."[62] His fullness of divinity, which thus elevates his human nature, also makes him the perfect medium of divine revelation. In him, we can see God because, in him, God is with us.

CONCLUSION

The commentaries compiled in this volume were written at different times in Thomas's teaching career—the commentaries on Isaiah in the early part, those on Job in the middle, and those on the Psalms at the end. They address a wide array of topics and questions and showcase the breadth of Thomas's learning and intellectual curiosity. His commentary on the Psalms highlights the glory of God in all his works of creation, governance, restoration, and glorification. His exposition of Job probes the mysteries of divine providence and human existence. He meditates on the nature of prophecy, revelation, and Christ in his commentary on Isaiah. Despite their topical variety and the different historical periods they represent in Thomas's career as a scholar, they cohere together in this collection in a way that demonstrates the continuity of Thomas's approach to the Old Testament throughout his career.

We can see, for instance, his overriding concern for the literal meaning of Scripture. Nevertheless, as we have seen, his understanding of the literal meaning is uniquely expansive due to his robust sense of the divine agency in and behind the human authorship of Scripture. In Thomas's interpretation, the literal sense of the Old Testament writings can thus be more overtly Christian than we are perhaps accustomed to assert today.

Again, Thomas's approach to Scripture is unrelentingly theological and philosophical. Although he demonstrates a keen interest in the historical and literary dimensions of the Old Testament Scriptures, his primary concern centers on the theological revelations they contain and express. Moreover, the theology of the Old Testament is speculative in a way that is nevertheless

61. "Prologue of Saint Thomas to Isaiah" 5 (12).

62. *On Isaiah* 7.2.254 (107).

profoundly pedagogical and practically vital. In the commentaries on Job and the Psalms, for instance, we see Thomas's concern to help his reader understand and orient his life to God within the order of creation and in the face of his eventual death. The theology of the Old Testament, for Thomas, is ordered to redemption, beatitude, and the eternal union of the human soul with God. This is to say that it is ordered to Christ, for Christ is the redeemer, the self-revelation of God, and the way to eternal life with him. Consequently, for Thomas, Christ is the essential truth revealed by God in the Old Testament.

The Prologue of Saint Thomas to the Psalms

In all his works, he gave thanks to the holy one and to the most High with words of glory.

—SIRACH 47:9

These words refer in the literal sense to David and are selected fittingly to show the cause of this work. In them, its four causes are shown—namely, the matter, the mode or form, the goal, and the agent. The matter is universal since, while individual books of the canonical Scriptures contain particular matter, this book contains the general matter of the whole of theology. And this is what Dionysius says: *The Sacred Scripture of the divine songs—that is, of the Psalms, intends to sing about all of the holy and divine actions.*[1] So the phrase ***in all his works*** designates the matter since he writes about every work of God.

Now the work of God is fourfold—namely, creation: *on the seventh day, God rested from every work* (Gen. 2:2); governance: *My Father is working still* (John 5:17); restoration: *My food is to do the will of him who sent me, and to accomplish his work* (John 4:34); and glorification: *The work of the Lord is full of his glory* (Sir. 42:16). And all these are treated completely in this teaching.

First is the work of creation: ***I will behold thy heavens, the works of thy fingers*** (Ps. 8:4). *Second* is the work of governance since all the histories in the Old Testament are treated in this book: ***I will open my mouth in parables. . . . How great things have we heard and known, and our fathers have told us*** (Ps. 77:2–3).

Third is the work of restoration, in regard to the head—namely, Christ—and in regard to all the effects of grace: ***I have slept and taken my rest, and I have risen up*** (Ps. 3:6). For all the things that pertain to faith in the Incarnation are related so plainly in this work that it seems to be a gospel rather than a prophecy.

Fourth is the work of glorification: ***The saints shall rejoice in glory*** (Ps. 149:5). And this is the reason why the Psalter is used so frequently in the Church since it contains the whole of Scripture. Or, according to the Gloss, it is to give us hope in divine mercy since, although David sinned, he was nevertheless restored through penance.[2]

Now, the matter is universal because it is ***all his works***, and because it looks to Christ, *for in him all the fullness of God was pleased to dwell* (Col. 1:19), and so the matter of this book is Christ and his members.

1. Pseudo-Dionysius, *Ecclesiastical Hierarchy* 3.3.4.
2. Cf. Peter Lombard, *Magna glossatura*.

The mode or form of Sacred Scripture is of many kinds. For example, narrative: *Hath not the Lord made the saints to declare all his wonderful works?* (Sir. 42:17 DRB). And this is found in the historical books. Another kind admonishes, exhorts, and commands: *Declare these things; exhort and reprove with all authority* (Titus 2:15); *remind them of this, and charge them before the Lord* (2 Tim. 2:14). This kind is found in the law, the prophets, and the books of Solomon. Another kind disputes, and this is in Job and in the Apostle: *I desire to argue my case with God* (Job 13:3). Then there is praying or praising, and this is also found in this book since everything said in the other books in the modes already mentioned is also here, in the mode of praise and prayer: ***I will give praise to thee, O Lord, with my whole heart; I will relate all thy wonders*** (Ps. 9:2). And so he says, ***he gave praise***, because he spoke in the mode of giving praise.

And from this comes the reason for the book's title: *The Beginning of The Book of Hymns* or *The Soliloquies of the Prophet David About Christ*. A hymn is the praise of God with song. Now, a song is the exultation of a mind dwelling on things eternal breaking forth aloud. Therefore, he teaches us to praise God with exultation. A soliloquy is a person's conversation with God alone or with just himself since this is fitting for praising and praying.

The goal of this scripture is prayer, which is the lifting up of the mind to God. *Prayer is the ascent of the intellect to God.*[3] ***The lifting up of my hands, as an evening sacrifice*** (Ps. 140:2). The soul is lifted up toward God in four ways: *first*, to admire the height of his power, and this is the elevation of faith: *Lift your eyes on high and see who has created these things* (Isa. 40:26). ***How great are thy works, O Lord*** (Ps. 103:24). *Second*, the mind is lifted up to stretch toward the excellence of eternal beatitude, and this is the elevation of hope: *You will lift up your face without blemish; you will be secure and will not fear. You will forget your misery. . . . And your life will be brighter than the noonday* (Job 11:15–17). *Third*, the mind is lifted up to cling to the divine goodness and holiness: *Rouse yourself, stand up, O Jerusalem* (Isa. 51:17). And this is the elevation of charity. *Fourth*, the mind is lifted up to imitate the divine justice in action, and this is the elevation of justice: *Let us lift up our hearts and hands to God in heaven* (Lam. 3:41).

And these four ways are implied when he says, ***to the holy one, and to the most High***, since the last two ways of being lifted up relate to ***the holy one*** and the first two to ***the most High***. And the Psalms teach that this is the goal of this Scripture.

3. John of Damascus, *An Exact Exposition of the Orthodox Faith* 3.24.

First, about ***the most High*: *From the rising of the sun . . . the Lord is high above all nations*** (Ps. 112:3–4). *Second*, about ***the Holy One*: *Let them give praise to thy great name, for it is terrible and holy*** (Ps. 98:3).

So, Gregory says that if it is carried out with the attention of the heart, the voice of psalm-singing prepares for Almighty God a way to the heart so that he may pour the mystery of prophecy or the grace of remorse into the attentive soul.[4] The goal is, therefore, that the soul may be joined to God as ***the holy one*** and ***the most High***.

Now, the phrase ***with words of glory*** indicates the author of this work. For it should be noted that Sacred Scripture differs from other kinds of knowledge. For other kinds of knowledge arise through human reason, but Scripture through the impulse of divine inspiration: *No prophecy ever came by the impulse of men but men moved by the Holy Spirit spoke from God* (2 Pet. 1:21).[5] So, in Sacred Scripture, the human tongue is like the tongue of a child saying the words another provides: ***My tongue is the pen of a scrivener*** (Ps. 44:2), and *The Spirit of the Lord speaks by me, his word is upon my tongue* (2 Sam. 23:2). And so, he says, ***the words of the Lord***, or ***of glory***, which are spoken through revelation. Thus 1 Kings 20:35 says, *In the word of the Lord: strike me* (DRB)—that is, in divine revelation.

And so, this Scripture[6] can be said to be the ***words of glory*** in four ways since it is related to glory in four ways. *First*, in regard to the cause from which it flows, since this teaching comes forth from the glorious Word of God, a voice coming down in this way from the excellent glory: *This is my beloved Son* (2 Pet. 1:17). *Second*, in regard to content, since this book contains the glory of the Lord that it announces: ***Declare his glory among the gentiles*** (Ps. 95:3). *Third*, in regard to the way it comes forth, since glory is equivalent to clarity, and the revelation of this prophecy was glorious because it was manifest.

For there are three modes of prophecy: *first*, through sensible things: *The fingers of a man's hand appeared . . . and the king saw the hand as it wrote* (Dan. 5:5). *Second*, through imaginary likenesses, as is made clear by the dream of Pharaoh and the interpretation made by Joseph (Gen. 41): *I saw the Lord sitting upon a throne* (Isa. 6:1). *Third*, through the manifestation of the truth itself.[7] And this latter mode befits the prophecy of Daniel, who put forth his prophecy solely by the impulse of the Holy Spirit without any exterior help. *For the other prophets*, as Augustine says, *prophesied deeds and words through certain images of things and verbal veiling (namely, through dreams and visions), but he was taught*

4. See Gregory the Great, *Homilies on the Book of the Prophet Ezekiel* 1.15.

5. Cf. Thomas Aquinas, *Summa theologiae* 1.1.3.

6. That is, the Psalms.

7. Cf. Thomas Aquinas, *Summa theologiae* 2-2.173.2; *On Isaiah* 1.1.

directly by the truth.[8] So when David said that *the Spirit of the Lord speaks by me*, he immediately added, *He dawns on them like the morning light, like the sun shining forth upon a cloudless morning* (2 Sam. 23:2, 4). For the sun is the Holy Spirit, illuminating the hearts of the prophets, who sometimes appears under the clouds when he illumines through the two modes of prophecy already mentioned and who sometimes appears without clouds, as here. And to this can be added, *How the king of Israel honored himself today, uncovering himself today before the eyes of his servants' maids* (2 Sam. 6:20).

The *fourth* way in which this Scripture relates to glory is that through it, God invites us to glory. Psalm 149:9, ***This glory is to all his saints***, aptly relates to *how the king of Israel honored himself today, uncovering himself* (2 Sam. 6:20).

Thus, we know the matter of this work: it concerns all the works of the Lord; its mode: praying and praising; its goal: so that, elevated, we may be joined to the ***most High*** and ***holy one***; and its author: the Holy Spirit revealing it.

But, before we come to the text, we should consider three things generally about this book. *First*, the translation of this work. *Second*, the way of explaining it. *Third*, its division.

There are three translations.[9] One is from the earthly Church's beginning at the time of the apostles, and by Jerome's time, this had been corrupted by copyists. So, Jerome corrected it at the request of Pope Damasus, and this is read in Italy. But since this translation did not agree with the Greek, Jerome translated it again from Greek into Latin at the request of Paula, and Pope Damasus had this sung in France, and it agrees word for word with the Greek. Later, a certain Sophronius was disputing with the Jews, who said that something was not as he cited it from the second translation of the Psalter, so he asked Jerome to translate the Psalter into Latin from Hebrew. Jerome agreed to his request, producing a translation that entirely agrees with the Hebrew but that is not sung in any church, though many still have it.

---

8. Cf. Augustine, *Letter 147*, 13.

9. Thomas actually mentions four translations here. The first, called the *Versio vetus Latina* (the Old Latin Version), comes from the Latin translation of the Septuagint that preceded Jerome's Vulgate. The second version, which he describes as "read in Italy," is the Roman Psalter, a corrected version of the Old Latin translation that more closely follows a common version of the Septuagint. The third version is the Gallican Psalter, which Jerome produced using the four Greek columns of his *Hexapla*—an immense text in which Jerome presented a line-by-line comparison of six different versions of the Bible. In the eighth century, Alcuin used the Gallican Psalter in the version of the Bible he created, and thus, by Thomas's time it was the most influential psalter, both for liturgical and scholarly use. Thomas relies on it as his default translation, and in the sixteenth century it was included in the Sixto-Clementine Vulgate. The fourth translation Thomas mentions is the *Iuxta Hebraeos*, the "Hebrew Psalter," the final translation of the Psalms that Jerome produced using pre-Masoretic Hebrew manuscripts instead of the Septuagint.

Second, regarding the way of explaining it, it should be known that in explaining the Psalter, as with other prophecies, we must avoid the error condemned in the Fifth Synod.[10] Theodore of Mopsuestia said that Sacred Scripture and the prophecies do not speak explicitly about Christ, only about other things, but that people have applied them to Christ.[11] Thus, ***They parted my garments amongst them*** (Ps. 21:19) in the literal sense was not about Christ but David. This theory was condemned by that Council, and anyone who insists that Scripture must be explained this way is a heretic. Therefore, blessed Jerome, writing about Ezekiel, gave us a rule that we will follow in regard to the Psalms—namely, that events should be explained as prefiguring something relating to Christ or the Church.[12] For, as it is said, *all these things happened to them in figure* (1 Cor. 10:11 DRB).[13]

Now prophecies are sometimes about things that took place in their own time; however, they are not about these things principally but insofar as these things prefigure future ones. This is why the Holy Spirit ordained that when such things are said, certain elements exceeding that event itself are inserted to lift the soul up to what is prefigured.

Just as in the book of Daniel, many things are said about Antiochus as a figure of the Antichrist—hence, we read some things there that were not fulfilled in him but will be fulfilled in the Antichrist. Similarly, some things are written about the reign of David and Solomon that were not to be fulfilled in the reign of these men but were to be fulfilled in the rule of Christ, in whose figure they were spoken. Take Psalm 71:2, for example: ***Give to the king thy judgment, O God.*** According to its title, this psalm is about the reign of David and Solomon, but there is material in it that exceeds the capacity of these men—namely: ***In his days shall justice spring up, and abundance of peace till the moon be taken away***, and further, ***He shall rule from sea to sea and from the river unto the ends of the earth*** (Ps. 71:7–8). Therefore, the psalm is about the reign of Solomon insofar as it prefigures that of Christ, in which all that has been said will be fulfilled.

10. The Second Council of Constantinople, held in 553.

11. Numerous passages from the writings of Theodore are excerpted in the acts of Constantinople's fourth session, including one that argued, concerning Psalm 21: "It is beyond doubt that the psalm does not at all fit the Lord." Instead, Theodore argued, the passages "were manifestly applied to him by the apostles because what had first been said hyperbolically by David on account of ills inflicted on him happened in actuality to Christ." *Acts of the Council of Constantinople of 553: With Related Texts on the Three Chapters Controversy* 4.28, trans. Richard Price, vol. 1 (Liverpool: Liverpool University Press, 2009).

12. The rule to which Thomas refers here, in fact, appears in the prologue of Jerome's *Commentary on Hosea*.

13. Cf. Thomas Aquinas, *Summa theologiae* 1.1.10.

Its *first* division is that there are one hundred and fifty psalms, and this has a hidden meaning since one hundred and fifty is composed of seventy and eighty. Seven, from which seventy is named, signifies the length of this time, which is measured by seven days. Eight, from which eighty is named, signifies the state of future life; for eight, according to the Gloss, relates to those who are risen.[14] So one hundred and fifty signifies that this book treats those things that pertain to the course of this present life and to future glory. Seven also signifies the Old Testament, for the Old Testament fathers maintained a sevenfold structure of observance. They observed the seventh day; the seventh week; the seventh month; and the seventh year of the seventh decade, which is called the jubilee (cf. Lev. 25:8–10). Now, eight signifies the New Testament because we celebrate the eighth day, the Lord's day, because of the solemnity of the Lord's Resurrection. And in this book of Psalms, the mysteries of the Old and New Testaments are contained.

The *second* division follows those who said that the Psalter is divided into five books by the five divisions of the psalms that say, ***So be it, so be it***; and this is in Greek, where the Hebrew has, ***Amen, amen.*** And according to them, this phrase marks the end of each book, and it is found first in Psalm 40:2, which begins, ***Blessed is he that understandeth.*** Again, in Psalm 71:2: ***Give to the king thy judgment, O God.*** And in Psalm 88:2: ***The mercies of the Lord I will sing forever.*** And in Psalm 105, whose first verse begins, ***Give glory.*** And so there are five books.[15]

But this division is not found among the Hebrews, who regard it as one book: for it is written in the book of Psalms, ***May their camp be a desolation*** (Ps. 68:26; Acts 1:20). For they say that ***So be it, so be it*** or ***Amen, amen*** does not refer to the end of a book, since it is used many times in the other books where it is not the end of a book.[16]

The *third* division is into three groups of fifty, and this division reflects the three states of the faithful people. *First,* the state of penitence, to which are directed the first fifty psalms, which end with the psalm beginning, ***Have mercy on me, O God*** (50:3), which is a penitential psalm. *Second,* the state of justice, which consists in judgment, and this group ends with Psalm 100, which begins, ***Mercy and judgment.*** The *third* concludes the praise of eternal glory, and so it ends in this way: ***Let every spirit praise the Lord*** (Ps. 150:5).

14. *Glossa Ordinaria.*

15. A division related to this theory is favored by contemporary scholarship, although in many forms it is more complicated, involving several original collections being split and layered around a central set of psalms. For a reference to this fivefold division, see *Oxford Companion to the Bible,* ed. Bruce Metzger and Michael Coogan (New York: Oxford University Press, 1993), 626.

16. Cf. Augustine, *Expositions on the Psalms* 150.2, and Judith 13:26 (DRB).

Now, about the order of the Psalms, it should be noted that although some psalms are about history, they are not in historical order. For the psalm that begins ***I will love thee, O Lord*** (17:2) pertains to the history of Saul, but the psalm that begins ***Why, O Lord, are they multiplied*** (3:2) pertains to the history of Absalom, which came later. So, they signify something other than merely history.

The first fifty pertain to the state of penitence, and so the tribulations and attacks against David and his deliverance are treated in them figuratively.[17] And in order that the division also be literal, King David prays against two kinds of attack or persecution.

First, against what was against the whole people of God, and this is in the fifth set of ten, beginning, ***As the hart panteth after fountains of water, so my soul panteth after thee, O God*** (Ps. 41:2). And *second,* the just person individually is afflicted in two ways: sometimes by those persecuting him in temporal affairs, and sometimes by those living unjustly: *they afflicted the soul of the just with unjust works* (2 Pet. 2:8); ***fainting hath taken hold of me because of the wicked*** (Ps. 118:53).

So, he puts first the psalms pertaining to the first kind of persecution against David, which signifies something against Christ and the Church, and next, the fourth set of ten, those pertaining to the second kind of tribulation: ***Blessed are they whose iniquities are forgiven*** (Ps. 31:1).

And David, while reigning, suffered two kinds of tribulation: by particular persons and by the whole people. Therefore, the psalms that are against an individual are first. Next are the psalms in which he prays against the second persecution, and this is in the third set of ten—namely: ***O God my God, look upon me*** (Ps. 21:2).

Now, he suffered persecution from two particular persons—namely, Absalom and Saul—and this signifies the persecution that the saints suffer either from those of their own household or from those outside. So, Christ was made to suffer by Judas and by the Jews.

Therefore, the psalms against the first are put first; those against the second are next, and these are in the second group of ten: ***Save me, O Lord, for there is now no saint, truths are decayed from among the children of men*** (Ps. 11:2).

17. For further discussion of this division of the first fifty psalms, see Thomas's discussion in the opening of Psalm 31, included at page 112 below.

The Prologue of Saint Thomas to Job

1 Just as things that are generated naturally reach perfection from imperfection by small degrees, so it is with human beings in their knowledge of the truth. In the beginning, they attained a very limited understanding of the truth, but later, they gradually came to know the truth in fuller measure. For this reason, many erred in the beginning due to an imperfect knowledge of the truth. Among these, there were some who excluded divine providence and attributed everything to luck and chance. Indeed, this opinion predominated among so many of these early philosophers that they held the world to have been made by chance and by what naturally arose from the positions of the ancient natural elements, which constituted only a material cause. Even certain later philosophers, such as Democritus and Empedocles, attributed most things to chance. However, by a more profound diligence in their contemplation of the truth, later philosophers showed by evident proofs and reasons that natural things are set in motion by providence. For such a sure course in the motion of the heavens and the stars and other effects of nature would not be found unless all these things were governed and ordered by some intellect transcending the things ordered.

2 Therefore, after the majority asserted the opinion that natural things did not happen by chance but by providence due to the order that clearly appears in them, a question emerged among them about human actions as to whether human affairs evolved by chance or were governed by some kind of providence or a higher ordering. This doubt was fed especially because there is no sure order apparent in human events. For good things do not always befall the good, nor evil things the wicked. On the other hand, evil things do not always befall the good nor good things the wicked, but good and evil befall both the good and the wicked indifferently. This fact, then, especially moved the human heart to the opinion that human affairs are not governed by divine providence. Some said that human affairs proceed by chance, except to the extent that they are ruled by human providence and counsel; others attributed their outcome to a fatalism ruled by the heavens.

3 This idea causes a great deal of harm to humanity, for if divine providence is denied, there will remain no reverence or true fear of God among people. The degree of indolence toward the virtues and inclination toward vices that would follow from this lack of reverence is sufficiently easy to assess, for nothing calls people back from evil things and induces them to good as much as the fear and love of God. For this reason, the first and foremost aim of those who had pursued wisdom inspired by the Spirit of God for the instruction of others was to remove this opinion from human hearts. So after the promulgation of

the Law and the Prophets, the book of Job occupies first place in the order of Holy Scripture, the books composed by the wisdom of the Holy Spirit for the instruction of human beings. The whole intention of this book is directed to this: to show that human affairs are ruled by divine providence using probable arguments.

4 The methodology used in this book is to demonstrate this proposition from the supposition that natural things are governed by divine providence. The affliction of the just is what seems especially to impugn divine providence in human affairs. For although it seems irrational and contrary to providence at first glance that good things sometimes happen to evil people, nevertheless, this can be excused in one way or another by divine compassion. But that the just are afflicted without cause seems to undermine totally the foundation of providence. Thus, the varied and grave afflictions of a particular just man called Job, perfect in every virtue, are proposed as a kind of theme for the question intended for discussion.

5 Nevertheless, there were some who had the impression that Job could not have been anything in reality but that it must have been a parable made up to serve as a particular case for a debate about providence, as people frequently invent cases to serve as a model for debate. Although it does not matter much for the intention of the book whether or not such is the case, it makes a difference for the truth itself. This aforementioned opinion seems to contradict the authority of Scripture. In Ezekiel, the Lord is represented as saying, *If these three men, Noah, Daniel, and Job, were in it, they would deliver but their own lives by their righteousness* (14:14). Clearly Noah and Daniel were men who really existed, and so there should be no doubt about Job, who is the third man numbered with them. Also, James says, *Behold, we call those happy who were steadfast. You have heard of the steadfastness of Job, and you have seen the purpose of the Lord* (5:11). Therefore, we must believe that Job was a real man.

6 However, as to the epoch in which he lived, who his parents were, or even who the author of the book was—that is, whether Job wrote about himself as if speaking about another person or whether someone else reported these things about him—is not the present intention of this discussion. With trust in God's aid, I intend to explain this book entitled the book of Job briefly, as far as I am able, according to the literal sense. The mystical sense has been explained for us both accurately and eloquently by the blessed Pope Gregory so that nothing further need be added to this sort of commentary.[18]

18. See Gregory the Great, *Moralia in Job*.

The Prologue of Saint Thomas to Isaiah

Write the vision and make it plain upon tables that he that readeth it may run over it. For as yet the vision is far off, and it shall appear at the end.

—HABAKKUK 2:2–3

1 From these words, we can understand three things about the book of the prophet Isaiah, which we have at hand: the author, the manner, and the subject matter. Regarding the *first*, three things are set out: the author, the author's minister, and the minister's office or gift.

The speaker's authority reveals the author; hence it says, *The Lord answered me, and said,* ***write the vision***. For the author of Holy Scripture is the Holy Spirit, as it says below: ***Now the Lord God has sent me and his Spirit*** (Isa. 48:16); *because no prophecy ever came by the impulse of man, but men moved by the Holy Spirit spoke from God* (2 Pet. 1:21); for it is the Spirit who *speaks mysteries* (1 Cor. 14:2).

The minister is shown in the act of writing, for he says, ***Write***. The tongue of the prophet was an organ of the Holy Spirit, as is said in Psalm 44:2: *My tongue is like the pen of a ready scribe*; and: *What then is Apollos? What is Paul? Servants through whom you believed* (1 Cor. 3:5).

The office of the minister is shown in the privilege of the vision, for it says, ***the vision***, as it says in 1 Samuel 9:9: *For he who is now called a prophet was formerly called a seer*; and in Numbers 12:6: *If there is a prophet among you, I the Lord make myself known to him in a vision, I speak to him in a dream*. Thus, therefore, the author is clear.

2 The manner is shown in ***make it plain***, for this prophet's manner of writing is plain and open. Hence, as is said in Jerome's preface, he seems *to be not prophesying about the future but composing an account of past events*.[19] Regarding the manner of writing, three things are set out: the explanation of the vision, the reason for the explanation, and the benefit that follows.

The *first* is shown where it is said, ***make it plain***. He makes plain what he has seen, or the vision, in three ways: *first*, through the use of similitudes; *second*, through the expression of thought; *third*, through the beauty of his words. And in these three ways, this prophet surpasses the other prophets.

He sets out beautiful and courtly similitudes, which indeed are necessary for us due to the connaturality of sense to reason. It is, thus, natural for our reason to receive from sensible objects; hence, it more clearly grasps things whose

19. "Preface of St. Jerome," in Thomas Aquinas, *Commentary on Isaiah* 2, trans. Louis St. Hilaire, Latin/English Edition of the Works of St. Thomas Aquinas, vol. 30 (Green Bay, WI: Aquinas Institute, 2021).

likenesses it sees by the senses. Likewise, Dionysius shows this in his second Letter to Titus—namely, that sensible figures are necessary in the Scriptures: *All those who hear plain things weave in themselves a certain figure, which conducts them to an understanding of theology.*[20] Again, in Hosea: *Through the prophets [I] gave parables* (12:10).

Isaiah also excels in the expression of thought, *so that he seems to compose not a prophecy but a gospel*, as is said in the Helmeted Prologue.[21] Thus it is said to him below: ***Lift up thy voice . . . fear not. Say to the cities of Judah*** (Isa. 40:9). He also excels in beauty of words as *a man of noble and urbane eloquence*, as Jerome says in the Prologue; *the tongue of the wise dispenses knowledge* (Prov. 15:2).

3 After this, the reason for this explanation is touched on when it says, ***upon tables.*** For there are the tables of the law, there are tables of a stony heart, and there are tables of a soft and fleshly heart: *You yourselves are our letter . . . written . . . not on tablets of stone but on tablets of human hearts* (2 Cor. 3:2–3).

The *first* tables of the law were written by God's finger, as is said in Exodus 31:18, and therefore Scripture is profound and obscure and filled with many mysteries. Thus, to explain them, it was necessary for plain prophecy to be written upon these tables by a human finger, as it says below: ***Take thee a great book and write in it with a man's pen*** (Isa. 8:1). But it was necessary to write plainly on the *second* tables, the stony hearts, in order to confound them: *Well did Isaiah prophesy of you, when he said: "This people honors me with their lips, but their heart is far from me"* (Matt. 15:7–8). But it was necessary to write on the *third* tables, the fleshly hearts, to instruct them: *They read from the book, from the law of God, clearly*, and it continues, *the people understood the reading* (Neh. 8:8).

4 The benefit of the explanation, however, is shown in what follows: ***that he may run over it.*** For to run over is to come to the end quickly by running. The end, moreover, is threefold: the end of the law, the end of the commandment, and the end of life.

For Christ is the end of the law that everyone who has faith may be justified (Rom. 10:4); *the end of the commandment is charity* (1 Tim. 1:5 DRB); the end of life is death: *He who endures to the end will be saved* (Matt. 24:13). Therefore, it says, ***that he that readeth it may run over it***, as if to say: that he who reads

20. Pseudo-Dionysius, *Letter 9*, 1.

21. The "Prologus Galeatus": Jerome's preface to Samuel and Kings. However, these words appear in Jerome's *Letter 53*, 8; cf. also, the "Preface of St. Jerome" to Isaiah (cited in 10n19 above), where he says, "Isaiah should be called not so much a prophet as an evangelist, for he describes all the mysteries of Christ and the Church so clearly that you think that he is not prophesying about the future but composing an account of past events."

it without the impediment of doubt may run over, believing in Christ, and believing may love, and in love may persevere.

5 The subject matter is touched upon in what follows: ***For as yet the vision is far off***; and the primary subject matter of this book is the appearance of the Son of God. Hence, in the Church, it is read during the season of Advent. Now, there are three appearances of the Son of God. The *first* is that in which he, having been made man, appeared in the flesh: *The goodness and loving kindness of God our Savior appeared* (Titus 3:4). The *second* is that in which he appeared by faith, believed by the world: *The grace of God has appeared for the salvation of all men* (Titus 2:11). The *third* is that in which he will appear by sight in glorification: *We know that when he appears we shall be like him* (1 John 3:2). And these appearances are the subject matter of this book. Thus, in the Prologue it is said that *all his concern is for the coming of Christ and the calling of the gentiles.*[22]

6 But certainly, the one who afterward was thus seen was still far off in Isaiah's own time. Indeed, he was far off because he was exalted in equality of majesty: *Man beholds it from afar. Behold, God is great, and we know him not* (Job 36:25–26). He was also far off because he was hidden in the Father's preordination: *What is the plan of the mystery hidden for ages in God* (Eph. 3:9). He was also far off because he was delayed in the expectation of the fathers: *These all died in faith, not having received what was promised, but having seen it and greeted it from afar* (Heb. 11:13).

7 But certainly what was then far off has come near because what was exalted has been made the lowest. For the Word *became flesh* (John 1:14). What was hidden has been made public because *the only-begotten Son, who is in the bosom of the Father, he has made him known* (John 1:18). What was delayed has begun even now to be possessed by the saints in glory: *Come, O blessed of my Father, inherit the kingdom prepared for you from the foundation of the world* (Matt. 25:34).

8 Thus, therefore, he was able to say, ***as yet the vision is far off, and it shall appear at the end.*** For the *first* appearance was at the end of the law, *but when the time had fully come, God sent forth his Son, born of woman, born under the law* (Gal. 4:4). The *second* appearance, however, was at the end of idolatry, as it says below: ***Behold, the Lord will ascend upon a swift cloud and will enter into Egypt, and the idols of Egypt shall be moved at his presence*** (Isa. 19:1). The *third* will be at the end of all misery, for *he will wipe away every tear from their eyes, and death shall be no more, neither shall there be mourning nor crying nor pain any more, for the former things have passed away* (Rev. 21:4).

---

22. "Preface of St. Jerome," in Thomas Aquinas, *Commentary on Isaiah* 5.

And these are the last things about which it is said of Isaiah: *By the spirit of might he saw the last things and comforted those who mourned in Zion. He revealed what was to occur to the end* (Sir. 48:24–25).

Chapter 1

DIVINE WISDOM, CREATION, AND THE COSMOS

Job 38:1–12

Divine Wisdom

On Job 38.1 (491–499)

38:1 *Then the Lord answered Job out of a whirlwind and said:*

38:2 *Who is this that wrappeth up sentences in unskillful words?*

38:3 *Gird up thy loins like a man. I will ask thee and answer thou me.*

38:4 *Where wast thou when I laid up the foundations of the earth? Tell me if thou hast understanding.*

38:5 *Who hath laid the measures thereof, if thou knowest? or who hath stretched the line upon it?*

38:6 *Upon what are its bases grounded? or who laid the corner stone thereof,*

38:7 *When the morning stars praised me together and all the sons of God made a joyful melody?*

38:8 *Who shut up the sea with doors, when it broke forth as issuing out of the womb:*

38:9 *When I made a cloud the garment thereof and wrapped it in a mist as in swaddling bands?*

38:10 *I set my bounds around it, and made it bars and doors:*

38:11 *And I said, hitherto thou shalt come and shalt go no further, and here thou shalt break thy swelling waves.*

38:12 Didst thou since thy birth command the morning and show the dawning of the day its place?

491 ***Then the Lord answered Job out of the whirlwind and said***: After the discussions of Job and his friends about divine providence, Eliud had assumed to himself the office of determining the answer, contradicting Job in one thing and his friends in others. But because human wisdom is not sufficient to understand the truth of divine providence, it was necessary that the dispute should be determined by divine authority. Job thought correctly about divine providence, but in his manner of speaking he had gone to excess because he had caused scandal in the hearts of others when they thought that he did not show due reverence to God. Therefore, the Lord, as the determiner of the question, contradicts the friends of Job because they did not think correctly, Job himself for expressing himself in an inordinate way, and Eliud for an inadequate determination of the question.

So, the text continues, ***the Lord answered Job***, because this answer is more on his account, although he had not spoken immediately before in the chapter. The text shows the manner of response, saying, ***out of a whirlwind***, which can certainly be understood according to the literal sense to mean that the voice of God was formed miraculously in the air by some disturbance of the air, as happened on Mt. Sinai in Exodus, or like the voice that spoke to Christ, of which some said *that it thundered* (John 12:29 DRB). Or, this can be understood metaphorically, so that this answer of the Lord is an interior inspiration divinely given to Job himself, and so the Lord is said to have answered him ***out of a whirlwind*** both because of the disturbance that he still suffered and also because of the darkness that accompanies a whirlwind, since we cannot perceive divine inspiration clearly in this life but with the darkness of sensible likenesses, as Dionysius says in chapter 1 of *The Celestial Hierarchy*. The Lord indicated this, even if he had made his voice sensibly heard from a corporeal whirlwind.

492 Once a dispute is determined by the opinion of the judge, nothing else remains to be said except to reject the statement of the determination. So the Lord first rejects the determination of the question that Eliud had made. He rejects it because Eliud had enveloped the true opinions that he had proposed with many false and frivolous words, and so the text continues, ***he said: Who is this that wrappeth up sentences in unskillful words?*** In his arguments, Eliud had accused Job of saying he wanted to dispute with God and said that his claim to be just was tantamount to detracting from the justice of the divine judgment. But he enveloped these opinions with many presumptuous and even false statements, as should be clear already, which are called here unskillful words because every lack of order proceeds from a defect of reason.

493 So, after the Lord rejects the determination of Eliud, he himself begins to determine the question. First, he gets Job's attention when he says, ***Gird up thy loins like a man***, which here is used as a metaphor. For men usually gird up their loins in preparation for a journey or work. The Lord, therefore, wanted Job to be ready to consider what he said to him by removing every impediment. So, he clearly tells him to gird up his loins because 'loins' metaphorically mean carnal desires, which block listening with the mind in a special way; as Isaiah says, *Whom will he teach knowledge, and to whom will he explain the message? Those who are weaned from the milk, those taken from the breast* (28:9).

494 First, he begins in his determination to accuse Job for having spoken presumptuously when he provoked God to discussion. Since Job had given God two options when he said, ***Call me, and I will answer thee***, and ***I will speak, and do thou answer me*** (13:22), and as Job had already said enough, the Lord, as though choosing the second alternative, says, ***I will ask thee and answer thou me.*** God certainly does not question to learn but to convince a human being of his ignorance. He questions him about his effects, which are easily accessible to the experience of the human senses. When a person is shown to be ignorant of these, he is much convinced that he does not have knowledge of the highest realities. Among other sensible effects, he begins to ask about the principal parts of the earth. Of these, earth is more known to us because it is more immediate to our experience. He begins to ask him about this and says, ***Where wast thou when I laid up the foundations of the earth?*** He rightly compares the earth to a foundation because, as a foundation is the lowest part of a building, so also the earth is the lowest of bodies, and it lies under everything. Since the earth is the principal matter of the human body, matter precedes in time that which is made from it, and even more, the plan of the artisan who created the matter precedes it. So, he clearly says, ***Where was thou when I laid up the foundations of the earth***, as if to say, 'You cannot know the plan of the foundation of the earth, because when the earth was laid on its foundation you did not yet exist as a really existing thing.'

495 Consider that some of the ancients did not attribute the position of the earth and of the other elements to some ordering plan but to material necessity, according to which the heavier elements sank under the lighter ones. So, to disprove this opinion, the Lord consequently compares the foundation of the earth to the foundation of a building, which is constructed according to the plans of the architect. In the same way, the foundation of the land was made according to divine providence, which human intelligence is not capable of understanding fully. He makes this clear when he says, ***Tell me, if thou hast understanding***—as if to say, 'Therefore, you cannot give the answer for these

things because your intelligence is not capable of grasping them.' Consider that an architect puts four things in order in the foundation of a building.

First, he orders the size of the foundation. In the same way, divine reason has disposed how great a quantity the earth should have, and not more or less. He expresses this, saying, ***Who hath laid the measures thereof***, in all its dimensions. He clearly says, ***laid the measures***, for earth, by its nature, does not require a certain quantity by necessity, but this quantity was only imposed on the earth from divine reason, which a human being cannot know. So, he says, ***if thou knowest***, since a human cannot know or tell this.

Second, an architect puts in order in his plans the determination of the site of the foundation, which he encompasses by the extension of the measuring line, and so he says, ***who hath stretched the line upon it?*** This means the plan of divine government, which clearly determined the place of the earth in the composition of the universe.

Third, after the architect has determined the size of the foundation and where it must be located, he determines how to make the foundation solid. As to this he says, ***Upon what are its bases***, of the land, ***grounded***, because it was founded on the center of the world.

Fourth, after these three things, the architect now begins to lay the stones in the foundation. First, he lays the corner stone, on which all the different walls are aligned. As to this he says, ***or who laid***, put down, ***the corner stone***, on which the very center of the earth is clearly determined, according to which the different parts of the land are aligned.

496 A person usually lays the foundation of a building because he needs a place to live. But to show that God does not lay the foundation of the earth from need, he adds, ***When the morning stars praised me***, which is as if he should say, 'Although heaven is my dwelling and the stars praise me, yet I founded the earth, not because I need the servants who live there, but only from my will.' He does not say this as though heaven was made before the earth, especially as we read in Genesis, *In the beginning God created the heavens and the earth* (1:1). For the text says that the stars that he mentions here were created on the fourth day (Gen. 1:14). But Genesis says this to show that in the order of nature, heaven and the stars are prior to the earth as incorruptible to corruptible and moving to moved. He says the ***morning stars***—that is, ones newly created, because we call morning stars the ones that usually appear at the beginning of the day. The fact that the morning stars praise God can be understood, in one way, materially inasmuch as they are the material of divine praise in their brightness and nobility. Even if they were not so fair to humankind, which did not yet exist, they were so for the angels who already existed.

In another way, according to those who call the heavenly bodies animated, the stars in the beginning of their institution praised God, not with vocal, but with mental praise. This can even be referred to the angels whose ministry is to move the heavenly bodies, as the text continues, ***and all the sons of God made a joyful melody***, which refers to the angels of the highest hierarchies, whom Dionysius says are located in the entrance court of God. Therefore, as he clearly attributes praise to the lower angels, so he attributes shouting for joy to the higher angels because this connotes greater excellence in praise.

497 After the foundation of the earth, he continues then speaking about the waters that are immediately placed over the land. The natural order of the elements requires that water covers the earth at every point like air covers earth and water at every point. Nevertheless, by the divine plan for the generation of human beings, animals, and plants, a part of the land remains uncovered by the waters, as God closes the waters of the sea within their certain limits by his power, and so he says, ***Who shut up the sea with doors***, with determined limits. There were some who thought the action of the sun dried a determined part of the earth, but the Lord shows that it was from the beginning, by divine disposition, that the sea does not everywhere cover the land. He describes the production of the sea using the comparison of the birth of a living thing, a child, because water is especially apt to be changed into living things. This is why the seeds of all things are moist.

The child *first* comes forth from the womb of its mother, and he means this when he says, ***when it broke forth as issuing out of the womb***. He uses the verb ***broke forth*** in the production of the sea because it is a property of water to move almost continually. He says water proceeds ***out of the womb*** not because it has its origin from some corporeal matter but because it proceeds from the hidden origin of divine providence as from the womb.

Second, a newborn child is dressed, and expressing this he says, ***I made a cloud the garment thereof***. For since the clouds are born from water vapor, clouds are much more numerous in maritime climates.

Third, a child who is born is wrapped in swaddling clothes, and expressing this, he says, ***I wrapped it in a mist as in swaddling bands***. The fog does not mean those high water vapors confined in the clouds, but the vapors that darken the air on the face of the sea, and perhaps he alludes to this when Genesis says, *Darkness was upon the face of the deep* (1:2).

498 Having described what pertains to the original production of the sea, he explains his conclusion as if by saying that when the sea was newly made, ***I set my bounds around it***. He puts three things here that pertain to the boundary of the sea. One of these is shown when he says, ***my bounds***—that is, those

placed by me. The second is when he says, ***I made it bars***, and the third when he says, ***and doors.***

These three things pertain to the rule of divine power, and so he explains them in this way: ***I said, hitherto thou shalt come***, which pertains to the concept of a boundary, for a boundary is a measure by which the forward motion of something is impeded: ***here thou shalt break thy swelling waves.*** This pertains to the gates that are placed for the purpose of not allowing entrance or exit, except according to a determined measure. Thus, even the sea does not change its shore at will, but according to the determined measure of the ebb and flow of the waves.

499 After the land and the water, he proceeds on to the air, which, according to appearances, is continuous in heaven. The first common disposition to the whole body that stretches over the waters and the land is the variation of night and day, which happens from the motion of the day, which is first of movements. Therefore, he says as a consequence, ***Didst thou since thy birth command the morning?*** as if to say, 'Do day and night succeed each other on this earth by your command?' For dawn is a kind of boundary between day and night. He clearly says, ***since thy birth***, as when he spoke about the earth before he had said, ***Where wast thou?*** (Job 38:4). For just as earth is the first material principle of human beings, so also the highest heaven, which varies its motion day and night, is the first principle of the human body among corporeal causes.

Consider that the clarity of the break of day or the dawn is diversified according to the diverse places of the intensity of signs that accompany the sun, because when there is the sign of a quick rising, in which the sun rises immediately, the dawn lasts only a little while. When the sun shows signs of a delayed rising, it endures longer. The measure of place is determined from where the brightness of the sun begins to appear when the sun is there, and expressing this, he then says, ***and show the dawning of the day its place?*** as if to say, 'Have you ordered the places in heaven from which the dawn will gives its light?' He implies the answer: 'No.' From all these things, you can understand that your reason cannot comprehend divine things, and so it is clear that you are not suited to dispute with God.

Psalm 8

Creation and the Transcendence of God

On Psalms 8 (52–56)

8:1 *Unto the end, for the presses: a psalm of David.*

8:2 *O Lord our Lord, how admirable is thy name in the whole earth! For thy magnificence is elevated above the heavens.*

8:3 *Out of the mouth of infants and of sucklings, thou hast perfected praise, because of thy enemies, that thou mayst destroy the enemy and the avenger.*

8:4 *For I will behold thy heavens, the works of thy fingers: the moon and the stars which thou hast founded.*

8:5 *What is man that thou art mindful of him? or the son of man that thou visitest him?*

8:6 *Thou hast made him a little less than the angels, thou hast crowned him with glory and honor*

8:7 *And hast set him over the works of thy hands.*

8:8 *Thou hast subjected all things under his feet, all sheep and oxen, moreover, the beasts also of the fields.*

8:9 *The birds of the air and the fishes of the sea that pass through the paths of the sea.*

8:10 *O Lord our Lord, how admirable is thy name in all the earth!*

52 Above, he put a psalm in which David prayed because of his persecution;[1] here, he puts a psalm of thanksgiving. *First,* he puts forward a psalm for the favors bestowed upon the whole human race; *second,* another for the favors he received in the destruction of his enemies and for the good things granted to him; and

1. See Thomas Aquinas, *On Psalms* 7 (not included in this collection).

a *third*, for the evil things that have been removed: ***I will give praise*** (Ps. 9:2). For here he expresses the feelings of a person who considers the favors of God bestowed upon the whole human race and gives thanks.

I will explain here only the last word of the title—***Unto the end, for the presses: a psalm of David***—since the rest of it has been explained above.[2] Here, what was said in Deuteronomy should be considered: *You shall keep the feast of booths seven days, when you make your ingathering from your threshing floor and your wine press* (16:13). For it should be known that David celebrated the feasts with special devotion, and he would do something special to praise God.

Now, the celebration of the Feast of Tabernacles was a command. And it took place during the grape harvest, in commemoration of the divine favors that occurred when God led the children of Israel out of Egypt in tents and into the promised land where there are fruits. And so it was appropriate that they have beautiful fruits at the time of pressing; and so it says, ***for the presses***. This is the meaning according to the literal sense. But in a spiritual sense, the wine press is the Church.[3] *He . . . planted it with choice vines; he built a watchtower in the midst of it* (Isa. 5:2). *There was a householder who planted a vineyard . . . and built a tower* (Matt. 21:33).

Therefore, he says, ***for the presses***—that is, for the churches of the world; and the Church is called a wine press because just as in a wine press the wine is separated from the grape skins, so in the Church the good are separated from the bad by the work of the ministers, although they are not separated physically but in disposition. The same principle also applies to the threshing floor since the wheat is separated from the chaff.

Likewise, the spiritual sense is separated from the words set down literally. Likewise, the presses are martyrdoms, in which the separation of soul from the body takes place, while the bodies of those who were crushed by affliction and persecution for the sake of Christ's name remain in the earth for a time, but their souls go forth to rest in the heavens.

This psalm is divided into two parts. The Psalmist *first* wonders at the divine excellence. *Second*, he wonders at his mercy, at ***What is man?*** Regarding the *first*, he makes two points. *First*, he shows that the majesty of God is wonderful; *second*, that it is clear, at ***Out of the mouth of infants***.

Regarding the *first*, he makes two points. *First*, he describes him as wonderful. *Second*, he shows the reason for saying this, at ***For I will behold thy heavens***. Therefore, he calls him ***Lord*** of all. *You are Lord of all* (Esther 13:11). But he is particularly ***our Lord***—'the Lord of us who worship and are devoted

2. See Thomas Aquinas, *On Psalms* 4.19 (not included in this collection).

3. See Augustine, *Expositions on the Psalms* 8.1.

to you.' Jerome has ***our ruler.***[4] *I will not rule over you, and my son will not rule over you; the Lord will rule over you* (Judg. 8:23).

How admirable is thy name—that is, of your divinity. ***Wonderful are the surges of the sea; wonderful is the Lord on high*** (Ps. 92:4). *Why askest thou my name, which is wonderful?* (Judg. 13:18 DRB; Gen 32:29). Likewise, the name of Christ incarnate is wonderful: *His name will be called Wonderful* (Isa. 9:6). But surely it is not wonderful only in Judah, as the Jews say, or in Africa, as the Donatists say.[5] No, but ***in the whole earth.*** *For from the rising of the sun to its setting my name is great among the nations* (Mal. 1:11).

The reason for wonder is given next: '***For thy magnificence is elevated***, since your greatness appears in the heavens.' Wonder occurs when someone sees an effect without knowing the cause.[6] Therefore, a cause can be wonderful in two ways, either because it is completely unknown, or because it produces an effect that does not manifest the cause perfectly.

The first does not apply to God since he produces the effect. *His invisible nature . . . has been clearly perceived in the things that have been made* (Rom. 1:20). I say he produces an effect, but one that does not perfectly manifest the cause, and so he remains wonderful. And this is why he says, ***thy magnificence***—that is, your praise or your power, which is able to do great things—***is elevated above the heavens***, disproportionately exceeding the making of the heavens.

Here he excludes the error of those who say that God is the form of the heavens. For if that were true, he would be proportionate to the heavens. He also excludes the error of those who say that he acts out of a necessity of his nature; if this were true, he would not extend himself beyond the heavens, but he can do more, to infinity.

Or ***the heavens*** is the Scriptures since he is even more than is told in the Scriptures. *Glorify the Lord as much as ever you can, for he will yet far exceed, and his magnificence is wonderful* (Sir. 43:32 DRB).

Or ***thy magnificence***—that is, the Son of God made man—***is elevated above the heavens***, in the Ascension. *He who descended is he who also ascended far above all the heavens* (Eph. 4:10).

53 Afterward, when he says, ***Out of the mouth***, he shows that God's magnificence is very clearly manifest. And *first*, he shows the manifestation; *second*, its reason: ***For I will behold thy heavens.***

4. The work referenced here is Jerome's *Iuxta Hebraeos* translation of the Psalms. See 4n9 above.

5. Peter Lombard, *Magna glossatura.*

6. Aristotle, *Metaphysics* 1.2.

He shows that it is manifest because what is manifest is imparted to all, however simple, as though by a kind of natural knowledge. For there are two kinds of people who follow the natural and correct impulses: the simple and the wise. That the wise should know God is not a great thing, but that the simple do is. But there are some who pervert natural impulses, and these reject the knowledge of God. ***They have not known***—that is, they desired not to know—***nor did they understand*** (Ps. 81:5). *They say to God, "Depart from us! We do not desire the knowledge of your ways"* (Job 21:14).

Now, God makes it so that, through them—that is, through the simple who follow natural impulses—those who pervert the natural impulses are confounded. By ***infants*** he indicates the simple. *Like newborn infants, long for the pure spiritual milk* (1 Pet. 2:2). Therefore, he says, ***admirable*** indeed ***is thy name***, so that ***out of the mouth of infants and of sucklings, thou hast perfected praise***, 'you who move people interiorly to this. And you have done this' ***because of thy enemies***, 'who oppose themselves to the knowledge and understanding of you,' *enemies of the cross of Christ* (Phil. 3:18) ***that thou mayst destroy the enemy and the avenger***—that is, whoever is a persecutor.

Or Pharaoh, who wishes to wreak vengeance against the one confessing your name: *We destroy arguments and every proud obstacle to the knowledge of God* (2 Cor. 10:5).

Or the tyrant, who fights with arms against your holy name: *By doing right you should put to silence the ignorance of foolish men* (1 Pet. 2:15).

Christ did this, for Christ answered in Matthew 21, referring to the children of the Hebrews, that praise would be perfected in their words, who praised by the movement of the Holy Spirit, although they seemed to act childishly. This takes place when the simple recognize God, and others pervert the tendency of their natural understanding so that they do not know God. The same was so in the case of the apostles, who were *uneducated, common men* (Acts 4:13), *sheep in the midst of wolves . . . innocent as doves* (Matt. 10:16), and destroyed all the enemies of Christ. *God chose what is foolish in the world to shame the wise, God chose what is weak in the world to shame the strong* (1 Cor. 1:27).

54 Next, he adds the reason for this manifestation, saying, ***I will behold thy heavens.*** In his book *On the Nature of the Gods*, Cicero says, as Aristotle also says (although it is not in the books of his that we have with us), that, upon entering a palace that appeared to be well laid out, no one would be so crazy to deny that someone had made it, even if he did not see how it had been made.[7] We come into the world, and we do not see how it was made; but from the fact

7. Cicero, *On the Nature of the Gods* 2.2.

that it is well-ordered, we should perceive that it was made by someone. And the order of the heavenly bodies especially shows this.

Indeed, there were some people in error who attribute the causes of things to the necessity of matter; so, they say that all things were made because of warmth and coldness, dryness and moistness, the elements that came together thus. Now, even if this appears to be the case regarding some things, it is in no way possible of the heavenly bodies since they cannot be attributed to the necessity of matter, which is so distant from them, and they complete their course in such a length of time. One can deduce from this only an intelligent cause. And so, when Scripture wants to show the power of God, it brings us back to the consideration of the heavens. *Lift up your eyes on high and see: who created these?* (Isa. 40:26). That is to say, ***I will behold thy heavens, the works of thy fingers.***

Now, he says, ***the works of thy fingers***, for three reasons: since what we make with our fingers, we make with attention and precision. And the things to be considered about the heavenly bodies can lead back only to an intelligent cause, and so he says, ***the works of thy fingers***. Psalm 135:5 says: ***Who made the heavens in understanding.***

Or it connects to ***elevated***. When someone elevates something heavy, he supports it on his shoulders, but when he elevates something light, he supports it on his fingers, and so he says, ***the works of thy fingers***, as if making the heavens was light work for him. *Who hath . . . weighed the heavens with his palm? who hath poised with three fingers the bulk of the earth?* (Isa. 40:12 DRB).

Or he says it because those things that we make with our fingers are intricate works. So he says, ***the works of thy fingers***, to show that these are more intricate than other works.

Now, he names the moon, but not the sun, because of the gentiles who believed that it was a high god, and so he particularly mentions ***the moon and the stars*** in which no reason for error was shown. *The glory of the stars is the beauty of heaven, a gleaming array in the heights of the Lord* (Sir. 43:9).

Mystically, the apostles or the Scripture are ***the works of thy fingers***. The three fingers are the three persons, as if to say, 'The works of the whole Trinity or of the Holy Spirit.' ***The moon*** is the Church; ***the stars*** are the doctors. And God founded them.

55 ***What is man?*** Above, the Psalmist marveled at the excellence of the divine majesty, and now he remembers two favors bestowed by God upon the human race. With the second of these, he ends the psalm in praise: ***O Lord our Lord, how admirable is thy name.***

Regarding the *first*, he makes three points. *First*, he shows the mercy of God to humankind, by comparison with those beings that are above humans.

Second, by comparison with the first man, at ***thou hast crowned him with glory and honor***. *Third*, by comparison with those beings that are beneath humankind: ***thou hast set him over the works of thy hands***.

Above human beings there are two natures: the divine and the angelic. *First*, therefore, he describes the favors by comparison to God; *second*, by comparison to the angels, at ***Thou hast made him a little less***. The *first* is explained in regard to what is fitting in relation to natural favors. *Second*, in relation to those of grace.

And according to the *first* way, and concerning it, he makes two points. *First*, he describes the special care of humankind by God; *second*, the special familiarity: ***or the son of man***. For it is wonderful that someone who is great should be joined with a particular familiarity to someone little.

Thus, the Psalmist first mentions a human being's smallness in view of his condition: ***What is man***, such a small thing? *Man that is born of a woman* (Job 14:1), and *man, who is a maggot, and the son of man, who is a worm* (Job 25:6). *Second*, he mentions his smallness in virtue of his origin, for it is vile. *Who can make him clean that is conceived of unclean seed?* (Job 14:4 DRB), and *Did you not pour me out like milk and curdle me like cheese?* (Job 10:10).

And so, he says, ***or the son of man?*** But to this one so little, so vile, he says that he does two things: namely, that he is mindful of him and that he visits him. The *first* pertains to care; the *second*, to particular familiarity.

The manner of speaking is this: it is as if an artificer were to make great things, and, among them, one small thing, a needle. When he made the needle, he showed that he had knowledge of it. However, in disposing his works, if he should have care for the needle, it would be very amazing, and so he says, ***what is man*** 'that you should be mindful of him among the great creatures?' *Do not say, "I shall be hidden from the Lord . . . for what is my soul in the boundless creation?"* (Sir. 16:17). God has not forgotten you because of your littleness.

What great work is this? For God has care for all. *For neither is there any god besides you, whose care is for all men* (Wis. 12:13). It should be said that he has special care for the human person because he rewards his deeds in judgment. *Do you open your eyes upon such a one?* (Job 14:3).

Moreover, for the human being, he has not only concern but also familiarity with him: ***that thou visitest him***. Only a rational nature is capable of God, by knowledge and love. Therefore, God visits us insofar as he is made present to us through love or knowledge. *Your care has preserved my spirit* (Job 10:12). Therefore, God's mercy is great in the comparison of humanity to God.

56 What follows is said about humankind in comparison to the angels, to whom the human being is found to be close: ***thou hast made him a little less than the angels***. The image of God is found in the angels through the simple

intuition of the truth without inquiry, while in humankind it is through discursive inquiry, and so it is in him only to a small extent. So it is that human beings are called angels: *They shall seek the law at his mouth because he is the angel of the Lord of hosts* (Mal. 2:7 DRB). Moreover, the human being is corruptible, but only a little, since in the end, the human being will know without discursive reasoning in the fatherland, and this will be because of his incorruptible body. *For this perishable nature must put on the imperishable* (1 Cor. 15:53).

Next, he shows God's mercy to humankind by comparison to humankind itself when he says, ***thou hast crowned him with glory and honor.*** To be crowned befits kings. God has made the human being, in a sense, the king of all below, and this is glory (that is, the splendor of the divine image), and a particular crown belonging to humankind. *Man . . . is the image and glory of God* (1 Cor. 11:7). ***The light of thy countenance, O Lord, is signed upon us*** (Ps. 4:7).

Now, he is honored who is not subjected to another. As far as the soul is concerned, a human being is subject to no natural corporeal creature, whether in its entry or in its moving on—not in its entry since it is not produced by any creature and acts freely. Nor does it perish with the body, and the honor of the human being consists in this. And so it is said, *Nor discern the prize for blameless souls; for God created man for incorruption and made him in the image of his own eternity* (Wis. 2:22–23). ***Man when he was in honor did not understand*** (Ps. 48:13).

Next, when he says, ***thou hast set him over the works of thy hands***, he presents God's mercy to humanity through comparison with the beings that are beneath because he willed for human beings to have dominion over these lower things. And he makes three points about this. *First*, he presents the dominion; *second*, the ability to dominate; *third*, the number of those subjected.

The *second*, at ***Thou hast subjected all things under his feet.*** The *third*, at ***all sheep and oxen.*** Therefore, he says that since the human being is a king, you have given him dominion ***over the works of thy hands.*** *Let them have dominion over the fish of the sea, and over the birds of the air, and over the cattle, and over all the earth, and over every creeping thing that creeps upon the earth* (Gen. 1:26). He has this dominion through his rationality because he surpasses all animals in this, and so, after ***glory and honor***, he immediately adds, ***you have set him over***—'you have given him dominion,' in other words.

But notice that he says that human beings have authority over the works of his hands, not of his fingers, since they are not as intricate as the heavens (which are the works of God's fingers). The human being cannot subject them to himself.

Thus, *second*, he presents the ability to dominate. ***Thou hast subjected all things***, he says, and thus the human being is preeminent over them and subjects them to his will. This is signified in Genesis 2, where God leads all the animals to Adam. This subjection was complete before sin, but some now resist as a punishment for sin.

Third, when he says, ***sheep and oxen***, he enumerates the subjects, and he mentions the animals in such a way that plants are also included.

Now, among the animals, some whole genera are subject—namely, animals tame and domesticated by nature (like sheep and oxen)—and he uses the feminine form of ***all*** [***universas***] here since herds are made up largely of female cows and ewes. There are other animals whose whole genera are not subject, and some of these are those that walk; and in regard to these, he says, ***the beasts also of the fields***—that is to say, boars, and deer, and animals of this kind; some flying creatures, like birds; and some swimming creatures, like fish.

Now these can also be referred to the favors of grace, and then all the mysteries of Christ are enumerated in these. *First*, the Incarnation: ***What is man?*** He touches on two things, the cause of the Incarnation and the Incarnation itself, and says, ***What is man that thou art mindful of him?*** Although he visited the whole human race, nevertheless, he particularly visited that man assumed in the unity of hypostasis. *For surely it is not with angels that he is concerned but with the descendants of Abraham* (Heb. 2:16).

Second is the mystery of the Passion: ***Thou hast made him a little less*** in the passion. *Who . . . was made lower than the angels* (Heb. 2:9). In the Hebrew it has, ***Thou hast made him a little less than God***, since he was joined to God in the unity of person but made less by the passibility he assumed.

Third is the favor of the Resurrection in the honor made known to the apostles, which is reckoned through the passion: *At the name of Jesus every knee should bow* (Phil. 2:10). *That all may honor the Son, even as they honor the Father* (John 5:23).

The *fourth* mystery is the Ascension: ***Thou hast set him over the works of thy hands***. *And made him sit at his right hand in the heavenly places, far above all rule and authority and power and dominion* (Eph. 1:20–21).

The *fifth* mystery is his coming to judge: ***Thou hast subjected all things under his feet***—that is, you have made him judge over all. *Now in putting everything in subjection to him, he left nothing outside his control. As it is, we do not yet see everything in subjection to him* (Heb. 2:8)—that is, to his humanity, since *the head of Christ is God* (1 Cor. 11:3) and his feet are his humanity. [*He*] *has given him authority to execute judgment* (John 5:27). And some of those judged are good people, and certain of these, who are subject, are signified by sheep. *These sheep, what have they done?* (2 Sam. 24:17). Certain of the good are prelates, and these are signified by the oxen. *Abundant crops come by the strength of the ox* (Prov. 14:4). Some of those judged are evil, and there are three types: *All that is in the world, the lust of the flesh and the lust of the eyes and the pride of life* (1 John 2:16).

First, he describes the impure, and these are ***sheep and oxen, moreover, the beasts also of the fields***, since they take delight in subhuman things: *The beasts have rotted in their dung, the barns are destroyed* (Joel 1:17 DRB). He says this since they walk in the wide way (Matt. 7:13).

Second among the evil are the proud: ***The birds of the air***. *The birds came and devoured them* (Matt. 13:4). *Birds shall devour them with a most bitter bite* (Deut. 32:24 DRB).

Third, the greedy, ***that pass through the paths of the sea***, literally, or of the earth, figuratively. ***The wicked walk round about*** (Ps. 11:9 DRB). *From going back and forth on the earth, and from walking up and down on it* (Job 1:7).

God is wonderful in the eminence of his majesty, and this is shown through his mercy. And so he concludes his wonderment with ***O Lord our Lord, how admirable is thy name in all the earth!***

Finally, it should be known that this psalm is circular since it has the same verse at its beginning and at its end. Some psalms are partially circular because they do not repeat the entire verse but only part of it, such as ***Bless the Lord, O my soul*** (Ps. 102:1), which ends, ***in every place of his dominion*** (Ps. 102:22).

Psalm 23[8]

The Earth Is the Lord's

On Psalms 23 (206–210)

23:1 *On the first day of the week, a psalm for David.*

The earth is the Lord's and the fullness thereof: the world, and all they that dwell therein.

23:2 *For he hath founded it upon the seas and hath prepared it upon the rivers.*

23:3 *Who shall ascend into the mountain of the Lord or who shall stand in his holy place?*

23:4 *The innocent in hands and clean of heart, who hath not taken his soul in vain, nor sworn deceitfully to his neighbor.*

23:5 *He shall receive a blessing from the Lord, and mercy from God his Savior.*

23:6 *This is the generation of them that seek him, of them that seek the face of the God of Jacob.*

23:7 *Lift up your gates, O ye princes, and be ye lifted up, O eternal gates, and the King of Glory shall enter in.*

23:8 *Who is this King of Glory? the Lord who is strong and mighty, the Lord mighty in battle.*

23:9 *Lift up your gates, O ye princes, and be ye lifted up, O eternal gates: and the King of Glory shall enter in.*

23:10 *Who is this King of Glory? the Lord of hosts, he is the King of Glory.*

8. Psalm 23, so numbered in the Douay-Rheims translation used here, corresponds to Psalm 24 in most modern editions, which follow the Masoretic numbering system.

206 Having described tribulations and divine help, the Psalmist commends his helper's power.[9] There is no new title in the Hebrew, but in the Latin ***on the first day of the week [prima sabbati]*** is added.[10]

Here, it must be observed that the third commandment, as Exodus says, is *Remember the Sabbath day, to keep it holy* (20:8). God made the heaven and the earth and all that is in them in six days, and on the seventh, he rested. Therefore, we too should rest on the seventh day out of reverence. Thus, all the days of the week are called the Sabbath, just as the Lord's day is called the first day of the Sabbath: *Now after the Sabbath, toward the dawn of the first day of the week* (Matt. 28:1). And, successively, the whole week is called a Sabbath: *I fast twice in a week [sabbatum]* (Luke 18:12). So, here, on the first day of the Sabbath, the Psalmist remembers those things that pertain to the first of the Sabbath—that is, to the Lord's day.

Three things were done on this day: the creation of the world, the production of light, and the Resurrection of Christ as described in the Gospel (Matt. 28). Therefore, the Psalmist treats these things: the power of the Creator and the glory of the Resurrection. And it may be that this psalm was sung on the first day of the Sabbath.

This seems out of place.[11] Nevertheless, it should be observed that, although in David's time God was worshiped in Judah alone, recognizing that God is the God of the whole earth, David composed this psalm because he saw in a prophetic spirit that God would come to be worshiped in all the world. And he writes about this here.

This psalm is thus divided into three parts. In the *first* part, the Psalmist describes God's universal dominion. In the *second* part, he describes or shows how people draw near to God: ***Who shall ascend into the mountain of the Lord?*** In the *third* part, he prophesies the future worship of God throughout the whole world: ***Lift up your gates.***

Concerning the *first*, God's universal dominion, he does two things. *First*, he shows that the Lord's dominion is universal. *Second*, he describes its sign or cause at ***he hath founded it upon the seas.***

---

9. See Thomas Aquinas, *On Psalms* 20–21, the latter of which is included below at page 120.

10. Instead of *hebdoma*, the Latin word for 'week,' the first verse of Thomas's Latin edition features a synonymous use of the word *sabbatum* (Sabbath). Below, he explains that, because the Sabbath represents the reference point for the whole Jewish week, each day is counted and named in relation to the Sabbath. A week as a whole is also referred to as a Sabbath as representing a passage from one Sabbath to the next.

11. Thomas takes the superscription "On the first day of the week" as a possible indication that this psalm was sung liturgically on the first day of the week (i.e., Sunday). However, because this psalm celebrates both the creation and the Resurrection of Christ (the Lord's day and the first day of the week), Thomas here addresses the objection that *this* (i.e., the allusion to the Resurrection of Christ in Jewish liturgy) is *out of place* (i.e., anachronistic).

In other terms, he treats three topics in this psalm: *first*, creation; *second*, illumination, at ***Who shall ascend***; and *third*, the Resurrection or the glorification of one resurrected, at ***Lift up your gates***.

He makes two points about creation. *First*, he describes the Creator's power; *second*, he adds the reason: ***He hath founded it upon the seas***.

Now, we must observe that ***the earth*** can be understood in two ways: either as one element or as the dwelling place of human beings, and in either sense, it is under divine dominion. About the *first*: some do not extend divine providence to corruptible things but only to the heavens. *The clouds are his covert, and he doth not consider our things, and he walketh about the poles of heaven* (Job 22:14 DRB). *The Lord has forsaken the land, and the Lord does not see* (Ezek. 9:9). [To this opinion,] this psalm says, 'you lie,' since ***the earth is the Lord's***—that is, the element itself over which he has dominion.

Or he speaks of ***the earth***—that is, the Church—that is the good earth that brings forth much fruit: [*He has*] *enclosed the dust of the earth in a measure and weighed the mountains in scales and the hills in a balance* (Isa. 40:12).

But he adds, ***the fullness thereof***. *The earth was without form and void* (Gen. 1:2) since it was not yet full of trees and the other things that belong to the ornamentation of the earth, like plants and herbs.

Or he says, ***the fullness of the earth***—that is, the fullness of the grace of the Church. And this is Christ who has brought all the fullness of grace in himself. *Your countenance is full of grace* (Esther 15:14). *From his fullness have we all received* (John 1:16).

In the second way, the sphere of the earth—that is, our habitable earth—is God's. ***He shall judge the world in equity, he shall judge the people in justice*** (Ps. 9:9). *He did not create it* [the earth] *a chaos, he formed it to be inhabited* (Isa. 45:18). The center is the lowest place in the world, toward which the earth inclines by its gravity, and all other things fall toward it. And the psalm says that he ***founded the earth upon its own bases*** (103:5) since it tends there by its weight and is upon nothing since it rests upon nothing. And he says, [*He has*] *enclosed the dust of the earth in a measure* (Isa. 40:12) by its coldness and the cohesion of its parts. But because earth is an element, a mixture occurs from it and other elements. Now, earth is dry and cold, so it is neither by motion nor flux that one part is made continuous with another. It needs a moist element to contain and connect it, and so it is founded or solidified upon the waters. And because in nearly every part of the earth there is a kind of generation of waters, the whole earth can be almost said to be founded upon water. For this reason, it says, ***He hath founded it upon the seas***.

Or, just as a foundation secures a building, the water secures the earth to prevent it from separating. Furthermore, the separations in the earth cause the water, which is liquid and heavy, to flow throughout almost the entire earth.

Again, ***the earth*** designates the Church and all those dwelling in it—namely, the faithful. And we are all Christ's. As the Apostle says, *If we live, we live to the Lord, and if we die, we die to the Lord* (Rom. 14:8). Consequently, he gives here the cause of what he said above [i.e., ***the earth is the Lord's***] since ***he hath founded it upon the seas*** means to say, 'What an artisan himself makes is his.' But God made the earth and all things in it. Therefore, ***the earth . . . and the fullness thereof*** are his.

But some say that the providence of God does not extend to earthly things. On the contrary, the relative arrangement of the waters to the earth is a sign of great providence since the lighter elements should be above the heavier ones. Therefore, just as the air encircles the water, the water should encircle the earth. And the philosophers give many reasons for this. However, the cause is divine providence, ensuring that there would be a habitation for humans and animals. Hence, when he described the creation of things in the beginning, Moses reported that the earth was first unformed: *The earth was without form*—that is, unformed—*and void* of trees. Thus, he described it as encircled or covered with water, *and the darkness*—water—*was upon the face of the deep*—that is, over the earth—*and the spirit of God*—the air—*was moving over the waters* (Gen. 1:2).

Or *The earth was without form*—that is, unseen under the waters—so it follows, *Let the waters . . . be gathered together . . . and let the dry land appear* (Gen. 1:9), as if to say, 'Since the earth is first in the order of the elements, it was made to rest upon the waters by divine providence, so that humans and animals could live on it, but let the waters, nevertheless, occupy the earth insofar as they continue as the seas.' Hence, he says, ***he hath founded it upon the seas***—that is, beside them—as is said in other places: ***Upon the rivers of Babylon***—that is, beside the river of Babylon—***there we sat*** (Ps. 136:1).

He hath founded it—that is, establishing it as firm so the sea would not overtake it: *I set bars and doors* [for the sea], *and said, "Thus far shall you come, and no farther, and here shall your proud waves be stayed"* (Job 38:10–11). *I placed the sand as the bound for the sea, a perpetual barrier which it cannot pass* (Jer. 5:22).

And hath prepared it upon the rivers—that is, next to the rivers—and he says, ***prepared***, not founded, since its preparation requires that a river water it: ***The river of God is filled with water, thou hast prepared their food, for so is its preparation. Fill up plentifully the streams thereof*** (Ps. 64:10–11).

Or it was the Church that was ***founded . . . upon the seas***—that is, upon tribulations. ***Wonderful are the surges of the sea*** (Ps. 92:4). And it is ***upon the***

rivers—that is, the persecutions that prepared the Church for the crowns of martyrs. Or it is ***upon the seas***—that is, upon sorrows—but his consolation he has prepared, rivers of consolations: ***The stream of the river maketh the city of God joyful*** (Ps. 45:5).

207 ***Who shall ascend into the mountain?*** It is as if to say, 'It is great. How will anyone ascend to it?' *What is man, said I, that he can follow the King, his maker?* (Eccles. 2:12 DRB). He thus teaches how to reach its height.

He does two things. *First,* he advances a question and, *second,* an answer at ***the innocent in hands.*** In his question, he asks two things: one about the way or movement: ***Who shall ascend?*** and another about the end: ***Who shall stand in his holy place?***

The mountain here signifies the height of divine justice or majesty: ***Thy justice is as the mountains of God*** (Ps. 35:7). Therefore, the mountain is the height of the divine majesty, or the sublimity of Christ, who is called a mountain: *It shall come to pass in the latter days that the mountain of the house of the Lord shall be established as the highest of the mountains and shall be raised above the hills* (Isa. 2:2).

Thus, ***who shall ascend*** so far as to come to Christ and God? The holy ones who prepare ascents in their heart, as the Psalmist says. Again, ***who shall be able to stand*** where he is, which is the ***holy place***, the place of glory? *The place of our sanctification . . . the hope of Israel* (Jer. 17:12–13 DRB). *The place on which you are standing is holy ground* (Exod. 3:5). This is to say, 'Who can stand there?' But in another place, he says, ***Our feet were standing in thy courts, O Jerusalem*** (Ps. 121:2). So hereafter, the answer is given.

208 ***The innocent in hands***: To the question ***Who shall ascend?*** he presents this answer, *first,* in general terms and, *second,* specifically: ***This is the generation.*** Addressing the *first* point, he does two things. *First,* he identifies the merit [of ***the innocent***] and, *second,* their reward at ***He shall receive.***

Concerning merit, one sort belongs to innocent action, and so he says, ***innocent in hands***: *He delivers the innocent man; you will be delivered through the cleanness of your hands* (Job 22:30). ***I have walked in my innocence*** (Ps. 25:1).

Another belongs to the purity of the heart, and relating to this innocence, he explains that a pure heart is guarded from inner concupiscence. Thus, he says, ***clean of heart***: *Blessed are the pure in heart, for they shall see God* (Matt. 5:8). Again, he is guarded from every desire for temporal things ***who hath not taken his soul in vain***—that is, who has not poured it into vain things nor vainly exults in his virtues nor allows his sensuality to go so far as to consent to sin. Jerome has, ***who has not exalted his soul in vain***, since some become proud because of the purity of their heart:[12] ***Lord, my heart is not exalted*** (Ps. 130:1). Likewise, it pertains to the truth of the lips, so it follows, ***nor sworn deceitfully to his neighbor.*** *Love no false oath* (Zech. 8:17).

209 ***He shall receive a blessing***: Here, he describes the reward. Now, a reward consists in two things: obtaining good things: ***He shall receive a blessing***—that is, good things—***from God.*** *Blessings are on the head of the righteous* (Prov. 10:6). *To this you have been called, that you may obtain a blessing* (1 Pet. 3:9). Also, it consists in deliverance from evils, so he says, ***mercy from God his Savior***, who delivers from misery.

Or we can take it in another way: The one who is ***innocent in hands*** can approach since he is able to be innocent because ***he shall receive a blessing from the Lord and mercy*** since he avoids sins. *It depends not upon man's will or exertion, but upon God's mercy* (Rom. 9:16).

Subsequently, he shows this way in general: ***This is the generation of them that seek*** the Lord—as if to say, 'In general, there are many of this sort, and these are the whole generation of those seeking God who are innocent.' Therefore, Scripture speaks about the good as if they are one generation. *This generation*—namely, of the good—*will not pass away* (Matt. 24:34).

He describes this generation in two ways: from its eagerness since it seeks nothing except God, so he says, ***of them that seek him***, even in this life. *Seek the Lord while he may be found* (Isa. 55:6). To what end? That they may come to the vision of him, so it follows: ***them that seek the face of the God of Jacob.*** *I have seen God face to face, and yet my life is preserved* (Gen. 32:30).

210 ***Lift up your gates***: This is the third part of the psalm, which prophesies how it would come to pass that God would be worshiped throughout the whole world, as the literal sense explains.

God is said to dwell in people by faith: *Christ may dwell in your hearts through faith* (Eph. 3:17); and through charity: *He who abides in love abides in God, and God abides in him* (1 John 4:16). Likewise, one is said to enter who begins to be where he was not before. Therefore, God enters into us when we begin to have faith in him.

Formerly, the whole world lacked faith in God, and this was the case because of two obstacles: the decrees of princes and ancient custom. The *first* obstacle was present because individual cities promulgated laws about idolatry and established particular gods. *Second*, this worship became rather ingrained; in this way, they were accustomed to ministering to demons. Likewise, angels were worshiped, whom they called the host of heaven. These obstacles were the ***gates*** or doors which, being closed, prohibited entry into the house.

12. The version Thomas ascribes to Jerome here is closest to the Hebrew Psalter.

Now, he makes three points. *First,* he announces what will come to pass. *Second,* he proposes a question. *Third,* he gives a response.

Therefore, he says, ***O ye princes***—that is, 'O evil persons' or 'O demons'—***lift up your gates***—that is, 'take away the obstacles you placed there to stop people from drawing near to God.' Jerome has ***elevate***—as if to say, 'remove': ***Thou that liftest me up from the gates of death, that I may declare all thy praises in the gates of the daughter of Zion*** (Ps. 9:15).

O eternal gates—that is, 'eternal and ancient obstacles'—***be ye lifted up***—that is, 'be removed.' ***Thou enlightenest wonderfully from the everlasting hills*** (Ps. 75:5). As if to say, 'You! Remove the ancient obstructions to human hearts, and then he, the ***King of Glory***, will enter the world through faith, charity, and worship.'

Alternatively, it can be said that there are two types of ***gates***: some are evil ones that shut off access to life, and others are good ones by which the way of life is opened: ***Open*** (Ps. 117:19) ***the ways of life*** (Ps. 15:11)—that is, of justice. The evil gates are sins, but the good ones are virtues.

Therefore, he says, ***Lift up your gates, O ye princes***—that is, 'open them, remove sin, and obtain ***the eternal***'—the eternal gifts from the eternal God. ***Be ye lifted up*** in your hearts, and ***the King of Glory shall enter in***. He speaks prophetically since, from the beginning, not all immediately believed, but some doubted. As if to say, 'In whom do you desire to believe and whom do you desire to obey? Surely not the God of the Jews?' *I do not know the Lord, and moreover I will not let Israel go* (Exod. 5:2). He shows this unbelief when he says, ***Who is this King of Glory?*** And he responds, ***the Lord who is strong and mighty.***

Any king appears glorious in three ways. *First,* he acquires glory through great strength, so the psalm says, ***strong.*** *The hand of the valiant shall bear rule* (Prov. 12:24 DRB). *If it is a contest of strength, behold him* (Job 9:19).

Second, he appears glorious by his power, and the psalm shows this when it says, ***the Lord mighty***, since he is most powerful in ruling. *God is mighty and does not despise any* (Job 36:5). *His dominion is an everlasting dominion* (Dan. 7:14).

Third, he appears glorious because he is a good warrior; hence, it says, ***the Lord mighty in battle***, since he conquered death and the devil in all things. *The Lion of the tribe of Judah . . . has conquered* (Rev. 5:5).

Or he is ***strong*** in his own nature, ***mighty*** in jurisdiction over his own, and ***mighty*** against adversaries. Therefore, when he says a second time, ***Lift up your gates, O ye princes, and be ye lifted up, O eternal gates, and the King of Glory shall enter in***, we should understand that this is a repetition so his hearers may not disagree about who this powerful one is.

Alternatively, the first phrase refers to the princes—that is, the demons—but this second one refers to the good angels who, too, were formerly worshiped by human beings for their dignity, not because they desired it from those who worshiped them. [*They*] *worshiped all the host of heaven* (2 Kings 17:16). As if to say, 'Remove the obstacles on account of which people worship you.' And so he says here, ***The Lord of hosts, he is the King of glory.***

In the Gloss, there is another explanation.[13] Christ descends to hell and ascends into heaven, and here he prophesies these two things. *First*, he admonishes the infernal regions to open, so he says, ***Lift up***, O infernal princes, open your gates, ***and be ye lifted up . . . and the King of Glory shall enter in.*** But, when the demons ask, ***Who is this King of Glory?*** he responds, 'He who is ***strong and mighty in battle*** against you.'

Second, he admonishes the citizens to open ***the gates*** of paradise for us. So Christ responds as though with the voice of a herald, bearing the repayment, directing his voice to heaven, saying, ***Lift up***—that is, open—***your gates, O ye*** heavenly ***princes . . . and the King of Glory shall enter in.***

And to those asking, he says, ***the Lord of hosts, he is the King of Glory.*** Now, it should be observed that, as Dionysius says, we are not to understand this in such a way as to imply that the angels were ignorant of the mystery of the Incarnation; rather, they were marveling when they said, ***Who is this King of Glory?*** since the glory of Christ surpasses all thought.[14] For sometimes Christ himself teaches about himself through Scripture. *It is I, announcing vindication, mighty to save* (Isa. 63:1).

Now here, not he, but others—that is, angels—respond, calling him ***the Lord of hosts***, since some angels receive illumination immediately from God.[15] *I saw the Lord sitting upon a throne, high and lifted up; and his train filled the temple* (Isa. 6:1). From these, other intermediate and lower angels receive it, and to these lower orders is this response given by the higher.

---

13. Peter Lombard, *Magna glossatura*.

14. Pseudo-Dionysius, *Celestial Hierarchy* 4.4.

15. Pseudo-Dionysius, *Celestial Hierarchy* 8.2.

Psalm 32[16]

Spiritual Joy and Praise

On Psalms 32 (306–323)

32:1 *Unto the end. A psalm for David.*

Rejoice in the Lord, O ye just; praise becometh the upright.

32:2 *Give praise to the Lord on the harp; sing to him with the psaltery, the instrument of ten strings.*

32:3 *Sing to him a new canticle, sing well unto him with a loud noise.*

32:4 *For the word of the Lord is right, and all his works are done with faithfulness.*

32:5 *He loveth mercy and judgment; the earth is full of the mercy of the Lord.*

32:6 *By the word of the Lord the heavens were established; and all the power of them by the spirit of his mouth:*

32:7 *Gathering together the waters of the sea, as in a vessel, laying up the depths in storehouses.*

32:8 *Let all the earth fear the Lord and let all the inhabitants of the world be in awe of him.*

32:9 *For he spoke, and they were made; he commanded, and they were created.*

32:10 *The Lord bringeth to naught the counsels of nations, and he rejecteth the devices of people and casteth away the counsels of princes.*

32:11 *But the counsel of the Lord standeth for ever: the thoughts of his heart to all generations.*

16. Psalm 32, so numbered in the Douay-Rheims translation used here, corresponds to Psalm 33 in most modern editions, which follow the Masoretic numbering system.

32:12 ***Blessed is the nation whose God is the Lord, the people whom he hath chosen for his inheritance.***

32:13 ***The Lord hath looked from heaven: he hath beheld all the sons of men.***

32:14 ***From his habitation which he hath prepared, he hath looked upon all that dwell on the earth.***

32:15 ***He who hath made the hearts of every one of them, who understandeth all their works.***

32:16 ***The king is not saved by a great army, nor shall the giant be saved by his own great strength.***

32:17 ***Vain is the horse for safety; neither shall he be saved by the abundance of his strength.***

32:18 ***Behold, the eyes of the Lord are on them that fear him and on them that hope in his mercy.***

32:19 ***To deliver their souls from death and feed them in famine.***

32:20 ***Our soul waiteth for the Lord, for he is our helper and protector.***

32:21 ***For in him our heart shall rejoice, and in his holy name, we have trusted.***

32:22 ***Let thy mercy, O Lord, be upon us, as we have hoped in thee.***

306 The title is not new. It is ***Unto the end. A psalm for David.***[17] In the preceding psalm, the Psalmist treated his justification;[18] now in this one, he treats the dignity of the just and does two things in this connection. *First*, he exhorts the just to spiritual praise. *Second*, he expresses their dignity, at ***Blessed is the nation.***

17. The superscription "Unto the end" (Lat. *in finem*; Gk. *eis to telos*; Heb. *lamnasseah*) appears before some fifty-five of the psalms. Its precise meaning remains a matter of ongoing debate among scholars. In his commentary *On Psalms* 4.19 (not included in this collection), Thomas interprets it Christologically: "It is clear that 'unto the end' should be understood to mean 'unto Christ.'"

18. See Thomas Aquinas, *On Psalms* 31 (featured at page 111 of this collection).

He does two things in regard to the first. *First*, he exhorts them to spiritual joy and praise. *Second*, he gives a reason for gladness and praise, at ***For the word of the Lord is right.*** He does two things touching spiritual joy and praise. *First*, he exhorts them to joy and praise. *Second*, he explains the manner of doing this, at ***Give praise to the Lord.***

He does two things regarding this exhortation. *First*, he gives the exhortation. *Second*, he assigns its reason: ***praise becometh the upright.*** For he had said, ***I said, "I will confess" . . . and thou hast forgiven . . . for this shall every one that is holy pray*** (Ps. 31:5–6). Therefore, ***O ye just***, who have been justified, ***rejoice in the Lord***, not in the world. 'Otherwise, you are not just, for he is not just who does not rejoice in justice.'

Now, God himself is the just one, and he is justice. ***The Lord is just*** (Ps. 10:8). And so, ***Rejoice in the Lord, O ye just.*** *I will rejoice in the Lord, I will joy in the God of my salvation* (Hab. 3:18). But why does he say, ***Rejoice in the Lord, O ye just***, and not, 'Rejoice in the Lord, everyone'? The reason is that ***praise***—namely, of God—***becometh the upright.*** Therefore, we must consider whether they are just and how praise becomes them.

A thing is not called just unless it is conformed to a rule and measure. Now, the divine justice and will is the measure and rule of the human will. Therefore, those who do not have rightly ordered affection cannot praise God well since they do not desire to conform their will to the divine will, but instead they want the divine will to conform to theirs. And so, God does many things of which they do not approve. But those who are adapted to the will of God rejoice in both prosperity and adversity. And so, he says it is ***united praise*** since they praise in regard to everything, not merely a few things.[19] So they praise unanimously. *A hymn of praise is not fitting on the lips of a sinner* (Sir. 15:9). *The pride and glory of the survivors of Israel* (Isa. 4:2).

307 Afterward, when he says, ***Give praise to the Lord on the harp***, he describes the manner of praise and rejoicing. Now, we should observe that the primary intention of praising God is to incline and direct a person's affection toward God. Now, the harmony of music changes human affection. So, Pythagoras, seeing that the young were maddened by the Phrygian melody, changed the musical mode so that the souls of those enraged adolescents could be brought back to a state of mental peace, as Boethius says in the introduction to his *On Music*.[20]

---

19. "United praise" literally translates the Vulgate's *collaudatio* (*con-* + *laudo*), the corporate sense of which is absent from the Douay-Rheims' rendering: "Praise becometh the upright."

20. Boethius, introduction to *On Music*. The story of Pythagoras using music to calm frenzied young people can be found also in Quintilian, *Institutio Oratoria* 1.11.32 and Sextus Empiricus, *Against the Musicians* 7.

Therefore, it is understood that in every type of worship, some musical harmonies are practiced to uplift the human soul to God.

Now, this harmony was usually practiced in two ways: sometimes with musical instruments and sometimes with singing voices. He shows the *first* way first, ***on the harp***, and he shows the *second* second, at ***sing well unto him.***

Now, human affection is directed by instruments and musical harmonies in three ways. Sometimes rectitude and firmness of soul are instilled, sometimes one is snatched up to the heights, and sometimes it brings sweetness and rejoicing.

In regard to this, the Philosopher in his *Politics* wanted to institute three categories of song.[21] The *first* is the Dorian song, which includes the first and second tone, as some desire. The *second* is the Phrygian, which is the third tone. The *third* is the Hypolydian song, which is the fifth and sixth tones. Others were invented afterward. And this division can be applied also to instruments since certain instruments belong to the first, like the flute and horn; some belong to the second, like the organ; and some belong to the third, like the psaltery and harp: ***The pleasant psaltery with the harp*** (Ps. 80:3).[22]

But since the Psalmist hopes that this will lead to rejoicing, he mentions none but these two, the psaltery and the harp. It is true that *all these things happened to them in figure* (1 Cor. 10:11 DRB), so these instruments were used not only for this purpose but also as figures.

The harp has a deep sound signifying the praise that surges up from the depths—that is, from earthly things—while the psaltery has a high sound and signifies the praise that belongs to heavenly goods. Therefore, he says, ***of ten strings***, since the ten precepts of the Decalogue, in which the whole spiritual teaching consists, are signified by them.

308 Afterward, when he says, ***Sing to him a new canticle***, he treats the song sung with the human voice. It should be observed that, according to the literal sense, there is a twofold way of singing. For one way is with a simple song, and another is with harmony. He touches on the *first* when he says, ***a new canticle***, and the *second* at ***with a loud voice.***

According to a spiritual understanding, people should rejoice for two reasons—namely, for the goods of grace received and for the goods of glory for which they hope. We are renewed through the first goods. *Be renewed in the spirit of your minds* (Eph. 4:23). *We too might walk in newness of life* (Rom. 6:4). Therefore, he sings ***a new canticle*** who rejoices in God because of the renewal of grace. *They sing a new song* (Rev. 14:3). He truly sings ***well . . . with a loud***

---

21. Aristotle, *Politics* 8.5–7.

22. The psaltery is an ancient ten-stringed instrument similar in design and sound to a dulcimer.

voice who sings a song about the goods of glory, and a person expresses in words the song that he conceives in his heart.

Or it is ***in jubilation*** or ***in rejoicing***, according to Jerome. Now, there is a rejoicing of ineffable gladness that words cannot express, but ***voice*** signifies joys immense in extent. Now, those things that cannot be expressed are the goods of glory: *What no eye has seen, nor ear heard* (1 Cor. 2:9). And so he says, ***sing*** [***psallite***: play the psalter] ***well unto him*** in jubilation, since they cannot be expressed in singing.[23]

Now, you may say that there were musical instruments in the Old Testament, as well as vocal song. Why, then, does the Church dismiss the former but accept the latter?

Mystically, the twofold reason is given: [the musical instruments] were figurative. Accordingly, the reason is that God is praised by mind and voice but not by instruments. Another reason comes from the words of the Philosopher, who said that it is against wisdom that people be instructed in lyres and music since they would occupy their souls in these works, but there should be simple music so that they may be drawn from bodily things and brought to the divine praises.[24]

309 Next, when he says, ***For the word of the Lord is right***, he gives the reason for rejoicing and praise. Now, the reason for praise and rejoicing is twofold. *One* concerns God, from whom rejoicing comes. The *second* concerns his effect, at ***the word of the Lord***.

He makes three points about this. *First*, he describes what concerns God. And first: ***For the word of the Lord***—that is, his instruction—***is right***. Psalm 118:105: ***Thy word is a lamp to my feet***. Or it is his promise. *All the words of my mouth are righteous; there is nothing twisted or crooked in them. They are all straight to him who understands* (Prov. 8:8–9).

Second is that ***all his works are done with faithfulness***—that is, they are faithful. ***The Lord is faithful in all his words and holy in all his works*** (Ps. 144:13). There is great rejoicing when a faithful person is found: *A faithful man who can find?* (Prov. 20:6).

Or he says ***with faithfulness*** [***in fide***] because the works of God have good merits. Now, nothing is meritorious unless done in faith, since *without faith it is impossible to please him* (Heb. 11:6). Or, ***the word of the Lord is right, and***

23. The Douay-Rheims translation of Psalm 32:3 obscures Thomas's interpretive move here, which highlights the Vulgate text's injunction to praise God both in vocal singing (*cantate*) and in the playing of a psalter (*psallite . . . in vociferatione*). A more suitable translation would be "Sing a new song to him; play well a loud song for him on the psalter." For Thomas, the injunction to play the psalter alludes to the ineffability of the joys or goods of glory (heavenly beatitude), which are so great that words, even when sung, cannot express them.

24. Aristotle, *Politics* 8.6.

all his works are done with faithfulness. But in whom are they? They are ***with faithfulness***—that is, in the faithful since the works of God and right words do not appear in the unfaithful.

Third is that the Lord ***loveth mercy and judgment.*** He makes two main points about this. *First,* he shows the affection of God when he says, ***the Lord loveth. Second,*** he manifests it by a sign, at ***the earth is full of the mercy of the Lord.***

Among all the things from the Lord that cause rejoicing, there are two in particular: mercy and justice. *Mercy and truth preserve the king* (Prov. 20:28 DRB). For through justice, those subordinate to him are defended. Take away justice, and no one will be secure or joyful. Likewise, without mercy, all would fear and would not love. This can be understood to be true about God when he says, ***He loveth mercy and judgment.*** For he loves them in himself, since they are found in all his works. ***All the ways of the Lord are mercy and truth*** (Ps. 24:10).

Likewise, he loves them in each one: *He has showed you, O man, what is good; and what does the Lord require of you but to do justice, and to love kindness* (Mic. 6:8). And so he says, ***rejoice***, because truly God ***loveth mercy***, for ***the earth is full of the mercy of the Lord.*** Behold, it is manifested through a sign. For the whole fullness of the earth comes forth from the mercy of God, since the earth is full not only of temporal but of spiritual goods, and it is especially so since the coming of Christ. *They were all filled with the Holy Spirit* (Acts 2:4). All these come from the mercy of God. *It depends not upon man's will or exertion but upon God's mercy* (Rom. 9:16). Therefore, he says, ***the earth***, and not heaven, since there is no misery in heaven and so mercy is not needed, but the earth, where human beings exist, requires much mercy as it is full of many miseries.

310 Afterward, when he says, ***By the word of the Lord***, the cause of rejoicing is described concerning the divine effects. Moses made mention of three things in the beginning of creation: the heaven, the water, and the earth. *In the beginning God created the heavens and the earth*, and a little later: *The Spirit of God was moving over the face of the waters* (Gen. 1:1, 2). Therefore, following this, the Psalmist speaks, *first*, of the effect of God in the heavens; *second*, in the waters, ***gathering together***; *third*, on the earth: ***Let all the earth fear the Lord.***

Therefore, he says, ***By the word of the Lord the heavens were established.*** According to the Gloss, this can be explained literally or mystically.[25] And these words of the Lord are considered in each sense: the ***Lord***, the ***word***, and the ***spirit of his mouth.*** The ***Lord*** is a name of power, and power is appropriated to the Father. The ***word*** is a concept of the mind, so it is said to be wisdom gen-

25. Peter Lombard, *Magna glossatura* (PL 191:910).

erated. And the Word is the Son. The ***spirit*** is the Holy Spirit. Now, it is called the ***spirit of his mouth*** because the mouth is appropriated to the word, so this expression should be read as though he said, 'the spirit of the word,' since he is the Spirit of the Son and of the truth. And although the works of the Trinity are indivisible in regard to the divinity, since *whatever* [*the Father*] *does, that the Son does likewise* (John 5:19), this is spoken according to appropriation.[26]

Now, there are two marvels in heaven: namely, its perpetual being, since it is incorruptible, and its power, through which the whole lower world is changed—that is, made hot in summer and cold in winter. Now, the perpetuity of heaven relies on its natural form, for the forms of the elements are particular and they do not fulfill the whole potency of the matter, so their matter remains in potency to another form. But the form of heaven totally fulfills the potency of its matter. (But artificial forms come from the forms of artisans.) Now, the form conceived in the heart of the Father is the Word. Therefore, the formation of all things is attributed to the Word, so he says, ***By the word of the Lord the heavens were established.***[27]

Now, the power of the heavens is in their moving. Every later movement is derived from an earlier as a cause. The first motion in things that are voluntary is the motion of love since every motion in those things that have volition is a voluntary movement. And so, Dionysius says that the divine love does not allow him to be without generation, but it moves him to act.[28] Therefore, it is necessary that the power of the heavens comes from the Spirit, and so he says, ***and all the power of them by the spirit of his mouth.***

Mystically, the apostles are understood by the heavens; they were established by the word of the Lord—namely Christ or the Son of the Lord—and this is his exhortation and teaching. *I have prayed for you that your faith may not fail* (Luke 22:32). Likewise, their power was established through the Holy Spirit. *Stay in the city until you are clothed with power from on high* (Luke 24:49).

311 Afterward, when he says, ***Gathering together the waters of the sea,*** he shows God's effect on the waters. Now, in the waters, there are two marvels to be considered. One is that the waters are gathered together in one part of the

---

26. "Appropriation" here names a rule of theological predication by which we may identify an attribute with one person of the Trinity in particular while recognizing that it must belong to the other persons as well, given the common essence shared by all three persons. Or to put it in the terms of Gilles Emery, "Appropriation is the name for the theological procedure in which a feature belonging to the nature of God, common to all three persons, is specially ascribed to one of the divine persons." Gilles Emery, "Appropriation," in *The Trinitarian Theology of St. Thomas Aquinas*, trans. Francesca Aran Murphy (Oxford: Oxford University Press, 2007), 312–337, at 312.

27. Cf. Thomas Aquinas, *Commentary on John* 1.2 (featured at page 47 of *Thomas Aquinas: Selected Commentaries on the New Testament*), ed. Jason C. Paone [Park Ridge, IL: Word on Fire Academic, 2022].

28. Pseudo-Dionysius, *Divine Names* 4.14.

earth and do not occupy its whole surface, which is marvelous for two reasons. The *first* is that in the natural order, water would encompass the whole earth, just as air encompasses the water. Likewise, the sea is deeper than the earth. The *second* is that, although the water continually evaporates through the heat of the sun, it remains in the same quantity.

And so he says two things about the fact that they are gathered together into one by the command of God. *I placed the sand as the bound for the sea, a perpetual barrier which it cannot pass; though the waves toss, they cannot prevail, though they roar, they cannot pass over it* (Jer. 5:22). *Who shut in the sea with doors* (Job 38:8).

And so he says, ***Gathering together the waters of the sea, as in a vessel.*** Waters gathered together in a vessel quiver and rise but do not flow out since they are held in by the walls of the vessel, so the waters gathered together in the sea swell but do not flow out because they are contained by the divine power. *Let the waters . . . be gathered together* (Gen. 1:9).

Another marvel is that they continually evaporate but are not diminished. And so, as certain philosophers say, naturally, all the waters would be dried up by the power of the sun.[29] And so, against this, he says, ***laying up the depths*** [***abyssos***] ***in storehouses*** [***thesauris***].

The depths [***abyssus***], according to Augustine, means the impassible depth of the water, and this has a twofold interpretation.[30] It comes from *a-*, which means 'without,' and *basi*, which is a foundation. So it is as though it is without foundation and without radiance since the deep is obscure.

Three things are conveyed by 'storehouse' [*thesaurus*]: *first*, 'storehouse' names some great quantity of gold; and what is deposited in a storehouse is kept safe—whence it is named as though it were an 'enclosure for gold' [*theca auri*]. It is deposited, moreover, in order to be withdrawn for use.[31] These are all true of the depths since in them there is the immense abundance or multitude of waters. *Second*, in the depths, water is kept safe, and it does not flow away. *Third*, it is drawn out for use when vapors are raised from it and the rains are generated and water the earth. ***The fountains of waters appeared*** (Ps. 17:16).

29. In his *Commentary on Aristotle's Meteorology* (2.1.142), Thomas ascribes this view to the fifth-century (BC) natural philosopher Anaxagoras and the third-century (AD) doxographer Diogenes Laërtius who wrote about him in his *Lives of Eminent Philosophers* 2.3.

30. Augustine, *Expositions on the Psalms* 103.5–6.

31. The Douay-Rheims translation of the Vulgate's *thesaurus* as "storehouse" here obscures Thomas's interpretation of the passage. The primary sense of *thesaurus* is 'treasury'—the kind of storehouse used specifically for storing objects of value. Thomas's interpretation takes this sense for granted as is especially clear in the folk etymology that he offers where he relates *thesaurus* to *theca auri* ('enclosure for gold').

Mystically, it can be explained in two ways: about the good and about the evil. It is explained about the good so that by ***the waters of the sea*** we understand the people. *The waters that you saw . . . are peoples and multitudes and nations and tongues* (Rev. 17:15). Therefore, it is as though the many waters of the people of this world gather together in the Church ***as in a vessel.***

Now, the Church is compared to a vessel because of its unity and because a vessel is made from the skin of a dead animal. Through this, it is implied that some come to the Church to mortify their members, which are upon the earth. For so the apostles, ***the heavens***, were strengthened, and by them, the people were gathered together into the Church.

He is ***laying up the depths***—that is, the profundity of the divine senses—***in his storehouses*** of the Sacred Scriptures. *Abundance of salvation, wisdom, and knowledge; the fear of the Lord is his treasure* (Isa. 33:6). Or those who previously were ***the depths***—namely, sinners, sunk deep and obscured by the darkness of vices—he makes ***the storehouses*** of the gold of the Church. Paul is a great storehouse of the Church, and so are Matthew and Magdalene, who were at first like the depths.

Now, among the evil, the water of the sea is understood to be the troubles of this life. ***The waters are come even into my soul*** (Ps. 68:2). Now, God strengthens the heavens [the apostles] but does not take away weaknesses from them since they are strengthened by interior grace, which does not remove exterior weaknesses. And so he says that he gathers their troubles—namely, those of the heavens—***in a vessel***—that is, in their bodies—***laying up the depths***—that is, the persecutors of the Church—***in a storehouse*** since he does not give them the freedom to rage against the Church as they desire.

312 *Third*, when he says, ***Let all the earth fear the Lord***, he shows God's effect on the earth.[32] *First*, he gives an admonition; *second*, he shows God's effect on the earth, at ***He spoke***.

Concerning the *first* point, he does two things. *First*, he gives an admonition; *second*, he explains it, at ***let all the inhabitants of the world be in awe of him***. Therefore, he says, ***Let all the earth fear the Lord.*** But why does he give an admonition here where he has been speaking only about the earth—about things effected by other means in which he uses no admonition? The reason is that all other creatures obey God at his nod except the earthly human being, and so he says, ***Let all the earth***—that is, every earthly human being—***fear the Lord.*** *Fear God, and keep his commandments, for this is the whole duty of man* (Eccles. 12:13). This speech is metonymic, and thus, the container is taken

32. God's effect on the earth here is third in the sequence, summarized in paragraph 310 above, of God's three creative effects in the heavens, in the waters (paragraph 311), and on the earth.

for the thing it contains, so when he says, ***earth***, he means the inhabitants of the earth.

Second, he explains the warning, saying, ***let all the inhabitants . . . be in awe of him***, with the good awe of the servants of God, since he alone evokes it. *No one can come to me unless the Father who sent me draws him* (John 6:44).

313 Afterward, when he says, ***He spoke and they were made***, he shows the twofold effect on the earth. *First* is the effect of creation, *second*, that of governance, at: ***The Lord bringeth to naught.*** Now, in creation, two things should be considered: its formation and creation itself. Both are found here. *First*, he shows its formation when he says, ***He spoke, and they were made.*** Creation itself is *second*, when he adds, ***He commanded, and they were created.***

Therefore, he says, ***He spoke.*** Augustine says, *The whole formation is through the word, since the created thing is related to God as the artifact to the artisan. So, just as every artificial form is conceived in the mind of the artisan, so the forms of all things are conceived from the divine word.*[33] So ***he spoke***—that is, he conceived the Word eternally—and all things were made according to it, as if to say, 'He generated the Word in which he made all things.' And such is the formation.

Second is creation, since ***he commanded and they were created.*** To speak is to bring forth a formed expression. To command is to bring forth a warning or simple emanation. So, to command implies the creation of the unformed matter. *His word is full of power* (Eccles. 8:4 DRB). Mystically: ***He spoke, and they were made*** by the seeds of grace; ***He commanded*** in the work of truth. ***Thou shalt send forth thy spirit*** (Ps. 103:30).

314 In this he truly speaks of the work of governance. ***The Lord bringeth to naught the counsels of nations.*** While remaining stable, he changes all. *First*, he describes the changing of all, *second*, his own stability, at ***The counsel of the Lord.*** Concerning the inhabitants of the world, it should be noticed that some are small, and some are great, and both are changed.

Regarding the small, he says, ***The Lord bringeth to naught.*** Here, he touches on two things: the intention that concerns the end and the counsel that concerns those things that lead to the end. And this is changed not according to the counsel taken but as God disposes. *Take counsel together, but it will come to nought* (Isa. 8:10). And this is what he says: ***The Lord bringeth to naught the counsels of nations.*** And he specially brings to naught the counsels of those wanting to destroy the law of Christ. ***And he rejecteth the devices of peoples***, of human knowledge, for such the Lord intends to condemn.

---

33. Thomas cites book 7 of Augustine's *The Literal Meaning of Genesis* as the source of this quote. The passages that best correspond to the quote, however, can be found in 2.6.12–13 and 1.8.13. In his *Commentary on John* (1.3.77), Thomas cites Augustine's *The Trinity* (6.10.11) in connection with a very similar point.

In regard to the great, he says, ***and he casteth away the counsels of princes***, as if to say, 'I cast away not only the counsels of the peoples but of the princes since there is in them no power to bring about the intended effect but rather in the divine ordinance.' *He leads counselors away stripped, and judges he makes fools* (Job 12:17).

315 Afterward, when he says, ***But the counsel of the Lord standeth forever***, the stability of God is described in that his counsel stands, and his thoughts continue. But is there counsel in God? It seems that there is not since it implies doubt.

I respond. It must be said that counsel is understood in one way in God and in another way in us. For knowledge in us requires discursive thinking, but in God, it is certitude. So the counsel that is in us involves questioning, but when it is said about God, it implies ordering of all in respect to the appropriate end. *My counsel shall stand, and I will accomplish my purpose* (Isa. 46:10). *If* [this plan or undertaking] *is of God, you will not be able to overthrow them* (Acts 5:39).

The thoughts of his heart—that is, the intention of his will—remain since even if he changes his sentence, he does not change his counsel: *For my thoughts are not your thoughts, neither are your ways my ways* (Isa. 55:8).

316 ***Blessed is the nation whose God is the Lord.*** Above, he exhorted the just to rejoice; here, he describes their dignity, and he makes two points regarding it. *First*, he describes their dignity; *second*, he gives evidence for it, at ***from heaven***.

The dignity of the saints is the greatest since they alone have attained what all persons naturally desire. If one or only a few people were to attain the one thing that all desire to attain, this would be a great dignity. Now, all desire to grasp happiness, which the just alone reach, since they will obtain it perfectly in the future, but now only in its beginning and in hope. Therefore, the dignity of the just is great.

He touches upon two aspects of this happiness that begins here and will be perfect in the future—namely, its matter and cause—at ***the people***. Therefore, he says, ***Blessed is the nation***. Different people think different things about happiness. And there are different philosophical sects according to these different opinions.[34] For some place it in bodily goods, as Epicurus.[35] Some place it in the works of the active life, as the Stoics.[36] Some place it in the contemplation of truth, as the Peripatetics.[37]

---

34. See Augustine, *City of God* 19.1.

35. See Epicurus, *Letter to Menoeceus* 7.

36. The Stoics, representing arguably the most influential school of Hellenistic philosophy, famously argued against Aristotle, claiming that "virtue is the sole good" and "all that is needed for happiness." Cicero relates these and other famous Stoic sayings in his *Stoic Paradoxes*.

37. "The Peripatetics" names the broad tradition of thought deriving from Aristotle and his school, which famously gathered at the Athenian Lyceum. 'Peripatetic' transliterates the Greek *peripatētikós* (walker), which may allude either to the walkways (*peripatoi*) of the Lyceum

It is vain to seek happiness in that which is below us since happiness is above us. Now, what is above us is God. Therefore, human happiness consists in clinging to God. For each thing is perfect if it clings to its own proper good. Now, God is the proper good of a human being: ***It is good for me to adhere to my God*** (Ps. 72:28).

Now, someone can cling to God with his mind—namely, with the intellect and will—but not with the senses since these are held in common with the beasts. Therefore, a person clings to God in two ways: through intellectual contemplation and knowing and through the affection of loving. And these are imperfect while on the way but will be perfect in the fatherland. So here, happiness is imperfect; there it will be perfect. So, he says, ***Blessed is the nation.*** And why? Because ***the Lord is their God***; that is, it is joined to God with its mind. Therefore, ***Blessed is the nation whose God is the Lord.*** *God is not ashamed to be called their God* (Heb. 11:16).

But what is the cause of this? Could it be nature, fortune, or their proper power? No. Divine election: *You did not choose me, but I chose you* (John 15:16). Likewise: *No one can come to me unless the Father who sent me draws him* (John 6:44). And so he adds, ***the people whom he hath chosen***, as if to say, 'Therefore, they are blessed because they are chosen by God.' *He chose us in him before the foundation of the world* (Eph. 1:4).

And he says this ***for his inheritance***—that is, that they might be his inheritance. Inheritance implies stable possession. Now, God possesses all through his dominion. But the just alone are subject to him in will, so he chose them for his inheritance—that is, to have justice forever. *Righteousness is immortal* (Wis. 1:15). *Israel my heritage* (Isa. 19:25). Therefore, the ***Lord*** is their ***God*** because they enjoy him. And these are the inheritance of God because they are subject to him.

317 Afterward, when he says, ***The Lord hath looked from heaven***, he shows their dignity through a discussion of the divine judgment. And he makes three main points about this. *First*, he proposes the certainty of the divine judgment. *Second*, he adds the vanity of human prosperity, at ***The king is not saved***; and *third*, the effectiveness of grace in the saints, at ***Behold, the eyes of the Lord.***

Touching the certainty of judgment, he does two things. *First*, he ponders the certainty of the divine justice from its height; *second*, from its causality. *First*, he shows its height from the *first* passage [at ***from heaven***]; *second*, from the *second*, at ***who hath made.***

He makes two points about its height. *First*, he shows the certainty of the divine judgment from its height. *Second*, he removes any doubt at ***From . . .***

---

or to Aristotle's alleged habit of walking while lecturing. Aristotle identifies happiness with contemplation in *Nicomachean Ethics* 10.7.

which he hath prepared. Therefore, he says, ***from heaven.*** To the degree that some power is higher among the order and kinds of power, to that extent, it is more effective in accomplishing those works that are appropriate to it. And so, to the degree that some cognitive power is more subtle, to that extent, it is more effective in knowing. Nothing is as sublime as the divine intellect, and so its ability to know is the highest. And so he says, ***from heaven***—that is, from the height of the divine majesty. For as no corporeal thing is higher than heaven, so no spiritual thing is higher than God. And so, since he looks from on high, ***he hath beheld all the sons of men*** since the higher the place is from which someone looks, the more he sees. *All the ways of a man are open to his eyes* (Prov. 16:2 DRB).

318 Afterward, when he says, ***From his habitation which he hath prepared,*** he removes any doubt. For some believed that God dwelt in heaven as though he were far away and did not know human things: *Thick clouds enwrap him so that he does not see* (Job 22:14). The Psalmist rules this out, saying, ***From his habitation which he hath prepared,*** as if to say, 'No one has prepared for himself a place that would impede him, although perhaps it could be so if another prepared it.' For a king would be foolish to prepare for himself a seat from which he would not be able to rule his kingdom. So this is what he says: ***From his habitation which he hath prepared***—that is, from heaven, which he has prepared to be his dwelling, not indeed as though it encompasses him, but rather that by his glory he shines brightly through it—***he hath looked,*** he says, ***upon all that dwell on the earth***—in the flesh, that is—by reigning over them. ***Who is as the Lord our God, who dwelleth on high and looketh down on the low things?*** (Ps. 112:5–6). ***The Lord hath prepared his throne in heaven*** (Ps. 102:19). Or, he says, ***from heaven***—that is, from Christ. He has looked upon the angels or apostles with the eye of his mercy to save human beings.

319 Afterward, when he says, ***He who hath made the hearts of every one of them,*** he proves the certainty of the divine knowledge from its causality. He makes two points about this. *First,* he describes what it causes; and *second,* he concludes about the certainty of his knowledge, at ***who understandeth.***

He is said to be foolish who does some work without knowing its purpose, for he will be frustrated since the purpose is the goal. And so he says elsewhere, ***He that formed the eye, doth he not consider?*** (Ps. 93:9). Therefore, how would he be able to make anything able to know particulars unless he himself could know them? For a person knows singular things through his understanding, soul, and heart. Therefore, God, who made the very heart, knows it. And notice that these words have this weight. Therefore, he says, ***hearts,*** as though to exclude a unified intellect belonging to all, for different human beings have different intellects.[38]

Also, he says, ***of everyone***, to show that the soul is not double. Otherwise, he would not have said that he has known ***everyone*** but one through which he would know all and each individual one. Therefore, he made souls singular in themselves since the soul is a substance existing through itself, not because of matter.

So he says, ***He hath made***, to show that it does not come from the substance of God; otherwise, he would not have said that it was made but consubstantial. And so he indicates that ***he hath made***, since making belongs to potters, who shape a beautiful form from base materials. So, God infused the soul into the mud of the body by creation: *We have this treasure in earthen vessels* (2 Cor. 4:7). *Will what is molded say to its molder, "Why have you made me thus?"* (Rom. 9:20). And so he concludes that ***he understandeth all their works***, for he who knows the cause, knows the effect. Now, the cause of every human effect is the human heart. God knows the heart. Therefore, he also knows its works.

He made should be understood about the image of grace, since all the gifts of grace are from him, each one of them, since *there are varieties of gifts* (1 Cor. 12:4). And so he ***understandeth all their works***, by helping and moving.

320 ***The king is not saved by a great army***: Above, the Psalmist showed the dignity of the saints from the certitude of the divine judgment, from which he intended to prove their dignity. Now, in this part, he shows the vanity of human prosperity. And he makes two points about this. *First*, he shows that no temporal power can bring people to the salvation of the just. *Second*, he shows that the mercy of God does this, at ***Behold, the eyes of the Lord***. Therefore, he says, ***The king is not saved.***

Secular power is threefold. There is one type that consists in having many subordinates, another in strength of body, and another in exterior riches. And so he shows that none of these can bring someone to salvation.

First, he treats the first power, and this is that of ruling. So he says, ***The king is not saved by a great army***. Jerome has, ***in a multitude***. Psalm 145:2–3 says, ***Put not your trust in princes, in the children of men in whom there is no salvation***. On the contrary, if some are saved, this comes through God, ***who givest salvation to kings*** (Ps. 143:10).

---

38. Here Thomas alludes to the view of Averroes (1126–1198), the Arabic Aristotelian who interpreted Aristotle's view of the soul as implying that all individual human persons share a single immaterial intellect. Averroes develops his argument for the unity of the intellect in book 3 of his *Long Commentary on the "De Anima" of Aristotle*.

Second, he shows that salvation is not found in strength of body, so he says, ***nor shall the giant be saved by his own great strength.*** *The giants were born there, who were famous of old* (Bar. 3:26).

Third, he shows that it is not found in riches. And he mentions two types of property: horses and an abundance of things.

Regarding the *first*, he says, ***Vain is the horse***—that is, even though someone may have a good horse, he cannot be saved either corporeally or spiritually. *The horse is made ready for the day of battle, but the victory belongs to the Lord* (Prov. 21:31).

Regarding the *second*, he says, ***neither shall he be saved by the abundance of his strength***—that is, by his abundance of exterior things. *He who trusts in his riches will wither* (Prov. 11:28). *Woe to those who go down to Egypt for help and rely on horses* (Isa. 31:1). It can be explained mystically, morally, and allegorically that a human being is not saved by his own power, whatever good he may obtain. For there are three goods through which he might seem to possess salvation.

The *first* is power, and regarding this he says, ***The king is not saved by a great army.*** It may be true that he has the power to rule others, but this does not come from his own power; rather, he has it from God.

The *second* is steadfastness, and he does not have this from his own power, so he says, ***nor shall the giant be saved by his own great strength.***

Third is a good disposition of body and courage, so he says, ***Vain is the horse***—namely, a strong and robust body is vain.

Or, ***by the abundance of his strength*** is said in general to mean that, no matter what aptitude for the good he has, he will not be saved unless God gives him salvation. ***In my abundance I said, I shall never be moved. . . . Thou turnedst away thy face from me, and I became troubled*** (Ps. 29:7–8). This is what is said: *Let not the wise man glory in his wisdom, let not the mighty man glory in his might, let not the rich man glory in his riches* (Jer. 9:23).

321 Afterward, when he says, ***Behold, the eyes of the Lord***, he shows the effectiveness of the divine mercy to save. *First*, he describes the saving mercy; *second*, the affection of the saints, which is engendered by considering this, at ***Our soul waiteth for the Lord.***

He makes three points about the effectiveness of mercy. *First*, he shows the divine mercy; *second*, those things in which the divine mercy has an effect, at ***on them that fear him***; *third*, what effect it has, at ***to deliver.*** Therefore, he says, ***Behold, the eyes of the Lord.*** He treats the divine mercy in respect to God. ***Look thou upon me and have mercy on me*** (Ps. 118:132).

In regard to those upon whom he looks down, he adds, ***on them that fear him.*** *You who are of purer eyes than to behold evil and cannot look on wrong* (Hab.

1:13)—'therefore, look down upon those who fear and hope.' One does not suffice without the other since fear without hope despairs, and hope without fear presumes.

Now, fear arises from the consideration of the divine power. *Who would not fear you, O King of the nations?* (Jer. 10:7). But hope arises from the mercy of God. Fear of sinning arises from the first; from the second, hope of forgiveness.

Now he shows the effect of the divine mercy when he says, ***To deliver their souls from death and feed them in famine.*** Here, he shows a twofold effect: since it delivers from evil, and in regard to this he says, ***to deliver from death.*** It also confirms in the good, and in regard to this he says, ***and feed them.***

Therefore, he says, ***To deliver their souls from death,*** from corporeal death and from the death of sin and from the death of future damnation in the resurrection. *I will deliver them out of the hand of death* (Hosea 13:14 DRB).

Now, he confirms them in the good, so he says, ***and feed them in famine***—that is, in their need—and this is said about the nourishment of the body. ***The eyes of all hope in thee, O Lord, and thou givest them meat in due season*** (Ps. 144:15). And it is about spiritual nourishment. *Man does not live by bread alone, but . . . by everything that proceeds out of the mouth of the Lord* (Deut. 8:3; Matt 4:4). And it is about sacramental nourishment. *For my flesh is food indeed* (John 6:55). ***He hath set me in a place of pasture*** (Ps. 22:2).

322 Afterward, when he says, ***Our soul waiteth for the Lord,*** he shows the effect that follows in them from this consideration. And it is twofold. The *first* effect is hope. The *second* is prayer, at ***Let thy mercy be upon us.***

He makes two points about hope. *First,* he shows how the effect of hope arises in them. *Second,* he assigns a reason, at ***for he is our helper.*** Therefore, he also says, ***the eyes of the Lord are on those who fear him.*** And so, ***Our soul waiteth for the Lord***—in other words, 'If evils are sent to us from the Lord, we will endure them patiently.' *You have heard of the steadfastness of Job* (James 5:11). Likewise, we do this by awaiting his promises. Therefore, he awaits punishment and the promise.

And there is a twofold reason. One is because of the experience of his favors; another is the hope for future things. ***For in him our heart shall rejoice, and in his holy name, we have trusted.*** The experience of his favors takes place in progress in goods, so he says, ***for he is our helper.*** It also takes place in protection from evils, and so he says, ***and protector.***

Now, we hope for future joy, so he says, ***in him our heart shall rejoice***—that is, in the vision of him. *You shall see, and your heart shall rejoice* (Isa. 66:14). *Then you will delight yourself in the Almighty* (Job 22:26). And this joy is imperfect here, but there—that is, in the fatherland—it shall be perfect. And this is so because ***in his holy name, we have trusted.*** Here, ***and*** is put to mean 'because.'[39] His holy name is the name of his mercy, as if to say, 'We shall rejoice because ***in his holy name, we have trusted***—that is, in his goodness or in his mercy and not in our own merits.'

323 Afterward, when he says, ***Let thy mercy, O Lord, be upon us***, he gives the effect of prayer, for prayer is the interpreter of trust, and so it follows trust.[40]

And although any particular favor may come from the divine mercy, there nevertheless are two that particularly come from it. The *first* is the favor of the Incarnation. *Through the tender mercy of our God* (Luke 1:78). ***Let thy mercy***—namely, that you take up flesh and deliver us—***be upon us***—that is, upon our merits.

Another favor is salvation, and this is ***upon us***, because *he saved us, not because of deeds done by us in righteousness, but in virtue of his own mercy* (Titus 3:5). *Who ever trusted in the Lord and was put to shame?* (Sir. 2:10).

39. I.e., "in him our heart shall rejoice ***and*** in his holy name we have trusted" (v. 21).

40. The Latin term here rendered "trust" (for consistency with the Douay-Rheims translation) is *spes*, which is usually rendered 'hope.' Thomas's point here is clearer in reference to *hope* than to *trust*. The idea seems to be that our prayers are expressions of the content of our hope, since we pray for what we hope will come about.

Chapter 2

DIVINE JUSTICE, HUMAN SIN, AND SUFFERING

Job 1:20–22

Suffering, Sadness, and Divine Providence

On Job 1.4 (31–37)

1:20 ***Then Job rose up and rent his garments and, having shaven his head, fell down upon the ground and worshipped.***

1:21 ***And said, Naked I came out of my mother's womb, and naked shall I return thither. The Lord gave, and the Lord hath taken away, as it hath pleased the Lord so is it done. Blessed be the name of the Lord.***

1:22 ***In all these things, Job sinned not by his lips, nor spoke he any foolish thing against God.***

31 ***Then Job rose up***: Having recounted the adversity of blessed Job,[1] the text treats the patience Job showed in adversity. As evidence of what is said here, know that there was a difference of opinion among the ancient philosophers as to corporeal goods and the passions of the soul. For the Stoics said that exterior goods were not human goods and that there could be no sorrow for their loss in the soul of the wise person.[2] But the opinion of the Peripatetics was that some human goods are truly exterior goods, though these are certainly not the principal ones.[3] Nevertheless, they are like instruments ordered to the principal human good, which is the good of the mind. Because of this, they conceded that the wise person is moderately sad at the loss of exterior goods; his reason is not so absorbed by sadness that he departs from righteousness. This opinion is the truer of the two and is in accord with the teaching of the Church, as is clear from Saint Augustine in his book *The City of God*.[4]

1. See Thomas Aquinas, *On Job* 1.2 (not included in this collection).
2. For more on the Stoics, see 48n36 above.
3. For more on the Peripatetics, see 48n37 above.
4. Augustine, *City of God* 9.4.

32 So Job followed this opinion and truly showed sorrow in adversity; yet this sadness was so moderated that it was subject to reason. The text therefore continues, ***Then Job rose up and rent his garments***, which is usually an indication of sadness. Note, however, that the text says, ***Then***—namely, after he heard about the death of his children—so that he might be understood to have been sadder over their loss than the loss of his possessions. For it is characteristic of a hard and insensible heart to not grieve over dead friends, but it is characteristic of the virtuous to not have this grief in an immoderate way; as Saint Paul says: *But we would not have you ignorant, brethren, concerning those who are asleep, that you may not grieve as others do who have no hope* (1 Thess. 4:13).

This was true in the case of blessed Job, and so the state of his mind has become apparent in his external act. Because his reason remained upright, the text fittingly says that ***Job rose up***, although people in grief usually prostrate themselves. Indeed, because he experienced sorrow that did not penetrate so far as to disturb his innermost reason, in exterior actions, he displayed a sign of his sadness as corresponding to two deprivations: corresponding to things external to the body's nature, it says, ***he rent his garments***; corresponding to things that proceed from the body's nature, it says, ***he shaved his head***, which practice usually indicates grief among those who cultivate their hair. These two signs, then, fittingly correspond to the adversities mentioned, for the tearing of the robe corresponds to the loss of his possessions, and the cutting of the hair corresponds to the loss of his children. Then the mind stands upright when it is humbly submitted to God. For each thing exists in a higher and more noble state to the extent that it stands firm in what perfects it more, like air when it is subject to light and matter when it is subject to form. Therefore, the fact that the mind of blessed Job was not dejected by sadness but persisted in its righteousness clearly shows that he humbly subjected himself to God. So, the text continues, ***he fell upon the ground and worshipped***, to show evidence for his devotion and humility.

33 Job revealed the state of his mind not only by deeds but also by words. For he rationally demonstrated that although he suffered sadness, he did not have to yield to sadness. *First*, he demonstrated from the condition of nature. So, the text said, ***He said: Naked I came out of my mother's womb***—namely, from the earth, which is the common mother of everything—***and naked shall I return thither***—that is, to the earth. Sirach speaks in the same vein, saying that *much labor was created for every man, and a heavy yoke is upon the sons of Adam from the day they come forth from their mother's womb till the day they return to the mother of all* (40:1). This can also be interpreted in another way. The expression ***out of my mother's womb*** can be literally taken as the womb of the mother who bore him. When he says next, ***naked I shall return thither***,

the term ***thither*** establishes a simple relation. For a person cannot return a second time to the womb of his own mother, but he can return to the state that he had in the womb of his mother in a certain respect—namely, in that he is removed from human company. In saying this, he reasonably shows that a person should not be absorbed with sadness over the loss of exterior goods since exterior goods are not connatural to him but come to him accidentally. This is evident since a person comes into this world without them and leaves this world without them. So, when these accidental goods are taken away, if the substantial ones remain, one ought not to be overcome by sadness, although sadness may touch him.

34 *Second*, he shows the same thing from divine action, saying, ***The Lord gave, and the Lord hath taken away.*** Here, his true opinion about divine providence in relation to human affairs must first be considered. When he says, ***The Lord gave***, he confesses that earthly prosperity does not come to people accidentally, either according to fate or the stars or as a result of human exertion alone, but by divine direction. When he says, however, ***the Lord hath taken away***, he confesses that earthly adversities also arise among human beings by the judgment of divine providence. This leads to the conclusion that a person does not have a just complaint with God if he should be despoiled of his temporal goods because he who gave freely could bestow them either until the end of his life or temporarily. So, when he takes temporal goods away from a person before the end of life, one cannot complain.

35 *Third*, he shows the same thing from the good pleasure of the divine will, saying, ***as it hath pleased the Lord so is it done.*** For friends will and do not will the same thing. Thus, if it is the good pleasure of God that someone should be despoiled of temporal goods, if he loves God, he ought to conform his will to the divine will so that he is not absorbed by sadness in this consideration.

36 These three arguments are put in the proper order. For in the *first* argument, it is posited that temporal goods are exterior to a human being. In the *second*, it is posited that they are a gift given to a person and taken away by God. In the *third*, that this happens according to the good pleasure of the divine will.

So, one can conclude from the *first* argument that one should not be absorbed by sorrow because of the loss of temporal goods; from the *second*, that he cannot even complain; and from the *third*, that he ought even to rejoice. For it would not please God that someone should suffer from adversity unless he wished some good to come to him from it. So though adversity in itself is bitter and generates sadness, nevertheless, it should be the cause of rejoicing when one considers the benefit in view of which it pleases God, as is said about the apostles, who *left the presence of the council, rejoicing that they were counted worthy to suffer dishonor for the name* of Jesus (Acts 5:41). For when taking a bitter medicine, one can rejoice with reason because of the hope for health, although he suffers sensibly. So, since joy is the matter of the action of thanksgiving, therefore Job concludes this third argument with an act of thanksgiving, saying, ***Blessed be the name of the Lord.*** The name of the Lord is truly blessed by human persons inasmuch as they have knowledge of his goodness—namely, that he distributes all things well and does nothing unjustly.

37 Then the text therefore concludes to the innocence of Job when it says, ***In all these things, Job sinned not by his lips***—namely, he did not express a movement of impatience in word—***nor spoke he any foolish thing against God***—that is, blasphemy—so that he did not blaspheme concerning divine providence. For foolishness is opposed to wisdom, which properly is knowledge of divine things.

Job 7:1–10

The Ultimate End Beyond the Present Life

On Job 7.1–2 (121–129)

7:1 *The life of man upon earth is a warfare, and his days are like the days of a hireling.*

7:2 *As a servant longeth for the shade, as the hireling looketh for the end of his work,*

7:3 *so I also have had empty months and have numbered to myself wearisome nights.*

7:4 *If I lie down to sleep, I shall say: When shall I rise? and again, I shall look for the evening and shall be filled with sorrows even till darkness.*

7:5 *My flesh is clothed with rottenness and the filth of dust; my skin is withered and drawn together.*

7:6 *My days have passed more swiftly than the web is cut by the weaver and are consumed without any hope.*

7:7 *Remember that my life is but wind, and my eye shall not return to see good things.*

7:8 *Nor shall the sight of man behold me: thy eyes are upon me, and I shall be no more.*

7:9 *As a cloud is consumed and passeth away, so he that shall go down to hell shall not come up.*

7:10 *Nor shall he return any more into his house, neither shall his place know him anymore.*

121 ***The life of man upon earth is a warfare***: Above (Job 5:17–27), Eliphaz, wishing to draw blessed Job from out of despair, had promised him a certain earthly beatitude if he would accept the rebuke of the Lord. Here then, having demon-

strated the reasonable causes of his sorrow, blessed Job wishes to show further that Eliphaz's promised consolation, based on a promise of earthly happiness, is unfitting. He first demonstrates this from the condition of the present life and then later (Job 7:5) from his own condition.

122 Opinions have differed about the situation of this present life. Some have held that ultimate happiness is in this life. The words of Eliphaz seem to follow this opinion. Moreover, a person's ultimate end is in that place where he expects final retribution for good or evil. So if a person is rewarded by God for good deeds and punished for evil deeds in this life, as Eliphaz is eager to prove, it seems necessary to conclude that the ultimate human end is in this life. But Job intends to disprove this opinion, and he wants to show that the present human life does not contain the ultimate end within itself but is compared to this end as motion is compared to rest and a journey to its destination. He, therefore, compares this state to those of persons who pursue some end—namely, the state of soldiers who pursue victory in military campaigns. So he says, ***The life of man upon earth is a warfare***, as if to say, 'The present life that we live on earth is not like a state of victory but like that of a military campaign.' He also compares it to the situation of a hireling, so he adds, ***his days are like the days of a hireling***—namely, the time of a person living on earth.

He compares the present life to these two situations, given the two things incumbent upon a person in this life. *First*, one must resist impediments and harmful things, and on this account, life is compared to ***warfare***. *Second*, one must do what is expedient to achieve the end, on which account he is compared to a ***hireling***. From both images, one is given to understand that the present life is subject to divine providence, for soldiers fight under a general, and hirelings anticipate recompense from an employer. Further, the falsity of the opinion that Eliphaz defended is plain enough in these examples, for it is clear that an army general does not spare vigorous soldiers from dangers or toils but that the whole nature of warfare demands that he expose them, at times, to greater labors and perils. But after the victory has been won, the general gives greater honor to those who proved more vigorous. In the same way, the head of a household entrusts the more difficult tasks to his better employees, but on payday, he gives higher salaries to them. Correlatively, neither does divine providence dispose things in this way to give good people a greater exemption from the adversities and labors of the present life; rather, it aims to give them a greater reward in the end.

123 Therefore, since these arguments undermine the whole position of Eliphaz, Job intends to strengthen them and demonstrates them with effective reasoning. For clearly, each thing rests when it attains its ultimate end. So once the human will has attained its ultimate end, it must rest therein and not be moved

to desire anything else. But we experience the contrary in the present life, for a person always wants the future as though not content with the present state of things. Thus, it is clear that the ultimate end is not in this life but that this life is ordered to another end, as warfare is ordered to victory and the hireling's day to his pay. Note, moreover, that the present state of things in this life is insufficient and that desire stretches into the future for two reasons.

First, because of the afflictions of the present life: and so Job introduces the example of the servant desiring shade, saying, ***As a servant***, worn out from the heat, ***longeth for the shade***, which refreshes him. *Second*, for want of the perfect and ultimate good, for one does not possess it here: and so he uses the example of the hireling, saying, ***as the hireling looketh for the end of his work***. For the perfect good is the human end. ***I . . . have had empty months***—that is to say, 'I considered the past months to have gone by in vain for me because I did not obtain final perfection in them'—***and nights***—that is, 'when I should have been resting from my afflictions.' ***I have numbered to myself wearisome nights***—that is, 'I considered them wearisome because in them I was delayed from attaining my end.'

124 He next explains how his months have been empty and his nights wearisome, adding, ***If I lie down to sleep***—that is, at night, when it would have been the time for sleeping—***I shall say: When shall I rise?*** longing for the day. ***And again***, when the day has come, ***I shall look for the evening***, as he always strives for the future in his desire. This desire is indeed the shared experience of all persons living on earth, but people feel it more or less as they are affected more or less by sorrows or joys. For he who lives in joy desires the future less, but he who lives in sorrow desires it more. So Job passionately shows that this desire for the future is in him as he continues, ***I . . . shall be filled with sorrows even till darkness***, for because of these pains, the present time is tedious for me, and I desire the future more.

125 ***My flesh is clothed with rottenness***: Blessed Job had demonstrated above that the consolation of Eliphaz was inept, based as it was on the promise of happiness in this earthly existence. He first showed this from the general condition of human life on earth. Now, he intends to demonstrate that the same consolation is inept in light of his own condition. He proposes two things that prevent him from hoping for prosperity on earth.

The *first* is the bodily infirmity that he was suffering. Nothing can happen to a person detained by grave infirmity that can make him happy in this life. And so he says, ***My flesh is clothed with rottenness***, as if to say, 'My body is covered on all sides with infectious sores like a body is covered on all sides by a garment.' And since wounds heal up when they are treated early on, he shows that his sores have been neglected when he says, ***the filth of dust***, for they had not been tended properly, because he was literally sitting in a dung heap, as was stated above (Job 2:8). With a robust natural constitution, one can sometimes hope for health even with sores that have been neglected, but in Job, vigor had departed from his natural constitution, and so he says, ***my skin is withered and drawn together***, because the natural moisture was already exhausted in it, whether by old age or infirmity: 'So there seems to be no place for me to hope for further happiness in this life.'

The *second* reason is that the greater part of his life had already passed, so only a short time remained, and he could not expect great happiness during that time. Because of this, he says, ***My days have passed more swiftly than the web is cut by the weaver.*** Indeed, a person's life is, in one respect, like a woven fabric. Indeed, just as a weaver weaves a fabric by connecting threads with threads to reach the completion of the web, which finished product he cuts off, so too, for the completion of a human life, days are added to days, and when a life has been completed, it is taken away. And yet he says that a person's days pass more swiftly than the web is cut away because the weaver rests from time to time in the work of weaving, but the time of a human life slips away continuously, without interruption.

126 But one might object that although the greater part of his life would have passed, Job could still hope to return to the state of his past life. Some, at any rate, have advanced the theory that after death, when many cycles of years have transpired, a person returns to the same course of life that had formerly played out. And so, for example, in the future, Plato will lecture at Athens and do the same things he did before.[5] So, although a person has lived the greater part of his life, he could hope to be restored to happiness in this earthly life. To remove this possibility, Job continues, ***My days . . . are consumed without any hope*** of returning to former days. He had already seemed to address God in the text, saying, ***The life of man upon earth is a warfare.*** Now, to prove his point, he adds, ***Remember that my life is but wind***—that is, like the wind, for as the wind passes by and does not return afterward, so a human life does not return when it has passed away.

He continues in this vein, ***My eye shall not return to see good things*** of the earth, 'which I once possessed but now have lost.' 'And just as I will not return to see earthly goods when my life has passed, so neither will I be seen by any eyes on earth.' Thus, he continues, ***Nor shall the sight of man behold me.*** He posits these two things to show that he will not return to human association, which consists chiefly in seeing and being seen, for sight holds authority in sensitive life as the most acute of the senses. But although he said that he would

5. Cf. Augustine, *City of God* 12.13.

not be seen by a human eye after death, he confesses that he will be seen by the eye of God, saying, ***thy eyes*** will be ***upon me***, for the dead are seen by God, who observes spiritual things, because the dead live according to the spirit, not according to the flesh, which a person can see with his eyes.

127 One could take this to mean that the eyes of God consider the dead not according to the present state but regarding future things, as though a dead person were going to return again to the life he lost. To exclude this, he continues, ***I shall be no more***, as if to say, 'I say that your eyes will be on me after death because, subsequently, I will not be present again in the state of this earthly life.' He proves this by a comparison when he adds, ***As a cloud is consumed and passeth away, so he who shall go down to hell shall not come up***. The dead are said to descend into the underworld either because, spiritually, all were descending into Sheol before the death of Christ or because, according to the flesh, they are laid down under the earth. As far as the discussion at hand is concerned, it makes no difference how it is explained, for he merely means to say that the dead do not return to their past life, and he proves this point in a kind of simile, a sufficient proof.

As Aristotle says, a kind of circular motion appears in both corruptible and incorruptible bodies.[6] But there is this difference. In heavenly bodies, the same one in number returns in the circular motion, as the same sun in number sets and returns at dawn. This is so because the substance is not corrupted in such a change, but only the place changes. But in the motion of generation and corruption, the same one in number does not return, but the same species does. It is clear that according to the annual circular motion of the sun, a kind of circulation happens in the disposition of the atmosphere, for in winter, there are clouds that are dispersed later in the summer. When the winter returns again, clouds return, yet they are not numerically identical but only of the same species because the clouds that existed before perish completely. It is so with human beings. Those who return through the generations are not numerically the same persons but only the same in species as those who lived before.

128 From this, the solution to the argument of those who posited a return to the same life and the same acts becomes clear. For they believed that lower things are disposed according to the motion of the heavenly spheres; hence, when the same constellation returned after a very long time, they believed that the same thing would return in number. But it is not necessary that numerically the same things return, as has been said, but only things like them in species. Those thinkers thought that a dead person, after a certain span of time, would not only return to life but also have the same possessions and houses he formerly

6. Aristotle, *De generatione et corruptione* 2.11.

possessed. To disprove this, he says, ***Nor shall he return any more into his house.*** They also held that he would do the same works he had done before and hold the same offices and dignities. To exclude this position, he adds, ***neither shall his place know him anymore***—that is, he will not return again to his place. Here, the term 'place' refers to a person's status in the same way that we are accustomed to say, 'that person has an important position in that city.'

129 It is clear from these verses that Job here does not deny the resurrection that faith asserts but only the return to carnal life that the Jews hold and certain philosophers also held. Nor is this contrary to scriptural narrative in which some have been brought back to the present life because the one happens miraculously, whereas the other, just as Job says here, happens in the course of nature. Consider also that in saying, ***Remember that my life is but wind***, he has not spoken as though God could forget; rather, he speaks hypothetically, putting himself in the position of his adversaries. For if God were to promise the goods of this earthly life to a person whose life had, as it were, already passed, he would seem almost to have forgotten that a human life passes away like a wind that does not return.

Job 7:16b–21

Human Helplessness and Divine Concern

On Job 7.4 (134–141)

7:16b *Spare me, for my days are nothing.*

7:17 *What is man that thou shouldst magnify him, or why dost thou set thy heart upon him?*

7:18 *Thou visitest him early in the morning, and thou provest him suddenly.*

7:19 *How long wilt thou not spare me nor suffer me to swallow down my spittle?*

7:20 *I have sinned: What shall I do to thee, O keeper of men? Why hast thou set me opposite to thee and am I become burdensome to myself?*

7:21 *Why dost thou not remove my sin, and why dost thou not take away my iniquity? Behold now I shall sleep in the dust: and if thou seek me in the morning, I shall not be.*

134 ***Spare me***: After Job has shown that the consolation of Eliphaz, based on the promise of earthly happiness, was leading him to despair and the desire for death,[7] he shows what remains for him to hope for from God: that the trial put on him should cease. He expresses this, saying, ***Spare me***—as if to say, 'I have abandoned the hope of earthly prosperity; it is sufficient that you spare me; cease to afflict me.' Since a person's unhappiness and weakness usually induces another to spare him, he continues, ***for my days are nothing***, which seems to refer to human weakness and brevity of life, both with respect to all human beings in general and to him in a special way, because his days were almost at an end.

135 Consequently, he pursues both points. *First*, he says of his weakness, ***What is man?***—that is, 'How small a thing and frail in body ***that thou shouldst magnify him*** by honoring him among the other creatures or ***set thy heart upon***

7. See Thomas Aquinas, *On Job* 7.3 (not included in this collection).

him by guarding him and protecting him with special care?' Here, note that all things are subject to divine providence, and all things in their state receive their greatness from God. Nevertheless, some receive it in one way, others in another. For, since all particular goods in the universe seem to be ordered to the common good of the universe as part is ordered to whole and imperfect to perfect, they are disposed by divine providence as they are ordered to the universe. Moreover, it must be observed that, in whatever way they participate in perpetuity, things seek the perfection of the universe essentially. However, in whatever way they lack perpetuity, they conduce to the perfection of the universe only accidentally and not of themselves.

Therefore, according as they are perpetual, they are ordered by God for their own sake, but according as they are corruptible, they are ordered for the sake of other things. Thus, things that are perpetual both in their species and as individuals are directed by God for themselves. By contrast, things that are corruptible as individuals and perpetual only in their species are disposed by God as species for themselves and as individuals only for the sake of their species. Accordingly, the good and evil that occur among brute animals—as, for instance, when a particular sheep is killed by this particular wolf or other occurrences of this sort—they are not dispensed by God on account of some merit or demerit on the part of this wolf or sheep but for the good of the species because a proper food has been divinely ordained by God for each species. He expresses this, saying, ***dost thou set thy heart upon him***—that is, 'you provide for his good.' He does not turn his heart to the good of individual animals but rather to the good of the species, which can exist perpetually.

136 He shows how God turns his heart toward him when he says, ***Thou visitest him early in the morning***—that is, from the day of his birth, you help him by your providence with things necessary for his life and glorification, whether they are corporeal or spiritual. ***And thou provest him suddenly*** by adversities in which he shows clearly he is disposed to virtue. As Sirach says, *The furnace trieth the potter's vessels, and the trial of affliction just men* (27:6 DRB). God is said to test a person not so that he may learn what kind of person he is but so to inform others and so that the one tested might know himself. These words of Job are not to be understood as expressing contempt for divine concern for human beings but as investigating and wondering. For if the human person is considered only as he appears exteriorly, he seems small, fragile, and perishable. So it would be astonishing for God to have such great care for him unless he should have something hidden that makes him capable of perpetual existence. Thus, by inquiry and wonder, the opinion of Eliphaz is refuted because if there were no other life for a human being except that on earth, he would not seem worthy of such great care as God has for him. Therefore, the very care that

God has especially for humankind demonstrates that there is another life for human beings after the death of the body.

137 Then he adds another reason that God should spare him, taken from the brevity of life. He puts it in question form, saying, ***How long wilt thou not spare me?*** This is like saying, 'The time of a human life is short and the greater part of the time of my life is already past. Therefore, what limit is forthcoming so that you might spare me, if you will not spare me now, so that I might have at least some brief time to rest?' He shows this meaning when he adds, ***nor suffer me to swallow down my spittle?*** For one cannot swallow saliva while speaking. It is necessary to pause briefly while speaking to spit out or to swallow saliva. He compares the time remaining in his life to this brief instant, as if saying: 'If you delay in sparing me, no rest will remain for me, not even the rest during which a speaker swallows his saliva.' This way of arguing presupposes the opinion of Eliphaz because if there is no other life for human beings except the one on this earth, there will not remain a time when God may spare Job if God does not spare him in this life.

138 Someone could object that Job was unworthy to be spared by God because his sins merit that he be afflicted even more. This follows also from the opinion of Eliphaz, who thought that he was scourged because of his sins. So he continues, ***I have sinned***, as if to say, 'Given that I have sinned and, because of this, merited to be afflicted, still, there remains a reason why you should spare me.'

To this, he adds three reasons derived from human weakness why God should spare him. The *first* is taken from our powerlessness to make satisfaction. A human being can do nothing from his own powers worthy to compensate for an offense committed against God. This is what he means when he says, ***What shall I do to thee, O keeper of men?***—as if to say, 'If you have such great care for human beings as their watchman that you require an accounting of their individual acts, my powers are not sufficient to perform some act for which you will remit my sins. If, then, this is expected, you would never spare me, so please spare me despite this powerlessness.'

139 The *second* reason is taken from human powerlessness to persevere. For a person cannot persevere after the corruption of human nature without the grace of God, and so it is customary even in Sacred Scripture to say that God hardens someone or blinds someone in the sense that he does not bestow the grace on him by which he may be softened and see. Job speaks here in this way, saying, ***Why hast thou set me opposite to thee?***—that is, 'Why did you not give me the grace of perseverance in this matter so that I might not be opposed to you by sin?' For whoever sins is opposed to God since he spurns the divine commandments, which are either handed down in the written Law or naturally inscribed in human reason.

Note that reason is the strongest of all the soul's powers. A sign of this strength is that reason commands the other powers and uses them for its own end. Yet it happens that reason is somewhat absorbed at times by concupiscence, anger, or the other passions of the lower part of the soul, and so a person sins. Nevertheless, the lower passions cannot hold reason bound, but rather, reason always returns to its nature, by which it tends to spiritual goods as its own proper end: Therefore, a kind of struggle goes on, even of a person against himself, when reason resists him because he has sinned, absorbed either by concupiscence or anger. Since a tendency to similar acts has been added to the lower powers from past sins as a result of habit, reason cannot freely make use of the lower powers to order them to higher goods or withdraw them from lower ones. Thus, a person becomes a burden even to himself in being opposed to God through sin. He shows this by saying, ***Am I become burdensome to myself?*** In this light it is clear that sin has its own immediate punishment. On these grounds, moreover, it seems to be easier to show mercy to a person after this punishment.

140 The *third* reason is taken from the powerlessness of the human being to cleanse himself from sin. For one sinks into sin by oneself, but it is only God's part to remit sin. So Job asks: 'If my punishment should not cease for as long a time as my sin remains and you alone can take away my sin, ***Why dost thou not remove my sin***, which I have committed against God or against myself? ***Why dost thou not remove my sin*** if any has been committed against my neighbor?' Remember, Job does not ask questions of this kind like a rash questioner of divine judgments but to destroy the falsity that his adversaries were eager to assert: that we should expect rewards and punishments for human deeds to come from God in this life only. If this view is asserted, the whole reason for divine judgments, by which he punishes people for sin in this life and remits sins in foreordaining them either to predestination or reprobation in the next, is thrown into confusion. If there is no future life but only the present one, there would be no reason why God should delay sparing those whom he intends to spare or justify or reward them. So, Job shows his own intention clearly, continuing, ***Behold now I shall sleep in the dust***—as if to say, 'The end of my life is almost here when I will die and decay to dust.' One cannot hope even to see tomorrow with certainty because of the uncertainty of death, so he says, ***if thou seek me in the morning, I shall not be***, 'for I cannot promise myself even a life until morning, much less a long span of life in which I can hope you would spare me if there will be no other life.'

141 Consider that Job proceeds in the manner of a debater, for whom it suffices at the beginning to disprove false opinion and afterward to explain what he himself thinks is true.

Note, too, that in these opening words, Job touched three reasons why someone should be afflicted in this life by God. The *first* is that his malice may be restrained so he cannot harm others. He touched on this reason in the text ***Am I a sea, or a whale, that thou hast enclosed me in a prison?*** (Job 7:12). The *second* is to try a person in order to manifest his virtue, and he touched this in the text ***Thou visitest him early in the morning, and thou provest him suddenly.*** The *third* reason is to punish sinners, and he touched on this when he said, ***I have sinned: What shall I do to thee, O keeper of men?***

Job 40:1–9

Human Pride and Divine Justice

On Job 40.1 (526–533)

40:1 ***And the Lord, answering Job out of the whirlwind, said:***

40:2 ***"Gird up thy loins like a man; I will ask thee, and do thou tell me.***

40:3 ***Wilt thou make void my judgment and condemn me, that thou mayst be justified?***

40:4 ***And hast thou an arm like God, and canst thou thunder with a voice like him?***

40:5 ***Clothe thyself with beauty, and set thyself up on high and be glorious, and put on goodly garments.***

40:6 ***Scatter the proud in thy indignation, and behold every arrogant man, and humble him.***

40:7 ***Look on all that are proud, and confound them, and crush the wicked in their place.***

40:8 ***Hide them in the dust together and plunge their faces into the pit.***

40:9 ***Then, I will confess that thy right hand is able to save thee."***

526 ***The Lord, answering Job out of the whirlwind***: In what he said before, the Lord demonstrated his wisdom and power by recalling the marvelous things that appear in his effects (Job 38; 39) so that he might make clear that no one can contend with God, either in wisdom or in power. Here, he proceeds further to accuse Job for invoking his own justice (Job 27:6), which to some sounded like a derogation of divine justice (Job 34). Also, the text prefaces this speech by explaining the manner of God's speech when it says, ***The Lord, answering Job out of the whirlwind, said.*** He excites his attention, saying, ***Gird up thy loins like a man***, and he demands an answer when he continues, ***I will ask***

thee, and do thou tell me. These things have already been explained (Job 38:1, 3), and so I will not explain them again.[8]

527 Consider that Job, in appealing to his own justice, did not intend to impute evil to divine judgment, as his three friends and Elihu wrongly supposed. Instead, he intended to show that he had not been punished in vengeance for his sins, as they charged, but as a test, as he had already said above: ***He has tried me as gold that passeth through the fire*** (Job 23:10). Nevertheless, even this was seen to be reprehensible because he commended his own justice in a way that was seen by others to pass over into a derogation of divine justice. And so God says, ***Wilt thou make void my judgment?***—as if to say, 'Do you not see that, in commending your own justice, you make my judgment to be reckoned void—that is, false—in human eyes?' Falsity of judgment is the cause of condemnation of the judge who expresses an evil judgment either from ignorance or malice, and so he then says, ***Wilt thou condemn me, that thou mayst be justified?***—as if to say, 'Do you want to show yourself just so that I will seem worthy of condemnation by others?'

528 Note here that if there are two equals and it is necessary to assign blame to one of them, it is not reprehensible if the one exculpates himself from an imputed fault even though the other may remain culpable in the opinion of others.[9] For a person naturally loves himself more than others. But when there is such a great distance as exists between God and a human being, the latter ought rather to suffer blame unjustly imputed to him rather than impute it unjustly to God. Therefore, in accusing Job, God proposes his own excellence over that of human beings, and this excellence is indeed manifested in his effects. But because he is here making a comparison of justice, which properly cannot be considered in relation to irrational things, to demonstrate divine excellence, he thus considers the effects produced by God in rational creatures. These effects can be considered in two ways. In one way, according to the operation of his power, and concerning this, he says, ***Hast thou an arm like God?***, for the arm expresses the power of God. He uses this arm to sustain the good, as Isaiah says: *He will gather the lambs in his arms* (40:11), and to punish evildoers, as Luke says: *He has shown strength with his arm, he has scattered the proud in the imagination of their hearts* (1:51). In another way, God works in rational creatures by the instruction of his wisdom, which, because of his excellence, is called thunder, and as to this he says, ***Canst thou thunder with***

8. See Thomas Aquinas, *On Job* 38.1 (included at page 15 above).

9. The example here seems to envision two defendants under suspicion for a crime committed by one person. Thomas's point seems to be that neither defendant would be morally wrong to prove his innocence even if the other suspect would be presumed guilty as a result. It is natural and thus morally appropriate, Thomas suggests, for a person to be more concerned to vindicate himself than another, even assuming the other is likewise innocent.

a voice like him? God uses this thunder to instruct the good: *We have heard scarce a little drop of his word, who shall be able to behold the thunder of his greatness?* (Job 26:14), and for the terrible rebuke of the wicked, as the psalm says: *The crash of your thunder was in the whirlwind*, and the text says after this, *The earth trembled and shook* (77:18).

529 From effects of this kind, he demonstrates the divine excellence as to three things. *First*, as to beauty, when he says, ***Clothe thyself with beauty***, as if to say, 'If you were as powerful in your works as God, you would attribute to yourself his beauty,' and so he clearly says, ***Clothe thyself***, for God does not clothe himself with beauty as something added beyond his essence, but his essence itself is beauty. This beauty includes his clarity or truth, his purity or simplicity, and the perfection of his essence. But a human being cannot have beauty unless he is clothed with it by participating in it from God as something added beyond his essence.

Second, he treats the divine majesty when he says, ***set thyself up on high***. The divine majesty is not in a place because God is not understood in a place but consists in his perfection and power because whatever is said about him is fitting to him in the highest degree. Majesty befits God essentially, and so he does not lift himself up to it, but it remains in him immovably. By nature, the human being is of the lowest condition, and so he cannot arrive at that divine height except by lifting himself up above himself, and so he clearly says, ***set thyself up on high***.

Third, he treats of his glory when he says, ***be glorious***. Glory includes the knowledge of another's goodness, and so Ambrose says that glory is *fame recognized and praised*.[10] However, the goodness of God is infinite, and no one knows this glory but God himself, and therefore, glory is only in God since he alone knows himself. A human being cannot arrive at this glory except by participation in divine knowledge, as Jeremiah says: *Let him who glories glory in this, that he understands and knows me* (9:24). And thus he clearly says, ***be glorious***, because a human being does have this glory by his essence.

530 Having explained what pertains to the excellence of divine power and nature, he proceeds further to call to mind the divine effects in rational creatures, both the good and the wicked. Understand that the effects that God works in the highest of the just are more attributed to his mercy, and those he works in the punishment of evildoers are properly attributed to justice. Thus, since the subject now is justice, first, he briefly treats the effects that God works in the good when he says, ***put on goodly garments***. For finally, all good angels and human beings are splendid from the participation of divine

10. This definition of glory, here misattributed to Ambrose, belongs in fact to Augustine, *Answer to Maximinus the Arian* 2.13.2.

wisdom and justice, and so, just as a person is adorned with splendid garments, so every beauty of holy angels and holy persons returns to the adornment of God because the goodness of God is commended by them, as Isaiah says: *You shall put them all on as an ornament* (49:18). Consider that it is characteristic of the mercy of God to make his saints splendid; but to use their beauty for his own glory is characteristic of his justice, about which he now speaks. So he does not say, 'make yourself precious garments,' but ***put on goodly garments.***

531 Then, he shows the effect of divine justice, which he causes in the wicked in a more extensive way. *First,* he does this as to human beings. Consider that every human evil has its beginning in pride; as Sirach says, *pride is the beginning of all sin* (10:15 DRB). Among all the vices, God detests pride most of all, and so the Epistle of James says, *God opposes the proud* (4:6). This is because the proud rebel against God when they refuse to submit humbly to him, and hence, they fall into every sin in their contempt for divine precepts. Earthly princes detest rebels most, and so the Lord especially calls to mind the effect of his power, which he exercises against the proud. There are two types of proud people. Some exalt themselves above others for the goods they have, like the man in Luke who said, *I am not like other men* (18:11). These are properly called the proud, as the name itself shows.

The specific punishment of the proud is lack of peace because when each person strives to be higher than the other and refuses to be subject to another, they cannot have peace with each other; and so Proverbs says, *Among the proud there are always contentions* (13:10 DRB). He shows this, saying, ***Scatter the proud in thy indignation***, saying in effect, 'Exercise the duty of God, which is to disperse the proud so that they cannot band together,' for the ***indignation*** of God here means grave punishment. Another type of proud persons are those who presumptuously claim for themselves what is above them. These are properly called the arrogant, and so Jeremiah says, *We have heard the pride of Moab, he is exceeding proud: his haughtiness, and his arrogancy, and his pride, and the loftiness of his heart* (48:29 DRB). Moreover, the proper punishment for these is to be cast down. Indeed, it follows that they should fall down perilously because they wished to elevate themselves above their ability, as the Psalm says: *You made them fall to ruin* (73:18); and so he says, ***behold every arrogant man and humble him***—that is, 'You should cast them down from the point of view of your providence.'

532 The *first* punishment common to both types of proud persons is confusion. Since they cannot attain the height to which they pretend, they are confounded when they see their inability, and so he says, ***Look on all that are proud, and confound them***, and he also said already, ***If his pride mount up even to heaven . . . in the end he shall be destroyed like a dunghill*** (Job 20:6–7).

The *second* punishment is destruction, which he shows, saying, ***crush the wicked in their place.*** He calls the proud wicked because, as Sirach says, *The beginning of man's pride is to depart from the Lord* (10:12), which is to oppose the divine worship that belongs to piety. The fitting punishment of the proud is that they are crushed because what is crushed is broken down into smaller parts by the force of a stronger body. It is just that the proud, who think themselves inordinately great, are reduced to the least by God's stronger power.

He plainly says, ***in their place***, to show that what they place their trust in cannot liberate them. Indeed, each thing is preserved in its own place, and so a multitude of riches, a status of dignity, or whatever else it may be that a person places trust in—this can be called 'his place.' God destroys the proud in spite of these so that they are seen to be destroyed in their place.

The *third* punishment is what occurs after they are reduced to the lowest place. Their reputation loses its luster, for it is just that he who sought the pomp of glory should be erased from human memory. As Proverbs says, *The name of the wicked will rot* (10:7), and so the text continues, ***Hide them in the dust***—that is, 'You will make them to be forgotten because of the state of evil to which they have succumbed.' He adds ***together,*** which can be interpreted in two ways. *First,* all the proud suffer the same end, and also, the proud do not perish successively but are cast down suddenly, all at once.

Their *fourth* punishment is that not only will they themselves remain unrecognized by others but also the goods for which they prided themselves will be unknown. Thus, he says, ***their faces***—which means their cognitive powers because a person's vision is situated in his face—***plunge into the pit***, into the depths of hell. He compares the damnation of the second death to the first death, in which people are reduced to bodily ashes and thrown into a ditch.

533 The Lord had treated these things first as proper to his own works. It is proper to him also not to need anyone else's help. A human being cannot attain this as he cannot do these works, and so he says, ***Then, I will confess that thy right hand is able save thee***, as if to say, 'If you can do these works that are proper only to God, you can reasonably attribute to yourself that you do not need divine help to be saved. But as you cannot do the former, you cannot do the latter. Thus, you ought not to glorify yourself in your own justice.'

Chapter 3

DIVINE REVELATION

Psalm 13[1]

Natural Revelation

On Psalms 13 (96–102)

13:1 *Unto the end, a psalm for David.*

The fool hath said in his heart: "There is no God." They are corrupt and are become abominable in their ways. There is none that doth good, no not one.

13:2 *The Lord hath looked down from heaven upon the children of men, to see if there be any that understand and seek God.*

13:3 *They are all gone aside, they are become unprofitable together. There is none that doth good, no not one.*

Their throat is an open sepulcher. With their tongues they acted deceitfully. The poison of asps is under their lips.

Their mouth is full of cursing and bitterness. Their feet are swift to shed blood. Destruction and unhappiness in their ways; and the way of peace they have not known. There is no fear of God before their eyes.

13:4 *Shall not all they know that work iniquity, who devour my people as they eat bread?*

13:5 *They have not called upon the Lord: there have they trembled for fear, where there was no fear.*

13:6 *For the Lord is in the just generation. You have confounded the counsel of the poor man, but the Lord is his hope.*

1. Psalm 13, so numbered in the Douay-Rheims translation used here, corresponds to Psalm 14 in most modern editions, which follow the Masoretic numbering system.

13:7 ***Who shall give out of Zion the salvation of Israel? When the Lord shall have turned away the captivity of his people, Jacob shall rejoice, and Israel shall be glad.***

96 Above, the Psalmist reproached the deceit of his enemies;[2] here, he describes their wickedness. The title is ***Unto the end, a psalm for David.*** And he considers two points regarding this. *First*, he shows their wickedness. *Second*, he describes his hope to be delivered from them, at ***Shall not all they know.***

He discusses two aspects of their wickedness. *First*, he shows their wickedness. *Second*, he makes certain that this wickedness really is within them, at ***The Lord hath looked down.***

He shows their wickedness in two steps. *First*, he describes the root of their wickedness; *second*, the progress of their wickedness: ***They are corrupt.*** *Pride is the beginning of all sin*, and *the beginning of the pride of man is to fall off from God* (Sir. 10:15, 14 DRB). To lack God in his heart is the beginning of a person's wickedness, and so he says, ***The fool hath said in his heart: "There is no God."*** *Wisdom will not enter a deceitful soul nor dwell in a body enslaved to sin* (Wis. 1:4).

But can this really be said? To speak in the heart is to think. But can it really be thought that there is no God? Anselm says that no one can do this.[3] Likewise, John of Damascus says, *Knowledge of God is naturally implanted in all*, and no one can think something to be nonexistent that he naturally knows to exist.[4]

But it must be understood that we can speak about the knowledge of God in two ways: either in itself or in relation to us. If we mean it in the *first* way, it is without a doubt true that no one can think that he does not exist. For no proposition can be thought false that is of the nature that the predicate is included in the definition of the subject.[5] It must be noted, moreover, that in God, existence is different than in other things, since the existence of God is his very substance. Therefore, he who speaks about God as he is in

2. Psalm 11:3–4 (DRB). See Thomas Aquinas, *On Psalms* 11 (not included in this collection).

3. Anselm, *Proslogion* 4.

4. John of Damascus, *An Exact Exposition of the Orthodox Faith* 1.1 and 1.3.

5. The proposition Thomas has in mind here is 'God exists.' His point, expressed somewhat tersely, is that anyone who could really grasp the meaning of 'God' would recognize that existence is entailed in it. As he goes on to explain, "The existence of God is his very substance." In other beings, what they are is irrelevant to the question of whether they are. But in God's case, what he is, if we could only grasp it, affirmatively answers the question as to whether he is. Consequently, the proposition 'God does not exist' seems intelligible only because and to the extent that we are ignorant of the meaning of its subject, 'God.' If we could adequately grasp the concept of God, we could no more think of him as nonexistent than we could conceive of a part being larger than its whole, for example.

himself says that he is existence itself; and so as he is in himself, no one can think that he does not exist.[6] Moreover, the words of John of Damascus are explained since that knowledge that is naturally implanted in man is known indeterminately—namely, that God is—but this is not the same sort of knowledge as the knowledge that God is that is held by faith.[7]

God is named from the word *Theos*, which means 'to burn every evil.'[8] Therefore, someone at some time says that there is no God when he thinks that he is not omnipotent and that he does not concern himself with human things. *What is the Almighty, that we should serve him?* (Job 21:15).

The fool hath said in his heart: "There is no God" can be understood as referring to the Jews who said that Christ was merely human and not God: *You, being a man, make yourself God* (John 10:33). These Jews, not believing what he had promised in the law, said that this one—namely, 'he who is preaching to us'—***is no God***. And this claim he called 'foolish' since they were unwilling to receive the wisdom of God and kept the eyes of their minds blinded: ***They have not known, nor understood*** (Ps. 81:5), *for their wickedness blinded them* (Wis. 2:21).

Alternatively, this verse rebukes the sinner, *first*, for the sin of the heart in consent, at ***The fool hath said in his heart***; *second*, for the sin of deed, at ***They are corrupt***; and *third*, for the habitual sin, at ***abominable***.

First, he calls the sinner a fool since he does not have wisdom, as he says. It is also because they do not understand spiritual things: *The unspiritual man does not receive the gifts of the Spirit of God* (1 Cor. 2:14). Afterward, the progression of wickedness is shown: ***They are corrupt and are become abominable***. Just as the two parts of justice are to do good and to avoid evil, so there are two parts to injustice—namely, to do evil and to avoid good. He describes the first part first and then the second.

He describes two aspects of doing evil: *first*, the depravity of the vices; *second*, their abomination. In physical things, corruption comes about through the exhalation of natural warmth driven out by alien heat. Now, the natural heat of the soul is the love of God. Therefore, when the alien heat of concupiscence and other sins enters in, God withdraws. And so, after he says, ***There is no God***,

---

6. Cf. Thomas Aquinas, *Summa theologiae* 1.2.1.

7. John of Damascus, *An Exact Exposition of the Orthodox Faith* 1.9. What Thomas means here by "indeterminately" seems to be that although we do naturally know that God exists, we only have a general and confused notion of the 'God' to which we thus ascribe existence. Elsewhere, he says of this "general and confused" natural knowledge of God that "this is not to know absolutely that God exists, just as to know that someone is approaching is not the same as to know that Peter is approaching" (*Summa theologiae* 1.2.1 ad 1).

8. Cf. Thomas Aquinas, *Summa theologiae* 1.13.8, obj. 1. Thomas borrows this folk etymology from John of Damascus, who relates the word *theos* with the Greek verb *aithein* ('to burn') in *An Exact Exposition of the Orthodox Faith* 1.9.

it immediately follows that ***they are corrupt.*** *They have denied the Lord and said, It is not he* (Jer. 5:12 DRB)—namely, the one who condemns sinners and rewards the just. *The mind of a fool*—namely, of the sinner—*is like a broken jar* (Sir. 21:14). Therefore, ***they***, the sinners, ***are corrupt***, through their evil actions. *Because their deeds were evil* (John 3:19), since after they lost, through consent, the goods given freely, their natural qualities became corrupted, and so punishment follows. ***A fire shall go before him and shall burn his enemies round about*** (Ps. 96:3).

Just as when a body putrefies, it becomes abominable, so a human soul is acceptable to God when the love of God is in it, but when it is corrupted through sin, it becomes abominable.[9] The abominable is that from which the human appetite flees, and so he says, ***they***—namely, sinners—***are become abominable*** to God and to human beings through the habit of sinning. *How exceeding base art thou become, going the same ways over again!* (Jer. 2:36 DRB). *They consecrated themselves to Baal and became detestable like the thing they loved* (Hosea 9:10).

And he said, ***in their ways***, since through them they became abominable. Or, according to Jerome, ***they did them eagerly.***[10] God detests the will that is eager to sin more than the sin itself: *They turned aside from following him and had no regard for any of his ways* (Job 34:27). Another text has, ***they have corrupted and detested the pursuit***[11]—of wisdom and instruction, that is—*because they hated knowledge and did not choose the fear of the Lord* (Prov. 1:29). *You will see still greater abominations* (Ezek. 8:6).

Next, he treats the ruin of the good: ***There is none that doth good***, since *there is not a righteous man on earth who does good and never sins* (Eccles. 7:20). ***One***—that is, Christ, who alone neither contracted nor committed sin. The Blessed Virgin had contracted sin.[12] *One man among a thousand I found, but a woman among all these I have not found* (Eccles. 7:28). Or, ***not one***, since there is not even one who does good perfectly. This is true, supposing that they have said, ***There is no God***, and that ***they are corrupt.***

97 ***The Lord hath looked down***: Here, he *first* makes certain of their guilt; *second*, explains it, at ***sepulcher.***

9. Cf. Thomas Aquinas, *Summa theologiae* 1-2.110.1 ad 1.

10. The reference here is to Jerome's Hebrew Psalter.

11. It is not clear what other text he might be referring to here. The rendering is similar both to the Hebrew and Gallican psalters.

12. Cf. Thomas Aquinas, *Summa theologiae* 3.27.1. Thomas's statement here, although it only concerns original sin, nevertheless conflicts with the dogma of the Immaculate Conception, officially defined by the Church in 1854 (Pope Pius IX, *Ineffabilis Deus*).

Now, sin is proven through wickedness, and so he records the inquiry of God, saying, 'You say that ***there is no God***, but this is false since ***the Lord hath looked down from heaven upon the children of men***.' *All the ways of a man are open to his eyes* (Prov. 16:2 DRB). Therefore, the Lord, the Father, has looked down by sending his own Son from heaven—that is, from the inner heart of his piety. *Heaven is my throne* (Isa. 66:1). Or ***the Lord hath looked down from heaven***—that is, Christ, through whom he will judge sinners. Or it can be taken in another way, so that some say that God does not know singular and changeable things since he is immaterial and simple and eternal. And so, he does not know in accordance with the movement of things but only according to the mode of his own ability to be known. The response is that, on the contrary, he knows material things immaterially, as Dionysius concludes.[13] And so he knows intellectually, and so he says, ***from heaven***—that is, from the height of his own dignity and nature—***he hath looked down . . . upon the children of men***. And he desires, with his antecedent will by which he desires all to be saved, to find in us that which belongs to salvation—namely, that we know God with our intellect and love him with our affections and desire him.[14]

And so, he says, ***to see***—that is, to cause sight since he himself always sees. —***if there be any that understand*** through the intellect: *If they were wise, they would understand* (Deut. 32:29), ***and seek God*** through the affection.

Will he find what he is seeking? On the contrary, he will find that ***they are all gone aside***. He describes three things: their going aside from God, their unprofitable action, and their ceasing to do good. Therefore, he says, ***They are all gone aside*** from God. *I know that after my death, you will surely act corruptly and turn aside from the way which I have commanded you* (Deut. 31:29). *There is no faithfulness or kindness, and no knowledge of God in the land* (Hosea 4:1). *They have not spoken rightly; no man repents of his wickedness* (Jer. 8:6). Also, because he has fallen away from God, he has become unprofitable, since that is unprofitable which does not attain that for which it was made. Now, humankind was made to enjoy God. *The prolific brood of the ungodly will be of no use* (Wis. 4:3). So, he says, ***they are become unprofitable together***. Likewise, they have ceased to do good since ***there is none that doth good***. This has already been explained.

98 ***Their throat is an open sepulcher***: Jerome says the Apostle Paul used the testimony of these verses and that he found it elsewhere in Sacred Scripture.[15] Where it appears in Romans 3, Jerome says that Paul has taken a certain part

---

13. Pseudo-Dionysius, *Divine Names* 7; cf. Thomas Aquinas, *Summa theologiae* 1.14.11.

14. Cf. Thomas Aquinas, *Summa theologiae* 1.19.6 ad 1.

15. Jerome, *Commentary on Isaiah* 16.1. There, Jerome identifies Psalm 5:9 as the source of "Their throat is an open sepulcher."

of it from Isaiah 59 and another part from other places in the Psalter but not so much from this psalm because he himself was a Hebrew and knew that this passage is not found in the Hebrew. It is included, however, in the Vulgate edition, which ordinary people use, which is not attributed to any specific translator.[16]

An open sepulcher emits a fetor, and thus, above, the Psalmist verified the wickedness or guilt of his enemies. Here, however, he explains it further, and he does two things: *first*, he shows the way in which sinners are harmful to others; and *second*, to themselves, at ***destruction and unhappiness.***

He describes two ways they hurt others. *First*, he shows how they hurt others by word; *second*, how they harm by deed: ***Their feet are swift.*** He makes two points about the harm they inflict with words. *First*, he describes their mouths' promptness to harm; *second*, the way they harm: ***With their tongues they acted deceitfully.***

Therefore, he says, ***Their throat is an open sepulcher.*** Now, just as a sepulcher is prepared for no other purpose than to receive corpses, so the mouth of the one who is always ready to kill through detraction is ***an open sepulcher***: *Fire and smoke and sulfur issued from their mouths* (Rev. 9:17). Again, notice their voracity, for the throat serves to consume.

But sometimes he harms by deceit, sometimes by wickedness, and sometimes by harshness. *First*, he describes the deceit that they have in their tongues: ***With their tongues they acted deceitfully*** by speaking with a superficial pleasantness—*Their tongue is a deadly arrow; it speaks deceitfully* (Jer. 9:8)—with deceit in their heart: ***The poison of asps is under their lips.*** Hidden poison is deadly, but the poison of asps is incurable, and asps cannot be charmed: ***Like a deaf asp that stoppeth her ears*** (Ps. 57:5), the poison of which kills by putting to sleep.

Wicked men are found among my people; they lurk like fowlers lying in wait. They set a trap; they catch men. Like a basket full of birds, their houses are full of treachery (Jer. 5:26–27). They draw birds to their snares with a sweet song. In this, their cruelty, their stubbornness, and their wickedness are shown. Their cruelty is shown because they strive to kill; their stubbornness, because hatred is always in their hearts, and so he says, ***the poison of asps.***

16. Thomas's comment here addresses the three final sentences of Psalm 13:3 of the Old Vulgate translation (and the Gallican and Roman psalters). These three sentences represent an interpolation of the material of Romans 3:13–18. Beginning in Romans 3:11, Paul presents an Old Testament quotation the beginning of which matches the first sentence of Psalm 13:3. But Jerome recognized that Paul's intent was not to offer a continuous verbatim quotation of Psalm 13:3. What Paul offers instead is a mosaic of phrases and motifs from several different Old Testament texts. Hence, as Thomas and Jerome explain, we should not suppose that Paul was misquoting the Psalm as though the Old Vulgate's interpolation were already present in his Hebrew edition of the text.

99 ***Their mouth is full of cursing***: Here, he shows how they harm openly since they detract by their words ***and bitterness***—that is, bitter words. *You shall not curse the deaf* (Lev. 19:14). Or this is when he speaks words against God to provoke to harshness or anger. *Their roaring is like a lion* (Isa. 5:29). Here, he shows how they harm by deeds: ***Their feet are swift to shed blood***: *For their feet run to evil, and they make haste to shed blood* (Prov. 1:16).

100 ***Destruction and unhappiness in their ways***: Here, he shows how they are harmful to themselves. Someone harms himself in two ways: by destroying the good that he has and by failing to attain that for which he hopes. Therefore, he says, ***destruction*** [*is*] ***in their ways***, since the good that they have is destroyed. ***And unhappiness***, since they do not reach the hoped-for good—namely, happiness. *Desolation and destruction are in their highways. The way of peace they know not, and there is no justice in their paths* (Isa. 59:7–8). Or their ***destruction*** is in this world, and their ***unhappiness*** is after death, which is the opposite of happiness. *The wicked man is reserved to the day of destruction, and he shall be brought to the day of wrath* (Job 21:30 DRB). This comes along with what is opposed to the love of neighbor since ***the way of peace they have not known***—they have not known what it is, in other words. Or, ***the way of peace they have not known***—that is, Christ, since his ways are the ways of peace. *Her ways are ways of pleasantness, and all her paths are peace* (Prov. 3:17). ***They have not known*** it because by sinning, they killed Christ himself.

Another action is against the love of God, so he says, ***There is no fear of God before their eyes***, and because of this they have sinned, since, as is said, *By the fear of the Lord everyone declineth from evil* (Prov. 15:27 DRB). Therefore, since they do not have this, they are ***an open sepulcher***.

101 ***Shall not all they know that work iniquity?***[17] Here, he discusses the hope of deliverance. *First*, he shows that the wicked do not have hope since ***they shall not know***. *Second*, he shows what sort of hope it is, at ***Who shall give out of Zion***. He discusses two aspects of the wicked's lack of hope. *First*, he shows that they do not know this hope. *Second*, he gives a sign of it: ***You have confounded the counsel***. *First*, he brings the question forward, and *then*, he interposes the guilt of the wicked.

He speaks in this way: 'I say that you are an open sepulcher and that God is not in your heart, but surely you know that ***the Lord is in the just generation***?' It is as if he were to say that the Lord is in it and that they ought to know this. *Yet you, O Lord, are in the midst of us, and we are called by your name* (Jer. 14:9). ***But thou dwellest in the holy place, the praise of Israel*** (Ps. 21:4). Therefore, the Lord is in it just as he is in the temple.

17. In other words: "Have they no knowledge, all the evildoers?" (RSV).

All they who work iniquity—namely, in regard to God—and ***who devour my people as they eat bread***—in regard to their neighbors, whom they devour by taking away their goods. *Let those that are left devour the flesh of one another* (Zech. 11:9). *Who eat the flesh of my people and flay their skin from off them* (Mic. 3:3). *The bread of the needy is the life of the poor; whoever deprives them of it is a man of blood* (Sir. 34:21).

They have not called upon the Lord—that is, they do not have hope from God. ***They have not called upon God*** (Ps. 52:6), and it follows from this that they do not have security, and so he says, ***They have trembled*** (Ps. 52:6). *The wicked flee when no one pursues* (Prov. 28:1). *Terrifying sounds are in his ears; in prosperity, the destroyer will come upon him* (Job 15:21). But those who call upon God are saved. *All who call upon the name of the Lord shall be delivered* (Joel 2:32). *The name of the Lord is a strong tower* (Prov. 18:10).

Therefore, this sort do not know that ***the Lord is in the just generation***. And he shows that they do not through a sign: that ***you have confounded the counsel of the poor man***—in other words, 'You considered him as one able to be shamed and blasphemed as much as you could.' And the counsel of the poor is that he knows ***the Lord is his hope***. Psalm 21:9: ***He hoped in the Lord, let him deliver him. Let him save him, seeing he delighteth in him*** (cf. Matt 27:43). It is he who says, *If you would be perfect, go, sell what you possess and give to the poor . . . and come, follow me* (Matt. 19:21). The rich always despise this counsel. *You have ignored all my counsel and would have none of my reproof* (Prov. 1:25). And where does the counsel of the poor come from? ***The Lord is his hope*** since he has nothing in this world in which he can hope except in God, who is the hope of the saints.

102 All of the ancients awaited this. *The scepter shall not depart from Judah* (Gen. 49:10). Moreover, they expected it to come from Zion—that is, from the Jews. *Salvation is from the Jews* (John 4:22). But when will it come? I respond: we will possess it when ***the Lord shall have turned away the captivity of his people***, who are in captivity to sin and the prison of hell. *Even the captives of the mighty shall be taken, and the prey of the tyrant be rescued* (Isa. 49:25). And then ***Jacob***—that is, the people of God—***shall rejoice*** interiorly, and ***Israel shall be glad*** exteriorly.

Isaiah 6:1–7

Revelation and the Ministry of Angels

On Isaiah 6.1 (204–223)

6:1 *In the year that king Uzziah died, I saw the Lord sitting upon a throne exalted and elevated: and the house was filled with his majesty,*[18] *and what was beneath him filled the temple.*

6:2 *Upon it stood the seraphim. The one had six wings, and the other had six wings: with two they covered his face, and with two they covered his feet, and with two they flew.*

6:3 *And they cried one to another, and said, "Holy, holy, holy, the Lord God of hosts, all the earth is full of his glory."*

6:4 *And the lintels of the doors were moved at the voice of him that cried, and the house was filled with smoke.*

6:5 *And I said, "Woe is me, because I have held my peace; because I am a man of unclean lips, and I dwell in the midst of a people that has unclean lips, and I have seen with my eyes the King, the Lord of hosts."*

6:6 *And one of the seraphim flew to me, and in his hand was a live coal, which he had taken with the tongs off the altar.*

6:7 *And he touched my mouth, and said, "Behold, this has touched thy lips, and thy iniquities shall be taken away, and thy sin shall be cleansed."*

204 ***In the year that king Uzziah died***: After he denounces the fault of the two tribes, adding the corrective punishment,[19] here he threatens the punishment of final condemnation—namely, the punishment of hardness of heart—and

18. The clause "et plena domus a majestate ejus" (and the house was filled with his majesty) appears in Thomas's Latin edition, but it is not found in contemporary critical editions of the Bible or in the Sixto-Clementine Vulgate used in the Douay-Rheims translation.

19. See Thomas Aquinas, *On Isaiah* 5.1, 3 (not included in this collection).

therefore, that punishment is foretold in the manner of a sentence and with the solemnity of a judgment.

Therefore, this chapter is divided into three parts. In the *first*, the author of the sentence is described—namely, the judge; in the *second*, the one who announces the sentence—the minister of the judge—where it says, ***I said, "Woe is me"***; in the *third*, the sentence itself is set out where it says, ***hearing, hear*** (Isa. 6:9).

Concerning the *first*, two things are presented: *first*, the time of the vision; *second*, the vision itself, where it says, ***I saw the Lord sitting.***

205 As to the *first*, he says, ***In the year that king Uzziah died.*** Uzziah, who is called Azariah in 2 Kings 15:6, was struck with leprosy by the Lord because he wanted to usurp the priestly office, as it says in 2 Chronicles 26:21. After he was stricken, his son Jotham governed the house of the king and the kingdom until his death. Nevertheless, he is not said to have reigned then but rather to have been the vice-regent of his father. Then, he first reigned when his father died. Hence, this vision was revealed when Jotham reigned, and the preceding vision, when Uzziah reigned.

206 ***I saw the Lord sitting***: Here, the vision is presented. *First*, he describes the judge's throne; *second*, the ministry of his assistants where it says, ***Upon it stood the seraphim.***

Now, some say this vision was imaginary; others say it was intellectual. Moreover, the prophet himself draws a figure from something similar. As Dionysius says in his letter to Titus, figures are placed around things that the prophets see plainly and without figures in order to guide those who hear the prophecy, who can more easily receive what the prophet has seen plainly through sensible figures.[20] However it may be, it is necessary to consider two things here.

First, the imagination of the figure, either seen by the prophet or composed by him; *second*, the signification of this figure, for sensible figures are introduced in Holy Scripture to signify something spiritually, as Dionysius says, and that will be the literal sense, just as in metaphorical speech the literal sense is not what is signified by the words but what the speaker wishes to signify by them.[21]

207 Concerning the *first*, therefore, we must note that the temple built by Solomon was one-hundred-twenty cubits in height, as is said in 2 Chronicles 3:3–4, and this height was divided into three houses, the highest of which was sixty cubits, while both lower ones were thirty cubits. Of these, 1 Kings 6:8

20. Pseudo-Dionysius, *Letter 9*, 1.

21. Pseudo-Dionysius, *Letter 9*, 1, as cited by Thomas Aquinas, *Commentary on the Sentences* 3.3.3.1, qa. 2; cf. Pseudo-Dionysius, *Celestial Hierarchy* 1.2, according to the translation of Eriugena as cited in Thomas Aquinas, *Summa theologiae* 1.1.9.

says, *One went up by stairs to the middle story, and from the middle story to the third*. Therefore, he saw the throne of the Lord in the highest room, because of which it says, ***exalted***—that is, high—as it is ***elevated*** above all rooms; and the middle room shines from the brightness of his face, because of which it says, ***The house was filled with his majesty***—that is, his glory; ***and what was beneath him***—that is, the adornments of his throne or also the splendor of his garments or the ranks of his subjects—***filled*** the lower room, in which the priests entered, because of which he says, ***the temple***.

Alternatively, others say that he saw the high throne in the middle room, which is called the house, which was filled with the middle members and arms of the Lord; the lower room, which is called the temple, was filled with his feet and legs, but his head and neck extended into the third story: *I saw the Lord sitting on his throne, and all the host of heaven standing beside him on his right hand and on his left* (1 Kings 22:19); *a king who sits on the throne of judgment winnows all evil with his eyes* (Prov. 20:8).

208 Concerning the *second*, it should be observed that the various interpreters assign three different meanings to this vision. Some say that the sitting on the throne signifies the coming oppression of their captivity; the filling of the house with majesty signifies that their enemies, who were under his direction, were to fill the temple. Moreover, the *Histories* touch on this.[22]

However, Jerome offers a better explanation: the seat signifies the majesty of the Son of God, because of which John 12:41 says, *Isaiah said this because he saw his glory and spoke of him*;[23] the throne signifies the angels, on whom God sits: *You who are enthroned upon the cherubim* (Ps. 80:1); the house signifies the Church Triumphant, which is full of his glory; the temple signifies the Church Militant, which is full of miracles or with the ranks of angels, who fill it like guards.

Dionysius explains this otherwise and better, as it seems.[24] The throne signifies the eminence of the divine nature, and it is called ***exalted*** because of its nobility, ***elevated***, as if raised above others insofar as it exceeds all things infinitely. He is said to sit on this throne on account of his immovability. Hence, Dionysius says, *What, then, are we to say regarding the divine station [as characterized here by the attributes] "resting" and "sitting"? Just that God remains what he is in himself, that he is established alone in his immovable sameness and definitive grounding.*[25] Moreover, ***the house*** is said to signify all creation, which

22. This is likely a reference to Josephus's *Antiquities of the Jews*, which in some medieval manuscripts is titled *Historiae Antiquitatis Judaice*.

23. Jerome, *Commentary on Isaiah* 3.3.

24. Pseudo-Dionysius, *Celestial Hierarchy* 13.4.

25. Pseudo-Dionysius, *Divine Names* 9.8.

is full of majesty since it is filled by participation, in its capacity, in goodness itself. By ***the temple***, he seems to understand the higher creatures, which are filled with those [goods] that are lower than [goodness] itself inasmuch as the goods received in them fall short of the goodness of God, to which they nevertheless seem to come close.

209 On the contrary, an objection is that, according to Exodus 33:20, *Man*—that is, one living in this mortal flesh—*shall not see me and live*. Again, 1 John 4:12 says, *No man has ever seen God*. Therefore, neither did Isaiah see God.

In response, it must be said that neither the interior nor the exterior vision can see unless a visual object moves it. The more perfectly the visible thing changes it, the better it sees, and it sees most perfectly when it receives the action of the visual object in its full power. It is on this account that the same thing is seen differently by different persons, both interiorly and exteriorly, and better by some and worse by others.

Therefore, nothing perfectly comprehends the visible object that is God except what grasps it whole, and for this reason, he alone sees himself in this way. Hence, Chrysostom says that the heavenly secret is not seen in its essence without a medium by those who achieve it in the perfection they possess by a reception of divine light—by, for instance, the blessed in heaven and those who are elevated by rapture to that mode of vision.[26] Those with less perfect vision see God according to certain similitudes of his goodness, whether in sensible things, images, or intelligible species. This is the kind of vision by which the prophets have seen by a prophetic light, by which we see by faith, and by which even the philosophers have seen by the light of reason who had come to know of God, as Romans 1:19–20 says.

210 Nevertheless, the question remains whether the prophets perceived such a vision immediately from God or by the mediation of angels. From his way of speaking, it appears to have been immediate, for he says, ***I saw the Lord***, and not 'I saw an angel.' Likewise, of Moses, Exodus 33:11 says, *The Lord used to speak to Moses face to face as a man speaks to his friend*. Again, as is commonly said, they saw in the mirror of eternity.[27] Therefore, some have seen God.

26. John Chrysostom, *Commentary on Saint John* 15.

27. With some basis in scripture (see Wis. 7:26) and the Fathers (especially Pseudo-Dionysius), the concept "the mirror of eternity" (*speculum aeternitatis*) seems to have appeared sometime in the Middle Ages (perhaps as early as the eleventh century) in theories about prophetic and other sorts of supernatural knowledge. In Thomas, the mirror of eternity represents a reflection of God's knowledge of all things past, present, and future that, as a reflection, remains distinct from God's knowledge itself. Thomas's doctrine of divine simplicity entails that God's knowledge is identical to his essence. Thus, Thomas insists on this distinction between the mirror of eternity and God's mind to avoid saying that, in viewing the former, a prophet views the divine essence or achieves the beatific vision.

To this, it must be said, according to Dionysius, that no mere human being—none among the fathers either of the New or Old Testament—received any revelation from God except by the mediation of angels.[28] And he calls it an inviolable law that the lowest things are led back by the first intermediaries, and he proves this by an argument *a maiori*,[29] for even Moses received the law through the mediation of angels, though he saw most excellently. This is confirmed by what Galatians 3:19 says: *Why then the law? It was added because of transgressions till the offspring should come to whom the promise had been made, and it was ordained by angels through an intermediary*; and Acts 7:53: *You who received the law as delivered by angels and did not keep it.*

211 Thus, to the *first* [indication of the possibility of an unmediated revelation of God cited above: ***I saw the Lord***], it should be said that an explanation can be given by appeal to the vision's end and its principle.

Appealing to the vision's end, [the explanation is] that the revealing angel intends to lead the human being to a knowledge of God and not of himself. He thus forms a vision of God, intending that something about God should be made known from things that are seen figuratively.

Appealing to the vision's principle, [the explanation is] that all the power by which angelic light makes something manifest is from God, the author and font of light. Likewise, in demonstrative inferences, the whole power of light or manifestation derives from first principles. Hence, in a gloss on Exodus 3, Gregory says: *The angel who is described as having appeared to Moses is sometimes reported as the Lord, sometimes as an angel. An angel, because he serves in speaking outwardly; the Lord, because inwardly, the director gives the efficacy of speaking. For since the speaker is directed from within, he is recounted both as an angel from his subservience and as the Lord from his inspiration.*[30]

212 To the *second* [indication of the possibility of an unmediated revelation of God referenced above: Exodus 33:11], it must be contended that [*The Lord used to speak to Moses face to face*] is said on account of the preeminent mode of vision by which Moses saw, surpassing all other prophets, as Numbers 12:6–8 states.

213 To the *third* [indication of the possibility of an unmediated revelation of God cited above: the common reference to the mirror of eternity], it must be said that God himself is not called the mirror of eternity but those species in

28. Pseudo-Dionysius, *Celestial Hierarchy* 4.3.

29. An argument *a maiori* (or *a maiori ad minus*), a kind of *a fortiori* argument, infers what must be true of a smaller, weaker, or more limited subject on the basis of what is held to be true of a larger, stronger, or more general one. For instance, here, Thomas ascribes to Dionysius the argument that, if even the revelation of Moses—the greatest of prophets—was mediated by angels, then all the more must we say that angels mediate the revelations of lesser prophets.

30. Gregory the Great, preface to *Moralia in Job* 1.3.

the prophet's soul. Moreover, they are called a mirror insofar as the disposition of eternal wisdom is reflected in them.

214 ***Stood the seraphim***: Here, he sets out the ministers' office. And *first*, he describes the order of the ministers; *second*, their praise: ***they cried one to another and said, "holy."***

Concerning the *first*, he sets out three things. *First*, he asserts the rank of the ministers, saying, ***Upon it***—namely, the temple—***stood the seraphim***, because the order of seraphim is supreme among all, as Dionysius says in a gloss on this passage.[31] Likewise, note that 'seraphim,' written with an 'm,' is plural in number and masculine in gender and signifies many of that order; written with an 'n,' however, it is neuter in gender and signifies the whole multitude of this order; but 'seraph' is singular in number and masculine in gender and signifies only one member of this order.[32] Below: ***Upon thy walls, O Jerusalem, I have appointed watchmen all the day and all the night, they shall never hold their peace*** (Isa. 62:6). And he says they ***stood***, upright in contemplation as if assisting.

Second, he sets out the adornment of the ministers in the number of their wings: ***six wings***. *Third*, the use of their wings: ***with two, they covered his face.*** In Hebrew, the statement is ambiguous. A possible explanation is that they covered the face of God, and Jerome understands it this way.[33] Another explanation is that they cover their own face, and Dionysius understands it this way.[34] According to him, the sense is that their heads were covered and their feet and the middle of their bodies, and ***with two, they flew***—namely, the middle two: *Each creature had two wings covering its body* (Ezek. 1:23), and below this: *I heard the sound of their wings like the sound of many waters* (Ezek. 1:24).

215 The signification of this vision can be interpreted in three ways. The Hebrew says that the twelve wings mean the twelve kings who ruled over the people from Uzziah, under whom the vision began, and those who followed him.[35] Only four of these were just—namely, Uzziah, Jotham, Hezekiah, and Josiah. On this account, they flew with four wings. The others, however, were ashamed in the sight of God, and thus, they covered their face. Four of these possessed

31. Cf. Pseudo-Dionysius, *Celestial Hierarchy* 7.1.

32. Thomas's morphological clarification is puzzling as it somewhat undermines his interpretation, according to which the passage indicates the supremacy, not of a plurality, but of the whole angelic order of seraphim. The distinction he highlights between the masculine and neuter plural implies that the neuter would be the appropriate form for ascribing supremacy to the *whole* order. Yet, the passage features the masculine form as if to indicate the supremacy of *some* but not all of the seraphim.

33. Jerome, *Commentary on Isaiah* 3.4.

34. Pseudo-Dionysius, *Celestial Hierarchy* 13.4.

35. Jerome, *Letter 18*, 10.

the kingdom freely—namely, Ahaz, Manasseh, Amon, and Jotham[36]—because the people made them kings, and these are signified by the wings that were on the head. The other four, in truth, possessed the kingdom under the servitude of others. Hence also they were made kings by others and not by the people, as Jehoiakim, made king by Pharaoh, Jehoiachin and Zedekiah and Gedaliah, about whom Jeremiah says: *Ishmael . . . and the ten men with him rose up and struck down Gedaliah . . . whom the king of Babylon had appointed governor in the land* (Jer. 41:2). For these last three were made king by Nebuchadnezzar, king of Babylon.

216 Jerome says that the seraphim are said to be winged either because they dwell above or because of the swiftness of their ministry. He understands the twelve wings to represent the ministry of perfection, which is betokened in the number twelve, as the twelve gems in the priest's crown, and thus concerning the others.[37] ***And with two they flew***, because they conceal from us those things that were before the world or after the world, and they show the things that happen in the six ages of the world; or because the past and the future are unknown to us, but we know the present: so this refers to the act of their ministry, and they ***stood***, in order to assist God.

217 Dionysius explains this otherwise. He explains that they are said to be winged because, similar to something that flies, they have deep and free contemplation.[38] Three pairs of wings are described, moreover, because the seraphim see those things that pertain to themselves, who are of the first hierarchy, and those things that pertain to the other two hierarchies more eminently than they who belong to them: so that by one wing is understood their natural capacity, and by the other, the light from God in which they participate, for by these two things they are elevated.

Now, those things that pertain to the hierarchies come from God as from a beginning and are ordered to God as to an end, and by neither manner can they be perfectly understood by the angels, which the veiling signifies. And they are also in themselves like a medium between the beginning and end, and they have perfect and free knowledge of them in this way, and therefore, with the two middle wings, they flew.

218 ***And they cried one to another***: Here, he presents their praise and does three things in connection with this theme. *First*, regarding their devotion, he shows their manner of praising, for ***they cried*** from the greatness of their affection; regarding their concord, that both cry out; regarding their order, that they

36. Jotham's inclusion in this list appears to be an error. Jehoahaz is the name most likely intended here, of whom 2 Kings 23:32 says, "He did what was evil in the sight of the Lord."

37. Jerome, *Commentary on Isaiah* 3.4.

38. Pseudo-Dionysius, *Celestial Hierarchy* 13; *Ecclesiastical Hierarchy* 4.

cry out ***one to another***, for one receives from the other, as Dionysius holds.[39] *Where were you . . . when the morning stars sang together, and all the sons of God shouted for joy?* (Job 38:4, 7).

219 *Second*, he sets out their song of praise, where it says, ***Holy, holy, holy***. And they praise three things: the Trinity of persons: ***Holy, holy, holy***; the unity of majesty: ***the Lord God of hosts***, who is before all things: *Holy, holy, holy is the Lord God almighty, who was and is and is to come* (Rev. 4:8); the liberality of his providence: ***all the earth is full of his glory***, for he also extends the diffusion of his goodness to the last creature, which is understood by ***the earth***: *Do not I fill heaven and earth? says the Lord* (Jer. 23:24). And this is according to Dionysius.[40] According to Jerome, ***all the earth is full*** through the knowledge of faith.[41] *Full of the glory of the Lord is his work. Hath not the Lord made the saints to declare all his wonderful works, which the Lord Almighty hath firmly settled to be established for his glory?* (Sir. 42:16–17 DRB).

220 *Third*, where it says, ***And the lintels***, he sets out the effect of their praise—namely, the punishment of sinners—below: ***Behold my servants shall eat, and you shall be hungry: behold my servants shall drink, and you shall be thirsty. . . . Behold my servants shall praise for joyfulness of heart, and you shall cry for sorrow of heart and shall howl for grief of spirit*** (Isa. 65:13–14). And the destruction of the temple is signified: ***The lintels of the doors were moved***: *Strike the hinges, and let the lintels be shook* (Amos 9:1 DRB); and the burning of the temple: ***The house was filled with smoke*** of burning by the Romans after the faith of Christ was known. Or by ***smoke***, the infidelity of the Jews is signified; by the movement of the hinges, the removal of their legal observances or ceremonies, which were like shadows enclosing the entrance to the truth.

221 ***And I said***: Here, the announcer of the sentence is presented. And *first*, his humility is shown; *second*, his purity: ***One of the seraphim flew to me***; *third*, his authority: ***and I heard*** (Isa. 6:8). His humility is shown in confession of sin. And he confesses a threefold sin.

The *first* is sin in speaking—a sin of omission: ***Woe is me because I have held my peace*** in not denouncing Uzziah the king, and thus he laments the fault; ***I have held my peace*** from praising God, and thus he laments the harm below in Isaiah 56:10: ***His watchmen are all blind, they are all ignorant: dumb dogs not able to bark, seeing vain things, sleeping and loving dreams.*** *A hymn of praise is not fitting on the lips of a sinner* (Sir. 15:9). Sin of commission:

39. Pseudo-Dionysius, *Celestial Hierarchy* 10.2; *Ecclesiastical Hierarchy* 4.3.9.

40. Pseudo-Dionysius, *Celestial Hierarchy* 7.4.

41. Jerome, *Letter 18*, 7.

I am a man of unclean lips. *Do not accustom your mouth to lewd vulgarity, for it involves sinful speech* (Sir. 23:13).

The *second* is a sin of association with the wicked: ***I dwell in the midst of a people that has unclean lips.*** *Bad company ruins good morals* (1 Cor. 15:33).

The *third* is a sin of presumption: ***I have seen with my eyes the King, the Lord of hosts***, as if to say: 'He who is impure cannot enter the Lord's temple; how much more can he not see the Lord himself?' *We shall surely die, for we have seen God* (Judg. 13:22), and this was from reverence. But Jacob said: *For I have seen God face to face, and yet my life is preserved* (Gen. 32:30); and this is from confidence. Jerome: *Happy conscience which has sinned in speech, not by his own vice, but only of a people that has unclean lips.*[42]

222 ***One of the seraphim flew to me***: Here, he shows his purity from the cleansing of his sins. And concerning this, he sets out three things. The minister of the cleansing: ***One of the seraphim flew to me.*** The instrument of cleansing: ***in his hand was a live coal . . . off the altar*** of holocausts. The inner altar was made of earth as is said in Exodus 20:24: *An altar of earth you shall make for me*; all around, however, was made of stone, where the fires of sacrifice were assembled; from these he took the coal. ***With the tongs***—that is, with an instrument having two arms by which receptive virtue may be signified—and by ***the altar***, divine light itself or goodness, and by ***the coal***, the gift received for the office of cleansing. Or by the fire, tribulation may be signified; by ***the seraphim***, Christ; by ***the tongs***, the two testaments; by ***the coal***, charity, which is in his hand—that is, his works.

Third, the manner of cleansing: ***He touched my mouth and said***—in the sacraments there is, likewise, an action and a form of words—***Behold this has touched thy lips*** expresses the act ***and thy iniquities*** against human beings ***shall be taken away, and thy sin*** against God. And he does not say, 'I shall take away,' for to forgive sins belongs to God alone, below: ***I am he that blot out thy iniquities for my own sake, and I will not remember thy sins*** (Isa. 43:25). Concerning all these things, Daniel 9:21–22 says, *The man Gabriel, whom I had seen in the vision at the first, came to me in swift flight at the time of the evening sacrifice. He came, and he said to me . . .*

223 But against this, it is objected that Dionysius says that those who belong to the higher orders are not sent in service,[43] but the seraphim certainly are the highest. Therefore, it does not seem true that they came to cleanse the prophet.

42. Jerome, *Commentary on Isaiah* 3.6.

43. Pseudo-Dionysius, *Celestial Hierarchy* 13.2.

To this, it should be said that Gregory touches on this question (in a certain homily concerning the hundred sheep) and leaves the matter in doubt.[44] Dionysius, however, expressly holds that only the inferior orders are sent to us, and he says this is by the order of divine law: lower things are restored through middle ones.[45] But he explains what is said here in two ways.[46] In one way, he says that this cleansing angel is called a seraph equivocally, not from his order but from the act that he was then carrying out because he cleansed with fire, and 'seraph' means 'fire'; in another way, he explains it saying that he is called a seraph properly because he is of this order and he is said to cleanse, not because he himself immediately cleanses, but because by his authority, or by an illumination received from him, a lower angel cleansed. And he gives an example: it is just as a bishop is said to absolve when another absolves by his authority. Therefore, because of reverence, the lower angel, who formed the vision, restores to God first and to the seraph second, as if he were saying: 'I cleanse you by light received from God, by the mediation of a seraph.' In verse 6, the Septuagint has ***carbuncle*** instead of 'live coal' because of their similarity to fire, for they have a flaming color.

44. Gregory the Great, *Forty Gospel Homilies* 34.13.

45. Pseudo-Dionysius, *Celestial Hierarchy* 4.3.

46. Pseudo-Dionysius, *Celestial Hierarchy* 13.2–3.

Job 4:12–5:1

Human Fallibility and the Varieties of Revelation

On Job 4.3 (81–92)

4:12 *Now there was a word spoken to me in private, and my ears, by stealth as it were, received the veins of its whisper.*

4:13 *In the horror of a vision by night, when deep sleep is wont to hold men,*

4:14 *Fear seized upon me, and trembling, and all my bones were affrighted:*

4:15 *And when a spirit passed before me, the hairs of my flesh stood up.*

4:16 *There stood one whose countenance I knew not, an image before my eyes, and I heard the voice as it were of a gentle wind:*

4:17 *"Shall man be justified in comparison of God, or shall a man be more pure than his maker?*

4:18 *Behold they that serve him are not steadfast, and in his angels, he found wickedness:*

4:19 *How much more shall they that dwell in houses of clay, who have an earthly foundation, be consumed as with the moth?*

4:20 *From morning till evening, they shall be cut down; because no one understandeth, they shall perish forever.*

4:21 *And they that shall be left, shall be taken away from them; they shall die, and not in wisdom."*

5:1 *Call now if there be anyone that will answer thee and turn to some of the saints.*

81 *Now, there was a word spoken to me in private*: Because Eliphaz had accepted that adversities in this life only happened to someone because of his sin, con-

sequently, he wishes to accuse Job and his family of being subject to sin. This accusation seemed contrary to what was apparent in Job and his family, and thus, he wishes to demonstrate that neither Job nor his family was immune from sin. Because Job's authority and reputation seemed to invalidate his word, he resorts to a higher authority, indicating that he had learned from revelation what he was preparing to report. Moreover, he indicates the revelation's elevation by asserting its obscurity, for the higher things are, the less perceptible they are from a human perspective. As Saint Paul says, *This man was caught up into Paradise . . . and he heard things that cannot be told, which man may not utter* (2 Cor. 12:3–4). In this way, Eliphaz also speaks, whether truthfully or fictitiously, saying, ***there was a word spoken to me in private.***

82 Consider that some truth, although hidden from human beings because of its exalted character, is revealed clearly to some and in a hidden way to others. To avoid being seen as boasting, he says that this truth was revealed to him in a hidden way: ***my ears, by stealth as it were, received the veins of its whisper.***

Here, he implies that there are three ways in which things are hidden in revelations. The *first* is when an imaginary vision reveals an intelligible truth to someone. As Numbers says, *If there is a prophet among you, I the Lord make myself known to him in a vision, I speak with him in a dream. Not so with my servant Moses. . . . With him, I speak mouth to mouth, clearly, and not in dark speech* (12:6–8). Moses, then, heard this hidden word in a clear voice. Others, however, hear in the manner of a whisper.

The *second* hidden manner is in the imaginary vision, when words are spoken that sometimes expressly contain the truth, as in the text of Isaiah: *Behold, a virgin shall conceive* (7:14); or sometimes under certain figures of speech, as in Isaiah: *There shall come forth a shoot from the stump of Jesse, and a branch shall grow out of his roots* (11:1). When, therefore, Isaiah heard *Behold, a virgin shall conceive*, he perceived the whispering itself, but when he heard, *There shall come forth a shoot from the stump of Jesse*, he perceived the veins of the whisper, for figures of speech are like veins derived from the truth itself through the likeness of a simile.

The *third* hidden way is when someone sometimes has a frequent and long-lasting revelation of God, as Exodus says about Moses: *Thus the Lord used to speak to Moses face to face, as a man speaks to his friend* (33:11). Sometimes someone has a sudden and passing revelation. Eliphaz shows the sudden character of his revelation when he says, ***by stealth***, for we hear those things almost stealthily that come to us quickly and in, as it were, a fleeting moment.

83 After he shows the high source of the vision in this way, he proceeds to the circumstances of the revelation. *First*, he speaks of the time, saying, ***In the horror of a vision by night, when deep sleep is wont to hold men*** because the

quiet night is more suitable for receiving revelations. During the day, the mind suffers noise from human commotions and the occupations of the senses so that it cannot perceive the whispering of a hidden word.

84 *Second*, he speaks of the recipient's disposition, adding ***Fear seized upon me***, for people usually are struck with fear at the unusual. Hence, when someone has strange revelations, he initially suffers fear. He adds, ***trembling*** to show the greatness of this fear, for the trembling of the body indicates the magnitude of fear. To emphasize this sort of trembling, he continues, ***and all my bones were affrighted***—as if to say, 'This trembling shows that the trembling was not superficial but violent, the kind that strikes even the bones.' Something similar is described in Daniel: *I . . . saw this great vision, and no strength was left in me; my radiant appearance was fearfully changed, and I retained no strength* (10:8). Consequently, he shows the cause of this fear, saying, ***When a spirit passed before me, the hairs of my flesh stood up***. For it is reasonable that one with lesser power is awestruck in the presence of one with greater power.

It is clear that the power of the spirit is greater than the power of the flesh, so it is not surprising that the flesh's hairs stand up in the spirit's presence, as happens when one is overcome by sudden fear. This is especially true when the presence of a spirit is felt in some strange corporeal phenomenon, for strange things usually lead to wonder and fear. Above, he said, ***In the horror of a vision by night*** so that the time expressed would correspond to this dread he recalls suffering. Indeed, at nighttime, any slight motion is liable to induce anxiety, as we suppose it to be something larger. This is what Wisdom says: *Whether there came a whistling wind, or a melodious sound of birds in wide-spreading branches . . . it paralyzed them with terror* (17:18–19).

85 *Third*, he presents the person revealing, when he says, ***There stood one whose countenance I knew not, an image before my eyes***. Here, he indicates three things that show for certain that it was a vision.

Note that, sometimes, due to an extreme disturbance of humors and vapors, either dreams do not appear at all because there are no phantasms, or they appear in a confused and disturbed way, as is often the case with those who have a fever. Such dreams, having little or no spirituality, exist entirely without significance. When, however, the humors and vapors have settled, quiet and ordered dreams appear, and as these are more spiritual, they emerge from the intellectual part of the soul with some strength. Dreams of this sort are usually truer. Therefore, he says, ***There stood***, which shows the stability of the vision.

Further, note that even when dreams are tranquil, they are the vestiges, for the most part, of thoughts of prior experiences. Hence, in a dream, one frequently sees those with whom he is accustomed to interact. Because such dreams have their cause in us and not in a higher nature, they have no great meaning. He shows this is not the case when he says, ***whose countenance I knew not.*** In this, he shows that this kind of vision did not originate from something he had already experienced but from a more hidden cause.

Third, consider that visions of this kind that arise from a higher cause sometimes appear to those who are asleep and at other times to those who are awake. Those seem to be truer and more certain that occur to those who are awake than those that appear to those who are asleep because reason is less restrained in someone who is awake and because, in sleep, one does not readily discern the difference between spiritual revelations and frivolous or ordinary dreams. To show that this revelation was not made to someone asleep but to one who was awake, he says, ***an image before my eyes.*** He means here that he saw this with the open eyes of someone awake. He also meant to express this before where he said, ***when deep sleep is wont to hold men*** and clarifies that he had not been seized by sleep.

86 Then he tells of the manner of the declaration made to him, saying, ***I heard the voice as it were of a gentle wind.*** Note here that apparitions of this kind are sometimes made from a good spirit, sometimes from an evil one. In both varieties, a person suffers fear in the beginning due to the unusual character of the vision. But when the apparition proceeds from a good spirit, the fear ends in consolation, as is evident with the angel who comforts Daniel (Dan. 10:18) and when Gabriel comforts Zechariah and Mary in Luke (1:13, 30). An evil spirit, however, leaves a person disturbed. The fact that he says, ***I heard the voice as it were of a gentle wind***, demonstrates a consolation that put his former fear to rest. This statement proves the vision to be from a good spirit, not a wicked one, by whom lying visions are often shown. The end of 1 Kings expresses the same thing: *I will go forth and will be a lying spirit in the mouth of all his prophets* (22:22).

The book of 1 Kings also speaks in this way of the apparition made to Elijah: *After the earthquake . . .* [*came*] *a still small voice* (19:12), and there was the Lord. However, we should note that sometimes one hears great disturbances and horrible voices even in visions that come from a good spirit, as is apparent in Ezekiel when it is said, *As I looked, behold, a stormy wind came out of the north* (1:4), and after many verses he adds, *I heard the sound of their wings like the sound of many waters* (1:24). Revelation says, *I heard behind me a loud voice like a trumpet* (1:10). This describes the threats or other grave dangers that these kinds of revelation contain. However, because something consoling must have been said here, the voice speaking is likened to a gentle breeze.

87 Finally, he expresses the words that he asserts were revealed to him when he says, ***Shall man be justified in comparison of God?*** He introduces these words

to confirm his opinion, which he already touched on (Job 4:7)—namely, that adversities do not happen to someone in this life except because of sin.

He presents three reasons to prove that no one can excuse himself when he suffers adverse things by asserting that he is free from sin. The *first* is drawn from a comparison of human beings to God and leads to an impossible conclusion: if a person is punished by God without being at fault, it follows that he is more just than God. The work of justice is to give each his due. So if God should inflict punishment on an innocent person who deserves no punishment, and if he, though afflicted by God, has inflicted punishment on no one—which we have to say if we suppose him to be innocent—it follows that this person punished by God would be more just than God because a human being is justified in comparison to God—that is, justified relative to God in comparison of justice. As perhaps this might not seem unfitting to someone, he carries the argument to another more obviously unfitting conclusion, saying, ***Shall a man be more pure than his maker?*** Each thing has purity according as its nature is preserved within it, which it receives from its proper causes. So, the purity of each effect depends on its cause, and it cannot surpass its cause in purity. Thus, human beings cannot be purer than their Creator, God.

88 His *second* argument comes from a comparison to the angels. It is an *a maiori* argument[47] when he says, ***They that serve him are not steadfast, and in his angels, he found wickedness.*** This opinion is clear according to the Catholic faith. The Catholic faith holds as certain that all angels were created good. Some of them fell through their own fault from the state of righteousness; some, however, attained a greater glory. The fact that the angels fell from the state of righteousness seems astonishing for two reasons, one relating to their contemplative power and the other to their active power. From the contemplative power, it seems that there should have been steadfastness in the angels. It is clear that the cause of mutability is potency; the cause of immutability is act. Moreover, to be disposed both to being and nonbeing belongs to the nature of potency. But as what is more perfected by actuality remains more fixed in one thing, what is intrinsically actual is completely unchangeable.

We must observe that just as matter is related to form as potency is to act, so the will relates to the good. What is good in itself—namely, God—is entirely unchangeable. However, the wills of other natures, which are not good in themselves, relate to him as potency to act. Thus, the more they cleave to him, the more confirmed they are in good. So, since the angels seem to cleave more to God and more closely than other creatures, as they contemplate him more keenly, they seem to be more steadfast than other creatures. Yet they were

47. For definition of *a maiori* arguments, see 87n29 above.

not steadfast. Thus, much less can lower creatures—humans, for instance—be judged stable however much they seem to cleave to God in worship, which is service to him. On the part of active power, it seems there could be little or no depravity in the angels, for the more a ruler approximates the first rectitude, the less crookedness it has. However, God, in whom the first rectitude exists, directs all things by his providence and orders lower creatures through higher ones.

Hence, as God sends them to direct others, there seems to be little or no perversity possible in the higher creatures who are called angels. So, if there can be perversity in them, one must believe that depravity could be found in any person, however great he may appear to be. However, one should take care that, from this opinion, he does not fall into the error of Origen, who asserts that even now, no created spirit is steadfast but all can be seduced into depravity.[48] For some, by grace, have gained the favor to cling to God unchangeably by seeing him in his essence. In this way, even some people, although lower in nature than the angels, by grace are granted immunity from the depravity of mortal sin even in this life.

89 Eliphaz takes his *third* argument from the human condition, to which he joins the conclusion of the preceding argument—hence, one could even form a single argument from the two. He does this when he says, ***How much more shall they that dwell in houses of clay.*** The human condition is such that the body is formed from earthly matter. He indicates this, saying, ***How much more shall they that dwell in houses of clay.*** The human body is said to be of clay because earth and water, the heavier elements, are more abundant in its constitution, as its motion indicates. So Genesis says, *God formed man of dust from the ground* (Gen. 2:7). This body of clay is called the house of the soul because the human soul is situated in the body, as a person in a house or a sailor on a ship, as the mover of the body. Because of this, some said that the soul was only accidentally united to the body, as a person is to clothes or a sailor on a ship. But he disproves this opinion when he adds, ***who have an earthly foundation.***

By this, we are given to understand that the human soul is united to the body as form to matter. Moreover, matter is said to be the foundation of form because it is the first part in the generation of a thing like the foundation is the first part in the building of a house. Now, he uses this manner of speaking to attribute to the human person what belongs to the soul, not that the soul is the human person as some held who said that a human being is merely a soul clothed with a body. He speaks this way, instead, because the soul is the more principal part of a human being. Each thing is usually called by what is more principal in it. These two things that he says about human weakness seem to be

48. See Origen, *On First Principles* 1.5.4.

set in opposition to what he had said above about the excellence of the angels. For the phrase ***they that dwell in houses of clay*** appears to be placed in opposition to what he said in ***they that serve him*** cling to him and live spiritually in him. However, when he says, ***who have an earthly foundation***, this seems to oppose ***in his angels***, for angels are incorporeal in nature according to the Psalm: *Who makest thy angels spirits* (Ps. 103:4 DRB).

90 From the premise of the human condition, he draws the conclusion of a miserable human destiny, saying, ***be consumed as with the moth.*** This can be understood in a prima facie literal sense to refer to bodily death, which a person necessarily suffers due to his earthly foundation. In this way, it can mean two sorts of death. First, it can mean natural death, by the expression ***be consumed as with the moth.*** For just as a moth corrupts the clothing from which it is born, so the natural death of the body arises from interior causes. However, it can also refer to violent death, for subsequently he says, ***From morning till evening, they shall be cut down***, for trees are cut down by a cause outside the tree itself. He says distinctly enough, ***From morning till evening***, because natural death can undoubtedly be foreseen before it happens by certain natural symptoms. Nevertheless, violent death is entirely uncertain, as though it were subject to different causes.

For this reason, a person cannot know if he will live from morning until evening. Yet note that this is not the meaning of the literal sense because, above, he addressed the defect of sin when he said he found wickedness in his angels. So, as the conclusion must follow from the premises, this passage must also refer to sin. Sin consumes the human life of justice in two ways. In one way, from interior corruption, to which he refers in saying, ***be consumed as with the moth.*** Just as clothing is eaten by the moth that is born from it, a person's justice is destroyed by things within him, such as the corruption of evil desires, evil thoughts, and other such things. In another way, it is corrupted by exterior temptation, which is indicated when he says, ***From morning till evening, they shall be cut down.*** Consider here that interior temptation does not suddenly overthrow someone but gradually overcomes him when, through negligence, he does not take care to restrain the first movements of sin in him: *He who despises small things will fail little by little* (Sir. 19:1). In the same way, clothing that is not shaken out is eaten by a moth. However, exterior temptation generally overcomes a person suddenly. In this way, David fell into adultery at the sight of a woman, and many denied the faith under torture.

91 However a person might fall into sin, he will obtain mercy if he acknowledges his sin and repents. But because no one could recognize all his sins, per the verse *Who can discern his errors?* (Ps. 19:12), it follows that many do not apply the remedy by which they might be freed because they are not cogni-

zant of their sins. In the next verse, he expresses this, saying, ***because no one understandeth***—the errors of sinners—***they shall perish forever***, for many are never freed from sin. Nevertheless, because some apply remedies against sins even though they are not aware of them, like David, who said, *Clear thou me from hidden faults* (Ps. 19:12), he adds, ***they that shall be left***—that is, excluded from the number of those who perish in eternity—***shall be taken away from them***, for they will be separated from their company. ***They shall die*** because, though a person may repent from his sin, he is still not free from the necessity of dying, but wisdom will not die in them.

This is what ***and not in wisdom*** means. Alternatively, this statement ***they shall die and not in wisdom*** does not relate to the phrase immediately preceding it [***they that shall be left shall be taken away from them***] but to what he had said above it: ***they shall perish forever*** such that sense is 'they will die without wisdom.' Or ***they that shall be left*** may mean the children who remain after their parents die and who, because of the sins of their parents, which they imitate, are borne away to death without wisdom. Eliphaz wants to establish from all the foregoing arguments that one easily falls into sin because the human condition is so fragile: without knowing it, a person and his children advance toward perdition. In the same way, although Job might not recognize himself as a sinner, [Eliphaz argued,] one had to believe that he and his children were perishing on account of some sins.

92 So, after Eliphaz has explained his revelation, since Job could not have believed this revelation, he adds, ***Call now if there be anyone that will answer thee***, as if to say, 'If you do not believe that this was revealed to me, you can invoke God if perhaps he will answer this doubt for you. If you do not think you can obtain this from God through your own merits, ***turn to some of the saints*** so that, by their mediation, you will be able to know the truth from God about this matter.'

Note that he says, ***to some of the saints***, because one should not diligently investigate hidden things through unclean spirits in just any way or using any technique. According to Isaiah, one may only do this through God or the holy ones: *When they say to you, "Consult the mediums and the wizards who chirp and mutter," should not a people consult their God? Should they consult the dead on behalf of the living?* (Isa. 8:19).

Chapter 4

CHRIST, REDEMPTION, AND THE CHURCH

Isaiah 7:10–25

Prophecies of the Incarnation

On Isaiah 7.2 (244–262)

7:10 *And the Lord spoke again to Ahaz, saying:*

7:11 *Ask thee a sign of the Lord thy God either unto the depth of hell, or unto the height above.*

7:12 *And Ahaz said: I will not ask, and I will not tempt the Lord.*

7:13 *And he said: Hear ye therefore, O house of David: Is it a small thing for you to be grievous to men, that you are grievous to my God also?*

7:14 *Therefore the Lord himself shall give you a sign. Behold a virgin shall conceive and bear a son, and his name shall be called Emmanuel.*

7:15 *He shall eat butter and honey, that he may know to refuse the evil and to choose the good.*

7:16 *For before the child know to refuse the evil and to choose the good, the land which thou abhorrest shall be forsaken of the face of her two kings.*

7:17 *The Lord shall bring upon thee, and upon thy people, and upon the house of thy father, days that have not come since the time of the separation of Ephraim from Judah with the king of the Assyrians.*

7:18 *And it shall come to pass in that day that the Lord shall hiss for the fly that is in the uttermost parts of the rivers of Egypt and for the bee that is in the land of Assyria.*

7:19 *And they shall come and shall all of them rest in the torrents of the valleys, and in the holes of the rocks, and upon all places set with shrubs, and in all hollow places.*

7:20 *In that day the Lord shall shave with a sharp razor by them*[1] *that are beyond the river, by the king of the Assyrians, the head and the hairs of the feet, and the whole beard.*

7:21 *And it shall come to pass in that day that a man shall nourish a young cow and two sheep.*

7:22 *And for the abundance of milk he shall eat butter: for butter and honey shall everyone eat that shall be left in the midst of the land.*

7:23 *And it shall come to pass in that day that every place where there were a thousand vines, at a thousand pieces of silver, shall become thorns and briers.*

7:24 *With arrows and with bows they shall go in thither, for briars and thorns shall be in all the land.*

7:25 *And as for all the hills that shall be raked with a rake, the fear of thorns and briers shall not come thither, but they shall be for the ox to feed on and the lesser cattle to tread upon.*

244 ***And the Lord spoke again to Ahaz***: Here, the sign of liberation is presented. And *first*, the sign is offered; *second*, a sign is given to encourage belief: ***Therefore, the Lord himself shall give.***

Concerning the *first*, three things are set out. *First*, a sign is offered: ***the Lord spoke again to Ahaz.*** Because he disdained the prophets, the Lord spoke on his own behalf. Because it seems hard [to believe] that such powerful kings should be destroyed so quickly, he says, ***Ask thee a sign***—that you might believe—***of the Lord thy God.***

From this expression, it seems that these would be the words of a prophet. It must be said, however, that it is a custom of Hebrew speech to use a noun for a pronoun. Hence, ***of the Lord thy God*** means to say, 'of me.' Or they are the words of the Lord through inspiration and of the prophet through declaration,

1. Thomas's edition differs here from the Douay-Rheims translation, which says, "the Lord shall shave with a razor that is hired by them that are beyond the river."

below: ***Should not the prophet*[2] *seek of his God?*** (Isa. 8:19). ***Unto the depth of hell***, so that the earth should be opened and hell exposed, as in the destruction of Dathan and Abiram (Num. 16:31–33). Alternatively, hell means the lower elements, as when Moses brought forth locusts and gnats from the earth (Exod. 8:16–19, 10:1–20). ***Or unto the height above***, as when the sun stood still for Joshua (Josh. 10:1–15): *For Jews demand signs* (1 Cor. 1:22).

245 *Second* comes the refusal of the offer: ***Ahaz said: I will not ask,*** either because he was trusting in idols or the king of the Assyrians, or because he was jealous of God's glory, or because he feared to offend God as he was in a desperate situation. Later in Isaiah, it says, ***Lord, they have sought after thee in distress*** (26:16). Hence, he says, ***I will not tempt the Lord***, relying on what Deuteronomy 6:16 says: *You shall not put the Lord your God to the test.* Nevertheless, he understood poorly, for he was allowed to seek a sign by the authority of the Lord, as Gideon did with the fleece (Judg. 6:36–40).

246 *Third*, the rebuke of the refusal is presented: ***And he***—namely, Isaiah—***said***: 'Since you are so rebellious,' ***hear ye therefore, O house of David***. He says this either on account of the king's consent in malice or because David was given as a sign foretelling of Christ: *One of the sons of your body I will set on your throne* (Ps. 132:11). ***Is it a small thing for you***—'that merits divine wrath'—***to be grievous to men***—'whom you plunder, or to the prophets, in whom you do not believe'—***that you are grievous***—'by your rebellion'—***to my God***—'not yours, whom you did not obey'? *You are the burden, for I will cast you away, saith the Lord* (Jer. 23:33 DRB).

247 ***Therefore, the Lord himself shall give you a sign***: Here, the sign is given to encourage belief. And *first*, a sign of liberation is conferred; *second*, he threatens unbelievers with the punishment of destruction: ***The Lord shall bring upon thee***. Moreover, this sign is of Christ's Incarnation. However, the Jews raise multiple objections against this claim.

The *first* is that the Lord was giving a sign of the Jewish liberation, to which Christ's Incarnation has no connection. To this, it must be said that the Incarnation of Christ signifies this liberation by an *a maiori* argument,[3] 'for if God is going to give his son for the salvation of the whole world, how much more is he able to save you from these enemies?' *He who did not spare his own Son but gave him up for us all* (Rom. 8:32). Alternatively, [Christ's Incarnation relates to the liberation of the Jews] as a motive cause, for it was as if this moved the Lord so that many good things would be given to this people, however unjust they were, because he had planned for his incarnate son to be from them.

2. Thomas's edition has "prophet" (*propheta*) here, although in the Vulgate (and hence, the Douay-Rheims) and most modern editions, the passage says "people" (*populus*).

3. For definition of *a maiori* arguments, see 87n29 above.

248 Again, they object that the following sign was given to those who were present but that the Incarnation did not happen in their time, and accordingly, it seems that [the Incarnation] would be no sign [for them]. In response to this, it must be said that, although [the Incarnation] would not occur while those persons were present, it did occur, nevertheless, while the house of David endured: hence he says, ***Hear . . . O house of David*** and not 'Hear, Ahaz.'

249 Likewise, they object that a sign ought to precede the thing signified, but the Incarnation happened long after the liberation, and therefore, it was not a sign of it. To this, it must be said that a sign sometimes follows the thing it signifies, as in Deuteronomy 18:22: *Thou shalt have this sign: whatsoever that same prophet foretelleth in the name of the Lord, and it cometh not to pass, that thing the Lord hath not spoken* (DRB);[4] sometimes it occurs at the same time: *When you hear the sound of marching in the tops of the balsam trees, then bestir yourself* (2 Sam. 5:24);[5] sometimes the sign precedes the thing it signifies, as in the case of Gideon in Judges 7:5–7, where, in the men who had lapped water with their hands, he was given the sign that he would obtain sure victory.

Moreover, [returning to the virgin birth,] it is necessary that this sign should follow what it signifies, even in the way they themselves explain it, for if it precedes what it signifies, then the child was born shortly before the death of Pekah, who reigned twenty years. In the seventeenth year of his reign, Ahaz began to reign, and Ahaz reigned sixteen years. Therefore, Ahaz reigned thirteen years after the death of Pekah, and in the twelfth year of Ahaz, Hoshea began to reign. In the ninth year of his reign, Samaria was captured, and this was six years after Ahaz's death. Therefore, at the capture of Samaria, the child would have been at least nineteen years old, and thus, what is said below in Isaiah 8:4, that the child did not know to call his father and mother, would be false.[6]

---

4. The sign here is evidently the fact that his prophecy proves false. The "thing signified," in turn, appears to be the fact of the prophet's fraudulence. Moreover, the thing signified precedes the sign, here, in the sense that the prophet was a fraud before the sign revealed his fraudulence.

5. The action ("bestir yourself") is the thing signified in this example of a sign that works as a kind of cue for what it signifies.

6. Thomas is arguing here against the objection described above in section 249 that the Incarnation could not have been the sign described in Isaiah 7:14–17 given that the latter is meant to be a sign of the liberation of Judah, which was to occur centuries before the Incarnation. The fact that the Incarnation followed the Jewish liberation cannot be a decisive objection against the Christian interpretation of this passage, Thomas argues, because even in the alternative interpretation favored by those who object to it, the sign of the young child (Emmanuel or Ma'her-shal'al-hash-baz, in Isaiah 8:3), necessarily follows the liberation of Judah that it signifies. Thomas pieces together a complicated timeline based on the succession of the last two northern Israeli-Samarian kings, Pekah and Hoshea, and the concurrent regency of King Ahaz of Judah. His purpose is to relate three events (or periods) in time: the oracle given to Ahaz, the birth and early childhood of the prophesied child (the sign), and the liberation of Judah from the oppression of Israel and Aram at the fall of Samaria (the thing signified). Thomas's timeline argument here seems

250 Likewise, they object that, in Hebrew, it does not say ***virgin***, but ***'almah***, which, according to them, signifies a marriageable young woman. It has this meaning in Genesis 24:16, concerning Rebekah, where we have *The maiden was very fair*, and they have *'almah*.[7] Moreover, even if [Isaiah 7:14] had used the term *betulah*, which does signify 'virgin' according to them, this would not necessarily mean that she had conceived while remaining a virgin because it could have happened that she who was a virgin at the time [of the prophecy] became corrupted thereafter and conceived by a man's seed.

To this, it must be said that it would have been no sign at all if a young woman or a corrupted virgin had conceived. And yet, the Lord wanted to signify something great when he said, ***unto the depth of hell or unto the height above***. For this reason, among us, ***'almah*** is used rather than 'young woman' because ***'almah*** signifies a virgin, according to the word's origin, and still more, it means one who is protected, about whom there can be no suspicion of evil. Nevertheless, *bethula* signifies a virgin according to a later manner of speaking.

251 Jewish interpreters, however, explain this verse in two ways. Some of them say that it concerns Hezekiah; others say it concerns a son of Isaiah, whom they imagine was named Emmanuel. Nevertheless, it is clear that the first explanation cannot stand since Hezekiah was twenty-five years old when he began to reign (2 Kings 18:2), and Ahaz reigned sixteen years (2 Kings 16:2). Hezekiah was thus nine years old when his father began to reign, and therefore, he was not the one about to be born who is being promised here. Moreover, how would he not know to call his father and mother when Samaria was captured in the sixth year of his reign?

It is clear that the second interpretation cannot stand either because it would not have been a sign at all.[8] Moreover, the son of Isaiah was not [ever] a lord of Judah, and yet, Isaiah 8:8 describes the land of Judah as a possession of Emmanuel. Therefore, it is necessary to understand this passage as speaking of the Son of God.

---

to be that if we suppose the sign of the child's birth and early childhood to have occurred shortly after the oracle was given, then the Emmanuel child would have been far too old by the time Judah was liberated since the oracle indicates that the liberation will come before he "knows how to refuse the evil and choose the good" (Isa. 7:16)—i.e., while he is very young. A longer interval of time, it seems, would need to have elapsed between the event of the oracle and the birth and childhood of the Emmanuel child in the Jewish interpretation that Thomas criticizes. Nevertheless, it is not entirely clear why and in what sense Thomas thinks the Emmanuel sign would have to *follow* the liberation it signifies.

7. Actually, the Hebrew word rendered "maiden" here is not *'almah* but *na'arah*, a term with a similar meaning.

8. That is, if Isaiah and his wife had conceived a son in the usual way, it would not have served as a sign that God was with Judah because there would be nothing distinctly divine or supernatural about it.

252 Following this, therefore, he does three things. *First*, he promises the sign: '***Therefore***, because you do not wish to ask, ***the Lord himself shall give you a sign*** of your liberation.' This sign is also given to the shepherds in Luke 2:12: *This will be a sign for you: you will find a babe wrapped in swaddling cloths.*

253 *Second*, he presents the sign itself: ***Behold a virgin.*** [In presenting the sign,] he *first* asserts a miraculous conception: ***Behold a virgin***—while remaining a virgin—***shall conceive and bear a son.*** *Second*, he discusses the naming of the miraculously begotten child, *first*, with reference to his divinity: ***shall be called***—that is, by the virgin or by you, Judah, in times of danger. ***His name shall be called Emmanuel***, which is translated 'God with us.' Matthew 1:23: *They shall call his name Emmanuel.* Moreover, all this has no parallel among other [cases of conception], for it is a new thing: *The Lord hath created a new thing upon the earth: a woman*—or a female—*shall compass a man* (Jer. 31:22 DRB)—hence, a human being, complete in conception, although not in size, as Augustine says, commenting on John 2:20: *It has taken forty-six years to build this temple.*[9] Therefore, he is higher than a human being, for there is *nothing new under the sun* (Eccles. 1:9). Hence, there cannot be found another event that corresponds to this prophecy besides this story: *Behold, you will conceive in your womb and bear a son* (Luke 1:31), who is signified in Ezekiel 44:2: *This gate shall remain shut; it shall not be opened, and no one shall enter by it; for the Lord, the God of Israel, has entered by it.*

254 *Second*, [he discusses the naming of the miraculously begotten child] with reference to his humanity: ***He shall eat butter and honey***—considered literally, the foods of men—because, from infancy, he was like others: *Being born, I drew in the common air and fell upon the earth that is made alike, and the first voice which I uttered was crying, as all others do* (Wis. 7:3 DRB). Alternatively, according to the fourth rule of Tyconius, [***butter and honey***,] as part, represent the whole, for by these, he understands all human foods.[10]

---

9. Augustine, *Eighty-Three Different Questions* 56, as cited by Thomas Aquinas, *Commentary on John* 2.3; cf. Augustine, *The Trinity* 4.5, 9. In the passage cited, Augustine relates the forty-six years of the temple's construction to the forty-six days in which a fetus develops to its complete form in his theory of conception. Having completed its formation by the forty-sixth day, the fetus's development throughout the remainder of the pregnancy consists only of growth but not transformation. For his part, Thomas holds a similar picture, in which an early process of progressive ensoulment (vegetal, animal, and human) produces a complete human conception that continues to grow in scale without further transformation throughout the final period of pregnancy. He interprets Jeremiah 31:22's "a woman shall encompass a man" in light of his view that Christ was the unique exception (hence, a "new thing") to this pattern. In his account, Christ never underwent a process of progressive ensoulment but was a fully formed (fully ensouled) tiny human being (a *homunculus*) from the first moment in Mary's womb. See *Summa theologiae* 3.33.2; cf. 131n42 below.

10. Tyconius, *The Book of Rules*, cited in Augustine, *Teaching Christianity* 3.34, and Isidore of Seville, *Sententiarum liber* 1.19.

That he may know: The ***that*** marks an attendant circumstance because even as a child who still feeds on such things [as ***butter and honey***], he ***knows to refuse the evil*** without experience ***and to choose the good*** without counsel because he has perfect knowledge of everything. The devil had promised this but did not fulfill his promise (Gen. 3:5), but God gave it freely: *For it is he who gave me unerring knowledge of what exists, to know the structure of the world and the activity of the elements* (Wis. 7:17).

Alternatively, ***that*** is causal: ***That he may know***—that is, '***He shall eat butter and honey*** to show that he knows,' since, by means of food, he was led to the perfect age at which to show that he knows. Augustine, on the *honey and milk* of Song of Songs 4:11, says that humanity is signified by butter because it comes from the nourishment of the earth; divinity is signified by honey because it is collected from the dew of heaven.[11] Moreover, he had a nature without corruption, like butter without curd, and he carried consolation without judgment, like honey without the sting. Bernard says, *Our little one chose to be newly conceived because he took the nature of our flesh without corruption. Similarly, the bee brings us honey without mingling in the sting.*[12] *For God sent the Son into the world, not to condemn the world, but that the world might be saved through him* (John 3:17).[13] Thus, ***that*** is also causal. And this is a sign from below on the part of the virgin giving birth and from above on the part of God being born: *The Lord will give what is good, and our land will yield its increase* (Ps. 85:12).

255 *Third*, the adaptation of the sign is presented: ***For before the child know***—that is, 'before he assumes created knowledge by being born'—***the land*** of Samaria and Syria (2 Kings 16:9, 17:3–5), ***which thou abhorrest, shall be forsaken.***

256 ***The Lord shall bring upon thee***: Here, he sets out the threat against those who do not believe the sign. And *first*, he shows the severity of the punishment; *second*, the order of punishment: ***And it shall come to pass in that day***; *third*, the effect of the punishment: ***And it shall come to pass in that day, that a man shall nourish a young cow.***

Moreover, he shows the severity of the punishment from the authority of the one who commands: ***The Lord***, who is powerful, ***shall bring***: *The Lord . . . Almighty is his name* (Exod. 15:3 DRB). Again, he shows the severity of the punishment by reference to its universality: ***upon thee***—through Tiglath-pileser—***and upon thy people and upon the house of thy father***—referring to 'your descendants'—through his tyrant sons.[14]

---

11. Perhaps Alain de Lille, *Elucidatio in Cantica canticorum.*

12. Bernard, *Sermons on Advent* 2.

13. Cf. John 12:47.

14. The threat of Isaiah 7:17, "The Lord shall bring upon thee," is directed not against the

Additionally, he shows the severity of the punishment by comparison with the past: The ***days*** are as evil [as those of the separation of Ephraim from Judah], and they are called evil on account of guilt: *Sufficient for the day is the evil thereof* (Matt. 6:34 DRB); *making the most of the time because the days are evil* (Eph. 5:16). Again, they are called evil on account of punishment: ***days that have not come since the time of the separation of Ephraim from Judah.***

Further, he shows the severity of the punishment in view of the power of those who execute it: ***the king of the Assyrians,*** Nebuchadrezzar, for the kingdoms of the Chaldeans and Assyrians were one under him. It had been one from the beginning, for the Assyrians had come forth from the Chaldeans (Gen. 10): *I will send for . . . Nebuchadrezzar the king of Babylon, my servant* (Jer. 25:9).

257 ***It shall come to pass***: Here, he presents the manner and order of punishment, and he sets out three things. *First,* the calling together of their enemies: ***The Lord shall hiss for***—that is, incite—***the fly***—that is, the king of Egypt who killed Josiah (2 Kings 23:29). He is compared to a fly because of the impurity of idols and decadence that thrives in Egypt. ***The fly that is in the uttermost parts of the rivers*** because they come even from the farthest parts of Egypt. ***The Lord shall hiss for . . . the bee***—namely, the Chaldeans and the Assyrians because they had the honey of defense from the former and the sting of persecution from the latter.[15] Earlier in Isaiah, it says, ***He will . . . whistle to them from the ends of the earth*** (5:26).

258 *Second,* in presenting the manner and order of their punishment, he describes the multitude of their enemies: ***They shall come and shall all of them rest in the torrents of the valleys***—for the benefit of water, which usually runs in valleys—***and in the holes of the rocks*** for fortification ***and, upon all places set with shrubs*** for wood, ***and in all hollow places*** for locations of homes. Later, he says: ***The stretching out of his wings shall fill the breadth of thy land*** (Isa. 8:8).

259 *Third,* he describes their captivity: ***In that day, the Lord shall shave with a razor***—that is, through the [Assyrian] king—***by them***—that is, through the Assyrians. Concerning the sharp ***razor,*** see Ezekiel 5:1: *Take a sharp sword; use it as a barber's razor and pass it over your head.* ***The Lord shall shave . . . the head***—the king [of Judah]—***the feet***—his artisans—***and the whole beard***—the soldiers, who exist for the king's adornment (2 Kings 25). In Isaiah 3:1–2,

northern kingdom of Israel but against the southern kingdom of Judah and its king, Ahaz, who at the time of the oracle was contemplating an alliance with the Assyrian king Tiglath-pileser III as a solution to the threat posed by Israel and its ally Aram. Isaiah's oracle warns against this alliance and threatens to turn Tiglath-pileser and his successors against Ahaz and his successors to the throne of Judah.

15. By "the former," here, he seems to be referring to Egypt, with whom Judah entered a defensive alliance against the threat of the Assyrians.

above, it says: ***The sovereign Lord of hosts shall take away from Jerusalem . . . the man of war, the judge, and the prophet.*** Alternatively, he says this against the Egyptians, who were their helpers: ***hired*** against ***them***—that is, the Egyptians.[16] *He shall carry off its wealth and despoil it and plunder it, and it shall be the wages for his army* (Ezek. 29:19).

260 ***It shall come to pass in that day that a man shall nourish a young cow***: Here, he presents the effect of the punishment or the sign of destruction. *First,* in the scarcity of animals: ***a man shall nourish a young cow and two sheep***, which will be the case because there will be so few animals. Earlier, Isaiah says, ***Strangers shall eat the deserts turned into fruitfulness*** (5:17).

Second, he presents the shortage of provisions as an effect of the punishment: ***butter and honey shall everyone eat*** due to the lack of bread: *Those who feasted on dainties perish in the streets* (Lam. 4:5).

Third, he shows the effect of the punishment in the scarcity of people, *first,* in the degradation of property: ***every place where there were a thousand vines . . . shall become thorns and briers***: *"Buy the field for money and get witnesses"—though the city is given into the hands of the Chaldeans* (Jer. 32:25); *I passed by the field of a sluggard, by the vineyard of a man without sense; and behold, it was all overgrown with thorns; the ground was covered with nettles* (Prov. 24:30–31). *Second,* he shows the scarcity of people in the multitude of thieves: ***With arrows and with bows***—namely, 'when you flee the place'—***they shall go in.*** Later, Isaiah says, ***Fear and the pit and the snare are upon thee, O thou inhabitant of the earth*** (24:17).

Fourth, he shows the effect of the punishment in [the people's] fear of enemies, for they will cultivate the mountains and abandon the plains: ***as for all the hills that shall be raked with a rake.*** *All her cities shall be perpetual wastes* (Jer. 49:13), and: [*You*] *hold the height of the hill* (Jer. 49:16).

261 Regarding the phrase ***his name shall be called Emmanuel***—that is, 'God with us'—we should observe that Christ is with us in many ways. *First,* as a brother, through a community of nature: *O that you were like a brother to me, that nursed at my mother's breast! If I met you outside, I would kiss you* (Song of Sol. 8:1). *Second,* as a bridegroom, through the bond of love: *If a man loves me, he will keep my word* (John 14:23). *Third,* as a shepherd, through the solace of an inner consolation: *Behold, I stand at the door and knock; if anyone hears*

16. It appears that Thomas is offering two different interpretations, possibly based on two slightly different versions of the verse in his editions. The two interpretations are possible, however, in virtue of the semantic range of the Latin preposition 'in,' which Thomas interprets here as indicating an instrument in one clause ("the Lord shall shave *with* [in] a razor") and an object in the next ("a razor hired *against* [in] them"). His interpretation of this latter clause is informed by Ezekiel 29:19–20, where the Babylonian (or Chaldean) army is described as hired by the Lord, who in turn, pays them with Egyptian plunder.

my voice and opens the door, I will come in to him and eat with him (Rev. 3:20). *Fourth*, as a savior, through the help of defense: *Fear not, O Jacob my servant, says the Lord, nor be dismayed, O Israel; for behold, I will save you from afar* (Jer. 30:10). *Fifth*, as a leader, through the example of his work: *The Lord alone did lead him* (Deut. 32:12).

262 Regarding the phrase ***Behold a virgin***, we should observe that he says ***behold*** on account of her singular eminence: *first*, because she is above other women on account of her virginity: hence he says, ***Behold a virgin***. *Second*, she is above other virgins because of her fruitfulness: hence, he says, ***shall conceive***. *Third*, she is above all angels because of the worthiness of her fruit: hence he says, ***shall bear a son***: *For surely it is not with angels that he is concerned but with the descendants of Abraham* (Heb. 2:16).

Psalm 31[17]

Sin and Penance

On Psalms 31 (295–305)

31:1 *To David himself, understanding.*

Blessed are they whose iniquities are forgiven and whose sins are covered.

31:2 *Blessed is the man to whom the Lord hath not imputed sin and in whose spirit there is no guile.*

31:3 *Because I was silent, my bones grew old whilst I cried out all the day long.*

31:4 *For day and night thy hand was heavy upon me. I am turned in my anguish while the thorn is fastened.*

31:5 *I have acknowledged my sin to thee, and my injustice I have not concealed. I said, "I will confess against myself my injustice to the Lord." And thou hast forgiven the wickedness of my sin.*

31:6 *For this shall everyone that is holy pray to thee in a seasonable time. And yet in a flood of many waters, they shall not come nigh unto him.*

31:7 *Thou art my refuge from the trouble which has encompassed me. My joy, deliver me from those that surround me.*

31:8 *I will give thee understanding, and I will instruct thee in this way, in which thou shalt go. I will fix my eyes upon thee.*

31:9 *Do not become like the horse and the mule, who have no understanding. With bit and bridle bind fast their jaws, who come not near unto thee.*

17. Psalm 31, so numbered in the Douay Rheims translation used here, corresponds to Psalm 32 in most modern editions, which follow the Masoretic numbering system.

31:10 ***Many are the scourges of the sinner, but mercy shall encompass him who hopeth in the Lord.***

31:11 ***Be glad in the Lord, and rejoice, ye just, and glory, all ye right of heart.***

295 Here begins the fourth set of ten within the first fifty psalms.[18] Moreover, just as in the first ten, there are psalms that mention the persecution of Absalom; in the second, the persecution of Saul; and in the third, the persecution of the people; so, in this fourth, the tribulation that the good endure from sinners is discussed. *As he lived among them, he was vexed in his righteous soul day after day with their lawless deeds* (2 Pet. 2:8).

Now, this group of ten is divided into two parts. In the *first* part, the dignity of the just is commended. In the *second*, help is sought against the persecutions of the wicked, beginning with Psalm 34:1: ***Judge thou, O Lord, them that wrong me.***

Concerning the dignity of the just, he recalls two things: the *first* is justifying grace; the *second* is the dignity of the just, at ***Rejoice . . . O ye just*** (Ps. 32:1); *third*, he advises the just to stand fast in justice, at ***I will bless the Lord*** (Ps. 33:2).

The title of this psalm [***To David himself, understanding***] is new.[19] Jerome has ***The knowledge of David.***[20] This title is found in many subsequent psalms. And in all the psalms named by it, it indicates a discussion of some general truth pertaining not merely to one person but related, instead, to God's providence or some other profound matter. Moreover, although there is something instructive in all of the psalms, these above all are intended for instruction.

Indeed, this psalm is titled for the ***understanding*** that the penitent should have, who ought to understand that he is a sinner and know God's liberating grace. If he *understandeth his offense, let him do penance* (Lev. 5:4–5 DRB). *Vexation alone shall make you understand* (Isa. 28:19 DRB).

This is the second penitential psalm. In the *first* (Psalm 6), he treated contrition of heart, but in this psalm, he treats confession. The psalm is divided into three parts. In the *first*, he describes the remission of sins. In the *second*, he describes the way to reach this remission at ***Because I was silent.*** In the

18. For further discussion of this division of the first fifty psalms, see Thomas's prologue to the Psalms, included at page 1 above.

19. He means "new" in the sense that the superscription "To David himself, understanding" did not appear in any of the preceding thirty psalms.

20. "Jerome" refers here to the Hebrew Psalter.

third, he describes the saints' desire for forgiveness, where he says, ***For this shall everyone that is holy pray.***

He makes two points [in the *first* part] about the remission of sin. *First*, he describes God's part; and *second*, the human part, where he says, ***in whose spirit there is no guile.*** For sin, first of all, is an offense against God; second, it is a stain; third, it is a state of liability for punishment. Against these three, he arranges three things: because God forgives the offense, covers the stain, and takes away the liability for punishment by not imputing the sin.

Regarding the *first*, forgiveness of the offense, he says, ***Blessed are they whose iniquities are forgiven.*** However, since blessedness is twofold—namely, in reality and hope—those ***whose iniquities are forgiven*** are blessed in hope but will later be blessed in reality. For he is blessed in hope in whom the cause of blessedness is already present and whose way is that of virtue and, especially, perfect virtue. So, he in whom perfect virtue appears can be called blessed in hope, like a well-flowering tree can be said to bear good fruit. After the corruption of the first human being, these flowers were lost and replaced by the thorns of sins. Therefore, the blessedness of the sinner in hope is not of this kind, but it is [the hope] that God will forgive his sins and make him fruitful. *Break up your fallow ground* (Jer. 4:3). ***Whose iniquities are forgiven.*** *Her iniquity is pardoned* (Isa. 40:2). *Forgive, and you will be forgiven* (Luke 6:37).

Regarding the *second* [God's covering of the stain of sin], he says, ***whose sins are covered.*** Sins are stains of the soul. *How exceeding base art thou become* (Jer. 2:36 DRB). When someone has something shameful in himself that is covered over, the shameful thing does not offend the eyes of the one seeing it. Now, God covers over the shamefulness of sin, but how? Totally, as though by washing the soul, for there is a double deformity in sin. One is the privation of grace by which the sinner is robbed, and this is totally taken away and not covered over since grace is given to him. Another stain comes from the action of past sin, and this stain is not removed since it is not given to him that he did not do it but that the guilt is no longer imputed to him.

Regarding the *third* [God's removal of the sinner's liability for punishment], he says, ***Blessed is the man to whom the Lord hath not imputed sin.*** This means that the punishment for his sin is not reserved for him: *Thou hast executed true judgments in all the things that thou hast brought upon us* (Dan. 3:28 DRB).

According to a gloss, three types of sin are suggested here: original sin, actual mortal sin, and actual venial sin.

The *first* kind is expressed by the word 'iniquity,' which is a kind of inequality, and this is present in original sin inasmuch as the powers of the soul lose the balance of innocence in original sin. This [original sin] is dismissed and diminished since it is removed as regards liability, but it remains in our action.

Moreover, he speaks ***iniquities*** in the plural since there are diverse original sins in different persons, yet one in each.

The *second* kind of sin, actual mortal sin, is signified [by ***sins***]. Now, actual mortal sins are said to be ***covered*** when not imputed to the sinner as his guilt.

Third, venial sin is signified [by ***sin***], which ***the Lord does not impute.*** Venial sin is not imputed as deserving of eternal punishment.

Alternatively, he says the *first* [***iniquities***] about sin before baptism, the *second* about the ***sins*** that come after baptism, and the *third* about those after confession, since then sin is ***not imputed*** as far as punishment is concerned. Nevertheless, on the part of a human person, it is required that he confess sincerely; otherwise, grace does not follow: *The Holy Spirit of discipline will flee from the deceitful* (Wis. 1:5 DRB). And so he says, ***in whose spirit there is no guile***, as when a person has one thing within him but outwardly pretends to have another.

296 ***Because I was silent, my bones grew old***: This is the *second* part of the psalm, where he presents the way of achieving remission of sins. He makes three points about this. *First*, he describes the state of sin; *second*, the conversion, which is the cause of the remission of sin, at ***I have acknowledged my sin***. Thus, he says, ***Because I was silent, my bones grew old whilst I cried out all the day long.*** This seems contradictory, for although he cries out all day, he claims to be silent.

To this, I respond by saying that he was silent about what should have been said but shouting what should not have been spoken, let alone shouted. There is sin, moreover, on both counts. About his *first* sin [of silence], Isaiah 6:5 says, *Woe is me, because I have held my peace* (DRB), for the sinner should declare his sins. *If I hold my peace it will not depart from me, but now my sorrow hath oppressed me* (Job 16:7–8 DRB). Therefore, ***because I was silent*** about my sins, ***my bones grew old***—that is, my interior strength failed. In Sacred Scripture, the members of the body should often be understood in reference to the interior powers. So, by ***bones***, in which there is strength, interior virtue should be understood. Furthermore, since what grows old fails—that is, fades away—he says, ***my bones grew old***. *Why is it, O Israel, why is it that you are in the land of your enemies?* (Bar. 3:10).

About his *second* sin [in speaking], Isaiah 5:7 says, *He looked . . . for righteousness, but behold, a cry!* And this is what he is saying [when he says]: ***whilst I cried out all the day long***, for he cried out that he was just and complained loudly about his punishment, and yet he was silent about his guilt. But what did the Lord do? The hand of the Lord converted him by intensifying the burden it imposed: ***Day and night thy hand was heavy upon me.***

The *second* point [regarding remission of sins] is the conversion that followed: ***I am turned in my anguish while the thorn is fastened.*** Therefore, he says, ***day and night***—that is, continually—***your hand was heavy.*** The hand of the Lord sometimes strengthens: *The hand of the Lord being strong upon me* (Ezek. 3:14). Sometimes it weighs down: *The hand of God was very heavy* (1 Sam. 5:11). *O Lord, in distress they sought you* (Isa. 26:16). For this reason, he says, ***I am turned in my anguish***—that is, 'in the misery I suffer for my sins'—***while the thorn is fastened*** or 'while the thorn'—that is, the remorse of conscience—'is fixed in my heart.' Or it is said about the spine of the back, which holds an entire person upright ***while it is fastened***, and it signifies pride, which, when inhibited, permits one to be corrected.

Alternatively, why do you cry aloud? 'Because of the weight,' he says, 'of your hand. Furthermore, this is because I am not turned to you but to sin.' And so, this takes place ***while the thorn*** of sin ***is fastened***—that is, while it is firmly in me—and thus should the thorn—that is, sin—be understood. Alternatively, we might interpret it as saying, 'while reason,' which is like a spine ruling the back, 'is suppressed.' Alternatively, according to the Hebrew, ***My moisture is changed into the dryness of summer***—that is to say, 'By the weight of your hand, whatever was carnal and moist in me has been changed to the dryness of summer.' Jerome has, ***I have been turned in my misery while the crops scorched***—that is, 'I have dried out the way crops do.'[21]

297 Afterward, when he says, ***I have acknowledged my sin to thee***, *first*, he makes his confession; *second*, he shows its effectiveness, at: ***I said, "I will confess."*** There are two things that a person should confess: the good things he has omitted and the evils he has committed. Thus, regarding the *first*, he says, ***my sin***—which is to say, 'I failed to do the good that I should have.' ***I have acknowledged . . . to thee***—not that God does not know, but when a person recognizes his sin, he wants God to know this so that he may forgive him. Regarding the *second*, he says, ***My injustice I have not concealed.*** *If I have concealed my transgressions from men, . . . oh, that I had one to hear me!* (Job 31:33–35). *He who conceals his transgressions will not prosper* (Prov. 28:13).

He shows the effectiveness of his confession when he says, ***I said, "I will confess."*** Confession is effective for the forgiveness of sins. Therefore, he says, ***I said***—that is, I proposed in my heart—***"I will confess . . . to the Lord"***—that is, to the honor of the Lord. *Give glory to the Lord, God of Israel, and confess* (Josh. 7:19 DRB). I will confess ***my injustice***, not 'my good deeds,' and ***against myself***, not 'for myself.' Someone may confess his sins but may confess against his neighbor, saying, 'Another led me to do it.' Alternatively, he may confess

21. The Hebrew Psalter.

against nature, saying, 'It happened out of weakness.' Or he may confess against God, saying, 'I was unable to resist.' *Behold, I have sinned, and I have done wickedly* (2 Sam. 24:17). Or I will confess ***against myself***—that is, that it was my intention by which I persisted in sin. Forgiveness follows: ***And thou hast forgiven***. *He forgives sins and saves in time of affliction* (Sir. 2:11).

On the contrary, the efficacy of confession is so great that forgiveness is given not only to someone who actually confessed but also to someone with the intention of confessing. Therefore, a person is forgiven before he confesses. *Before they call, I will answer* (Isa. 65:24).

What, then, does confession accomplish?

It should be said that the intention of acting works by the power of the thing intended so that it is carried out. So, if one desists from doing that thing, the effect ceases. Thus, it is necessary to carry the intention through. Nevertheless, in the confession of actual sins, the punishment is remitted through absolution by the power of the keys, and greater grace is bestowed on him because of his sense of shame, and many good things follow.

298 Here, he makes a *third* point [about the remission of sin], describing the saints' desire for remission of their sins, and he makes three points about this. *First*, he describes the saints' desire; *second*, he warns sinners: ***Do not become like the horse***; and *third*, he concludes the psalm with thanksgiving: ***Be glad***.

He makes two points about the desire of the saints. *First*, in general terms, he expresses the saints' desire to be forgiven of their sins. *Second*, he shows his own refuge, specifically, where he says, ***Thou art my refuge***.

He says two things about the general desire for forgiveness. *First*, he describes the desire of the saints through the sign of a prayer. *Second*, he shows the effect of the prayer where he says, ***In a flood of many waters, they shall not come nigh unto him***. Therefore, he states, ***I said, "I will confess." . . . For this***—that is, for the forgiveness of sins—***shall everyone that is holy pray to thee in a seasonable time***.

He explains three things. *First*, why we must pray: so that we may find forgiveness, for we have all sinned: *If we say we have no sin, we deceive ourselves* (1 John 1:8). Therefore, we must seek forgiveness: *Pray to the Lord, and he will heal you* (Sir. 38:9). *Forgive us our trespasses* (Matt. 6:12). *Second*, he explains who should pray: ***every one that is holy***. *The prayer of a righteous man has great power in its effects* (James 5:16). *Third*, he tells us when we should pray: ***in a seasonable time***—of grace and of the present life because, in the end, *the door was shut* (Matt. 25:10). *Behold, now is the acceptable time* (2 Cor. 6:2). *Night comes, when no one can work* (John 9:4).

299 Afterward, when he says, ***And yet***, the effect of the prayer is shown, since it is ***in a flood of many waters***. Here, water can be understood in three ways. In

one way, it is pleasures: *Unstable as water* (Gen. 49:4). In another way, it is false doctrine: *Stolen water is sweet* (Prov. 9:17). *Third*, it is tribulations: ***The waters are come in even unto my soul*** (Ps. 68:2). ***They shall not come nigh unto him*** follows. ***Unto him*** can be understood in two ways. In one way, ***him*** refers to a saint, as if to say, 'Although he suffers in many waters, they will not overwhelm him, whether they are the waters of pleasure or false doctrine or of tribulations.' *When you pass through the waters, I will be with you; and through the rivers, they shall not overwhelm you* (Isa. 43:2). ***We have passed through fire and water*** (Ps. 65:12). In another way, ***him*** can refer to God, and so he changes person in this speech since first he spoke to God and now he speaks to others, as if to say, 'Those who are in the flood of many waters, as was said above, will not approach God.'

300 Next, when he says, ***Thou art my refuge***, he expresses the desire of the saints in specific terms, and he says two things about it. *First*, he expresses their desire to be delivered; *second*, the effect of the desire, at ***I will give thee understanding.*** He considers two aspects of the desire. *First*, he shows the source of his prayer's hope. *Second*, he adds the petition, ***My joy, deliver me from those that surround me.***

Moreover, he finds the hope to pray in two facts. The *first* is that God is the special refuge of the just. The *second* is that he is their special refuge in tribulation. Therefore, he says, ***Thou art my refuge from the trouble which has encompassed me.*** Tribulation encompasses when it oppresses on all sides so that there does not seem to be a refuge anywhere: ***Evils without number have surrounded me*** (Ps. 39:13). But in this tribulation, there is no refuge but God. *We do not know what to do* (2 Chron. 20:12). ***He who dwelleth in the aid of the Most High*** (Ps. 90:1). He says, 'I have one to whom I may flee and in whom I may be consoled,' because, '***my joy*** is him *who comforts us in all our affliction*' (2 Cor. 1:4). ***According to the multitude of my sorrows in my heart, your comforts have given joy to my soul*** (Ps. 93:19). Afterward, he expresses what he asks for when he says, ***Deliver me from those that surround me***—that is, from ***the trouble which has encompassed me.*** And since tribulation comes from someone else, if trouble encompasses him, then those threatening him—the demons and persecutors—are surrounding him, and so he says, ***from those that surround me.***

301 Next, when he says, ***I will give thee understanding***, he shows the effect of his prayer. God is the one who speaks: ***I will give thee understanding.*** It is as though God says, 'You ask me to deliver you, and I will do three things for you: ***I will give*** you the gift of understanding, ***I will instruct*** you, and I will guard you.'

Three things that come from God are necessary for a person. The *first* is that he receive the gift of grace so that, through it, a person's soul may be perfected so to act promptly. Nevertheless, even though a person may have this free gift, it is not enough unless God moves the soul to do a good work. Thus, it is necessary that, after prevenient grace, God works to move him to do good. However, grace and this gift are received according to the mode of our nature, and it does not belong to this mode to be able to avoid all harmful things, and so God's protection and defense are also needed.

Thus, he *first* mentions the gift of understanding when he says, ***I will give thee understanding.*** The Lord *will fill him with a spirit of wisdom and understanding* (Sir. 15:5 DRB). This is necessary for a person to know his own sins and because it is impossible to be saved except through God. *Second,* he describes the need to use this gift when he says, ***I will instruct thee.*** *All your sons shall be taught by the Lord* (Isa. 54:13). *Third,* he describes the protection when he says, ***in this way***—namely, of the commandments ***in which thou shalt go. I will fix my eyes upon thee***—that is, I will protect you. *The eyes of the Lord move back and forth throughout the whole earth to show his might in behalf of those whose heart is blameless toward him* (2 Chron. 16:9).

302 Afterward, when he says, ***Do not become like the horse and the mule,*** he turns to sinners to bring them to penance, and he makes two points about this. *First,* he gives a warning; *second,* a threat, where he says, ***with bit and bridle.***

So, he says that God gives understanding to the human being, who surpasses the animals in understanding. Therefore, those unworthy to receive the gift of wisdom are compared to animals, and so he says, ***Do not become like the horse and the mule.***

According to the Gloss, the horse is a proud animal, but the mule is lazy, so it does not run.[22] Therefore, those are like horses who are elevated by pride. *Everyone turns to his own course, like a horse plunging headlong into battle* (Jer. 8:6). Those are like the mule who are slow to come to the way of God. *The soul of the sluggard craves and gets nothing* (Prov. 13:4).

Alternatively, the mule can be taken to mean the lustful. The mule is lustful even though it cannot generate, just as the sins of lust are unfruitful. *What return did you get from the things of which you are now ashamed?* (Rom. 6:21).

Alternatively, the horse carries any rider indifferently, and the mule carries any burden, just as sinners carry both a rider—the devil—and a burden, sin. Therefore, do not be like a horse, failing to discriminate between riders—between Christ and the devil. Do not be like the mule, which carries any burden of sin without caring.

303 Afterward, he adds a threat when he says, ***with bit and bridle.*** *First,* it is in the manner of a request, but *second,* it is in the manner of an announcement where he says, ***Many are the scourges.*** Therefore, he says, ***With bit and bridle bind fast their jaws, who come not near unto thee.*** This is metaphorical. If a

22. Peter Lombard, *Magna glossatura.*

human being acts like one, God treats him as such, warning and teaching him, but when he turns away from his human dignity, he is treated like a brute animal, which is coerced by punishments and force—namely, ***with bit and bridle***—as if to say, 'I warned you not to act like a horse or a mule, but if you do not acquiesce, I will act toward you as to a horse and mule.' Namely, ***with bit and bridle bind fast their jaws*** by subduing their speech and restricting food, which they enjoy to the point of voracity. Indeed, the jaws serve for speaking and eating. *I will put my hook in your nose and my bit in your mouth* (Isa. 37:29). Or, ***with bit and bridle***—that is, with great and small troubles.

304 Next, when he says, ***Many are the scourges***, he makes an announcement. *First*, he announces what is in store for the evil: ***many are the scourges***. They come from God: ***I will reprove thee and set before thy face*** (Ps. 49:21). They come from one's own conscience: *Pricked as it were with a sword of conscience* (Prov. 12:18 DRB). They come from the powerful: *The servant of God to execute his wrath on the wrongdoer* (Rom. 13:4). *A whip for the horse, a bridle for the donkey, and a rod for the back of fools* (Prov. 26:3).

Second, he tells what is prepared for the good: ***but mercy shall encompass him who hopeth. Mercy*** can be taken in the nominative case so that it is understood that mercy will encompass the one who hopes in the Lord. Alternatively, it can be taken in the ablative case to mean that the Lord will encompass one who trusts in him with mercy. Moreover, this takes place when he is fully submerged in human miseries. ***Who crowneth thee with mercy and compassion*** (Ps. 102:4).

305 Finally, the psalm is concluded with thanksgiving when he says, ***Be glad in the Lord, and rejoice, ye just***. Now, the custom in penitential psalms is that they begin with grieving and end in gladness since penance causes this.

Now, in this conclusion, he exhorts the just and the righteous to do good works and to have a right intention, saying, ***Be glad in the Lord, and rejoice, ye just***, as if to say, 'Two things are necessary for a person—namely, right action, and this brings about justice, and right intention, and this brings about gladness.' Therefore, he says, ***Be glad in the Lord and rejoice, ye just***. According to a gloss, *to be glad is to be silent with the sweetness of joy; to rejoice is to be excited in soul from the fervor of joy*. So, rejoicing comes from interior joy. But in what? ***In the Lord***, he says, not in the world. *Rejoice in the Lord always; again, I will say, Rejoice* (Phil. 4:4). There follows, ***Glory all ye right of heart***. The right of heart are those who conform their will to the divine will. It belongs to these to glory in God. *Let him who boasts, boast of the Lord* (2 Cor. 10:17).

Psalm 21[23]

The Suffering of Christ

On Psalms 21 (176–202)

21:1 *Unto the end, for the morning protection, a psalm for David.*

21:2 *O God, my God, look upon me: why hast thou forsaken me? Far from my salvation are the words of my sins.*

21:3 *O my God, I shall cry by day, and thou wilt not hear: and by night, and it shall not be reputed as folly in me.*

21:4 *But thou dwellest in the holy place, the praise of Israel.*

21:5 *In thee have our fathers hoped: they have hoped, and thou hast delivered them.*

21:6 *They cried to thee, and they were saved: they trusted in thee and were not confounded.*

21:7 *But I am a worm and no man: the reproach of men and the outcast of the people.*

21:8 *All they that saw me have laughed me to scorn: they have spoken with the lips and wagged the head.*

21:9 *He hoped in the Lord; let him deliver him: let him save him, seeing he delighteth in him.*

21:10 *For thou art he that hast drawn me out of the womb: my hope from the breasts of my mother.*

21:11 *I was cast upon thee from the womb. From my mother's womb thou art my God,*

23. Psalm 21, so numbered in the Douay-Rheims translation used here, corresponds to Psalm 22 in most modern editions that follow the Masoretic numbering system.

21:12 *Depart not from me. For tribulation is very near: for there is none to help me.*

21:13 *Many calves have surrounded me: fat bulls have besieged me.*

21:14 *They have opened their mouths against me, as a lion ravening and roaring.*

21:15 *I am poured out like water, and all my bones are scattered. My heart is become like wax melting in the midst of my bowels.*

21:16 *My strength is dried up like a potsherd, and my tongue hath cleaved to my jaws: and thou hast brought me down into the dust of death.*

21:17 *For many dogs have encompassed me: the council of the malignant hath besieged me. They have dug my hands and feet.*

21:18 *They have numbered all my bones. And they have looked and stared upon me.*

21:19 *They parted my garments amongst them and upon my vesture they cast lots.*

21:20 *But thou, O Lord, remove not thy help to a distance from me; look toward my defense.*

21:21 *Deliver, O God, my soul from the sword: my only one from the hand of the dog.*

21:22 *Save me from the lion's mouth; and my lowness from the horns of the unicorns.*

21:23 *I will declare thy name to my brethren: in the midst of the church, I will praise thee.*

21:24 *Ye that fear the Lord, praise him: all ye seed of Jacob, glorify him.*

21:25 ***Let all the seed of Israel fear him: because he hath not slighted nor despised the supplication of the poor man. Neither hath he turned away his face from me: and when I cried to him he heard me.***

21:26 ***With thee is my praise in a great church: I will pay my vows in the sight of them that fear him.***

21:27 ***The poor shall eat and shall be filled: and they shall praise the Lord that seek him: their hearts shall live forever and ever.***

21:28 ***All the ends of the earth shall remember and shall be converted to the Lord: And all the kindreds of the gentiles shall adore in his sight.***

21:29 ***For the kingdom is the Lord's; and he shall have dominion over the nations.***

21:30 ***All the fat ones of the earth have eaten and have adored: all they that go down to the earth shall fall before him.***

21:31 ***And to him my soul shall live: and my seed shall serve him.***

21:32 ***There shall be declared to the Lord a generation to come: and the heavens shall show forth his justice to a people that shall be born, which the Lord hath made.***

176 The tribulations David endured from his son and Saul are seen to have been treated in the previous psalms.[24] Treated here, in the third set of ten, is the persecution he suffered from the whole people who cast him out at Saul's command. Therefore, these psalms [21–30] are divided into three parts. In the *first* part, he narrates his tribulation [21–23]. In the *second*, a prayer is poured out to God for deliverance [24–27]. In the *third*, thanksgiving is given [28–30]. The *second* set of psalms begins, ***To thee, O Lord, I have lifted up*** (Ps. 24:1). The *third* starts at ***Bring to the Lord*** (Ps. 28:1). He does two things with regard to his tribulation. *First*, he describes it; *second*, he shows how he is helped by God in the tribulation: ***The Lord ruleth me*** (Ps. 22:1).

24. Cf. Thomas Aquinas, *On Psalms* 11.87 (not included in this collection), where Thomas explains that the first ten psalms are dedicated to Absalom's persecution of David and the second set of ten (Pss. 11–20) to Saul's persecution of him.

As was said above, here, as in the other prophets, certain then-contemporary circumstances are treated insofar as they were figures of Christ and belonged to prophecy itself. And again, at times, other things are put forward about Christ that go beyond, as it were, the capacity of the historical events.[25] And among these is this psalm in particular, which treats the passion of Christ, and indeed, this is its literal sense. This is why he spoke this psalm specifically during his passion when he cried out, *"Eli, Eli, la'ma sabach'-thani?" that is, "My God, my God, why have you forsaken me?"* (Matt. 27:46), which begins this psalm. And thus, although figuratively this psalm is said to be about David, it refers specifically to Christ in its literal sense. And at the Synod of Toledo (589), Theodore of Mopsuestia, who explained this as being about David in the literal sense, was condemned for this and many other things, so it must be interpreted as concerning Christ.[26]

It must be observed that five psalms treat the passion of Christ in detail and that this psalm is foremost among them. The others touch upon the passion of Christ more briefly. The *second* begins, ***Judge thou, O Lord, them that wrong me*** (Ps. 34:1); the *third*, ***Hear, O God, my prayer, and despise not my supplication*** (Ps. 54:2); the *fourth*, ***Save me, O God, for the waters are come in*** (Ps. 68:2); and the *fifth*, ***O God, be not thou silent in my praise*** (Ps. 108:2). And this is because of the five wounds of Christ or because of the five sheddings of his blood.[27] And they all progress in the same way, beginning with groaning and ending with the salvation of the people, since the passion accomplished the salvation of all. Jerome's title is ***To the victor, for the stag of the dawn.***[28] Our text says, ***To the victor, for the assumption*** or ***for the doe of the dawn.***

In this psalm, the passion of Christ is treated principally. His Resurrection is treated secondarily since understanding of the passion is given through it.

---

25. Connected with his view of the Psalms as prophetic in character, Thomas's point here seems to be that this psalm tells us more about Christ than what could be true of the events of David's story. Thus, although the psalm purports to be about the persecution of David, for Thomas, it refers primarily and literally to the future events of Christ's passion and only secondarily and figuratively to those of David's persecution.

26. In fact, the Third Synod of Toledo merely confirmed the canons of the Second Council of Constantinople (553), at which the doctrines of Theodore of Mopsuestia (c. 350–428), including the one mentioned here, were originally condemned. See 5n11 above.

27. The ambiguous "this" here refers to the fact that there are five psalms that treat the passion of Christ.

28. The version of this psalm's superscription that Thomas here identifies with Jerome appears to be the Hebrew Psalter, the last of the Latin translations of the Psalms that Jerome produced (c. 392) using Hebrew manuscripts. The two variants in the subsequent sentence that he designates "our text" (*nostra littera*) resemble Jerome's earlier (c. 384) Roman Psalter. Originally, the "The Stag of the Dawn" seems to have been the name of a well-known tune to which the psalm was sung in Jewish tradition.

Moreover, the passion is ordered to the Resurrection in the same way that if I were to say, 'He has been freed,' it would show that he had been a slave. Therefore, this is ***a psalm for David***—that is, for Christ. And it is ***for the assumption***—that is, the Resurrection, which was in the morning. Hence, it is ***for the doe***—that is, for human nature—or ***for the stag of the dawn***—that is, Christ. ***I will arise in the morning*** (Ps. 107:3).

This title comes from when David was a fugitive hiding in deserted places like a stag. So it was said above: ***Who hath made my feet like the feet of harts*** (Ps. 17:34). So, this psalm is titled for this tribulation, which prefigured the passion. Nevertheless, this applies better to Christ since, by the stag, the human nature in Christ can be understood, since a stag moves through the thorns without tearing its feet just as Christ moved through this present life without contaminating himself with iniquity. Likewise, a stag leaps very well, just as Christ ascended from the pit of death to the glory of the Resurrection. And so he is called a stag and is said to be of the morning because it was then that he rose.

This psalm is divided into three parts. The *first* part is a lament. The *second* is a narration of the passion, at ***I am a worm***. The *third* is a prayer for deliverance, at ***Thou, O Lord, remove not thy help to a distance from me***.

He makes three points regarding the lament. *First*, the lament or question is put down. *Second*, its explanation is given, at ***Far from my salvation***. *Third*, the reason for the lament is presented at ***Thou dwellest in the holy place***. This [the form of the lament] is the Septuagint translation. But the Greek and Hebrew editions exclude ***Look upon me***, thus retaining ***O God, my God, why hast thou forsaken me?*** because these were the words of Christ on the cross, whereas ***Look upon me*** was interposed.[29] Therefore, he makes a petition when he says, ***O God, my God, look upon me***. Now, ***God*** is repeated twice for greater certitude: *The doubling . . . means that the thing is fixed* (Gen. 41:32). ***Look upon me***—that is, 'have mercy on me': ***Look thou upon me and have mercy on me; for I am alone*** (Ps. 24:16).

Why hast thou forsaken me? These were the words of Christ on the cross (Matt. 27:46). Now, from these words, Arius took occasion for an error—namely, that the divinity and humanity of Christ were separated in his death. So, according to him, the Lord laments because of this, saying, ***Why hast thou forsaken me?*** But this is wrong. We should note that someone is said to be

29. Thomas's concern relates to his view of this passage as prophesying Christ's cry of dereliction on the cross (see Matt. 27:46). In light of the report of Matthew, Thomas here argues that the phrase "look upon me," which appears in editions of the Psalter that were based on the Septuagint, is an interpolation that was inserted to a text that thus originally matched Christ's cry of dereliction exactly.

forsaken by God when God does not aid him, just as he seems to be near when he protects him and fulfills his petition: *The Lord is with me as a dread warrior; therefore, my persecutors will stumble, they will not overcome me* (Jer. 20:11). And since Christ was not delivered from bodily suffering during his passion, he is thus said to be abandoned to the hour—that is, exposed to the passion: *He . . . did not spare his own Son* (Rom. 8:32). Also, his petition, *Father, if it be possible, let this chalice pass from me* (Matt. 26:39), does not seem to have been fulfilled since it took place in the flesh: *For a brief moment I forsook you*—that is, 'I exposed you to your passion'—*but with great compassion will I gather you* (Isa. 54:7) in the Resurrection. And so he says, ***Why hast thou forsaken me?***—that is, 'You have exposed me to the passion.'

Far from my salvation are the words of my sins: Here the lament or question is set forth, *first*, in general terms, and *second*, in specific ones: ***O my God, I shall cry***. Therefore, he says, ***Why hast thou forsaken me?*** and this because ***far from my salvation are the words of my sins***—that is, 'the words of me, a true man as possessing a human nature.' ***Salvation is far from sinners*** (Ps. 118:155). And these words, ***hast thou forsaken me?*** and ***far from my salvation*** and ***why?*** do not seem to apply to a just man or justice but seem to be ***the words of my sins***—namely, of a sinful man; that is, they show that 'I am unjust, a sinner.' So Christ spoke these words in the person of a sinner or of the Church. And this is one of the rules put down at the beginning of the Psalter: that things pertaining to his members are said of Christ about himself because Christ and the Church are one mystical body, and so they speak as one person.[30] Christ transforms himself into the Church, and the Church is transformed into Christ: *We, though many, are one body in Christ* (Rom. 12:5). Now, in the members of Christ—that is, in the Church—there are sins or transgressions. In truth, there is no sin in the head, in Christ, but only the likeness of sin. *Sending his own Son in the likeness of sinful flesh and for sin, [God] condemned sin* (Rom. 8:3). *He made him to be sin who knew no sin so that in him we might become the righteousness of God* (2 Cor. 5:21).

As his passion approached, Christ prayed, *Father, if it be possible, let this chalice pass from me* (Matt. 26:39). But these words of Christ can be explained in two ways. In one way, Christ pronounced them as personifying the weak in the Church, because it would come to pass that certain of its faint-hearted members would succumb to fear when threatened by suffering. In another way, it can be explained by saying that, in uttering this petition, he was exercising the office of weak flesh, which naturally fears and flees death. Thus, what he sought to be freed from was the word belonging either to those members in

30. Thomas seems to be speaking, here, of a point he makes in the prologue to his *Commentary on the Psalms* (see page 1 above).

whom sin is found or to his flesh, in which there is a similitude of sin or transgression. And thus, he says, ***the words***, by which he asks to be delivered, are ***of my sins***—that is, 'belonging to the faithful, for whose sins I suffer, or to the infirm flesh, which bears a likeness to sin.'

'I am ***far from*** bodily ***salvation***, since the chalice, the passion, does not pass from me as I asked,' as if to say, 'I am not in possession of the salvation I seek. If you were going to grant my petition, Father, this chalice would have passed from me.' And so, Jerome's text has, ***The words of my moaning are far from my salvation***. In his book *On the Grace of the New Testament*, Augustine explains it in another way: *These words, by which I ask to be delivered from the Passion and complain that I am abandoned to suffering, are far from my salvation which I, God, must accomplish*, for, as Matthew says, *He will save his people from their sins* (Matt. 1:21).[31]

He gives the reason why he is forsaken. Salvation is twofold. One is of the body, which is common to humans and beasts: ***Men and beasts thou wilt preserve, O Lord*** (Ps. 35:7). Another is spiritual and eternal, and this is proper to Christ, and so he says, ***my***, since the salvation of the New Covenant was accomplished through Christ: *Israel is saved by the Lord with everlasting salvation* (Isa. 45:17). And these two forms of salvation differ since the first is sought in the Old Covenant and the second in the New. Why, then, is he forsaken and made subject to suffering? Because he came in the New Covenant and the words he spoke here are ***far from my*** spiritual ***salvation*** since they concern the salvation of the body.

Far: Christ speaks in the person of sinners who are sometimes forsaken by God on account of their sins, so he says, ***the words of my sins***—those of sinners, that is—are ***far from*** spiritual ***salvation*** because the reason why sinners are not saved is that they are sinners: *God does not listen to sinners* (John 9:31). Or, according to Augustine, it says ***from me*** as if to say, 'By forsaking me, you have made me far from my salvation—of the body, that is—and these are the words of my sins.'[32]

177 ***O my God, I shall cry***: These specific outcries follow.

We can understand ***day*** and ***night*** in two ways. In one approach, they refer literally to a temporal day and night, and to cry out day and night is to lament incessantly. So, he says, ***thou wilt not hear***, as if to say, 'Although I cry out incessantly, you still do not hear.' Jerome's text has, ***Even during the night, there is no silence for me***, as to say, 'I am not silent but praying day and night.'[33]

31. Augustine, *Letter 140*, 6, 17.

32. Augustine, *Letter 140*, 6, 17.

33. "Jerome's text," here, is a reference to the Hebrew Psalter.

In another way, by ***day***, we can understand 'prosperity,' and by ***night***, 'adversity.' And according to Augustine, the ***words*** uttered for the salvation of the body are brought forth by day for prosperity and by night so that adversity might be taken away.[34] Therefore, Christ cries by day when he is prospering but is not heeded since he pleads to live, and he prays by night that adversity might be taken away, but it is not taken away.

But on the contrary, it is said about Christ that *he was heard* (Heb. 5:7). And it should be observed that prayer is an act of reason. Hence, every prayer of Christ proceeding from the judgment of reason was heard. But the case is different of a prayer expressing the weakness of passible nature and the proper motion of its members since he does not himself desire that it be heeded: *Now is my soul troubled. And what shall I say? "Father, save me"?* (John 12:27).

Moreover, he shows why he is heeded neither in prosperity nor adversity: ***it shall not be reputed as folly in me*** 'since this petition does not pertain to the salvation of the New Covenant, the eternal salvation that I intend, but it belongs to the salvation of the Old Covenant. Therefore, so that you may learn this wisdom, know that temporal salvation does not pertain to the New Covenant but to the Old.' This is the wisdom that is foolishness among human beings: *We are fools for Christ's sake* (1 Cor. 4:10); *has God not made foolish the wisdom of this world?* (1 Cor. 1:20).

178 ***Thou dwellest in the holy place***: Christ's question about the cause of his passion was presented above. Here, however, he shows that such a question is reasonable and that it is reasonable because he was abandoned. *First,* he says that this is remarkable on God's part. *Second,* he demonstrates this by ancient experience, at ***In thee have our fathers hoped***.

This statement bears a threefold relation to what was said before by three interpretations.[35] One is that he is far from temporal salvation and, thus, the latter separation obtains. Consequently, this fact, as it relates to God, is remarkable on two counts.

It is remarkable, *first,* that God should dwell in the saints and yet not defend them: *If the Lord is with us, why then has all this befallen us? And where are his wonderful deeds which our fathers recounted to us?* (Judg. 6:13). And so, he says, ***Thou dwellest in the holy***.[36] *You, O Lord, are in the midst of us* (Jer. 14:9),

---

34. Augustine, *Letter 140*, 7, 19.

35. "What was said before" refers to Christ's dereliction. Thomas here addresses the question of how God's indwelling, asserted here in verse 4 (the referent of "this statement"), is compatible with God's departure and abandonment of Christ emphasized in the preceding verses.

36. The phrase "in sancto habitas" of Thomas's Latin edition can refer either to a holy *place*, as it does in the Douay-Rheims rendering ("Thou dwellest in the holy place"), or to a holy *person* or *saint*, as Thomas seems to take it here (i.e., "in the holy one"). Thomas's point is that it is remarkable that God should allow the suffering of Christ in whom he so intimately dwells.

but he dwells especially in Christ. *Second*, it is remarkable because whatever good we have is all for the praise of God. And thus, God is praised by us all the more when things are well with us. And so, ***the praise of Israel*** follows: *Heal me, O Lord, and I shall be healed; save me, and I shall be saved, for you are my praise* (Jer. 17:14).[37]

According to another explanation:[38] ***Why hast thou forsaken me?***—that is, because ***the words of my sins*** are ***far from my salvation***, spiritually, but I cry for temporal things. You who truly ***dwellest in the holy place*** and are, therefore, ***the praise of Israel***, do not hear, because you do not hear someone when he does not cry for spiritual salvation. Or, according to a *third* explanation, Christ prays in this way in the person of a sinner, as if to say, 'Therefore, you are ***far from my salvation*** because you do not dwell in sinners but in the holy.'

179 ***In thee have our fathers hoped***: Here he gives another reason to find Christ's abandonment remarkable, from ancient tradition and the experience of the holy fathers who were delivered from tribulations when they called upon God, as is seen in Exodus 14 when they were delivered from the persecution of the Egyptians. Again, Susanna was delivered from the wicked judgment of the elders (Dan. 13). Daniel was delivered from the mouth or den of lions (Dan. 14). 'How, then, is it that I am forsaken by you and not delivered from the passion?'

He makes two points about this. *First*, he mentions the evil of bodily affliction; *second*, the evil of being confounded. Regarding deliverance from the first evil, he makes two points.

The *first* is that he hoped in him; so he says, ***In thee***, not in the world, ***have our fathers hoped.*** *You have hoped in the Lord for evermore, in the Lord God mighty forever* (Isa. 26:4 DRB). ***Thou hast delivered them***, and this is the fruit of hope, that you have delivered them.

Second, they cried; so he says, ***They cried to thee***, from the great affection of their heart, ***and they were saved.*** Psalm 119:1: ***In my trouble, I cried to the Lord.*** Regarding the *second* evil—namely, being confounded—he says, ***they trusted in thee and were not confounded.*** But on the contrary,[39] *there is no confusion to them that trust in thee* (Dan. 3:40 DRB). *Hope confoundeth not* (Rom. 5:5 DRB). It should be said that the ***fathers*** belonged to the Old Covenant, in which temporal things were given. Thus, to show that divine providence orders

37. Thomas's point here seems to be that the Father's abandonment of Christ is remarkable because no praise or glory redounds to him from Christ in his state of suffering and dereliction.

38. Thomas is returning, here, to the question the meaning of the divine indwelling implied in the "thou dwellest" of verse 4, which might be seen to contradict the prior "Why hast thou forsaken me?" of verse 2.

39. These passages seem to contradict the Psalmist's experience, not that of the patriarchs.

temporal things, he delivered them with a temporal deliverance. However, Christ promises and gives spiritual things, and so, to show that we ought to give little value to temporal things in our hope for the eternal, his reason indulged no desire for temporal deliverance. Nevertheless, some in the New Covenant are freed with a temporal deliverance, and in the Old Covenant, some were taught through spiritual afflictions to show that God is the author of both testaments.

180 ***I am a worm***: Here, he describes his passion. And *first*, he describes the shame he suffered. *Second*, he explains it, at ***All they that saw me***. *Third*, he gives a reason for it, at ***For thou art he***.

The *first* part can be read in two ways. In the *first* reading, he first presents an image of his shame; and *second*, he explains the disgrace. Therefore, he says, 'Whereas these others were delivered, I have not been delivered from shame but am crushed so vilely as if I were ***a worm and no man***.' *Man . . . is a maggot, and the son of man . . . is a worm* (Job 25:6). *I have become the laughingstock of all peoples, the burden of their songs all day long* (Lam. 3:14).

He explains that he is ***the reproach of men and the outcast of the people***. *Those who passed by derided him . . . "You who would destroy the temple"* (Matt. 27:39–40). *Those who were crucified with him also reviled him* (Mark 15:32). *He saved others; he cannot save himself* (Matt. 27:42). *And the soldiers plaited a crown of thorns and put it on his head* (John 19:2). And so 'I have become ***the reproach of men***,' in their words, as has been said, ***and the outcast of the people***, since they scorned him and, rejecting him, asked for Barabbas in Matthew 27. *You have made us offscouring and refuse among the peoples* (Lam. 3:45).

In a *second* way, ***I am a worm*** pertains to the dignity of Christ, for a worm is not generated from sexual intercourse but from the earth, from the heat of the heavenly sun alone. *He was like the most tender little worm of the wood* (2 Sam. 23:8 DRB). Likewise, Christ came from the virgin by the work of the Holy Spirit alone: ***The Lord will give goodness, and our earth shall yield her fruit*** (Ps. 84:13). Therefore, he says, ***I am a worm and no man*** only but also God.

Or this can be taken in another way, according to Augustine.[40] By ***man***, the old man should be understood—namely, Adam, who was a man but not the son of man. By ***worm***, Christ should be understood, who was a man because he was the son of man—that is, of the virgin. Therefore, he says, ***I am a worm and no man*** who rejoices in temporal things but the son of man who rejoices in spiritual things.

The outcast of the people: here [the theme] continues.

Afterward, he describes the derision. *First*, he shows that it is universal; *second*, that it is manifold. That it is universal is shown when he says, ***All they***

40. Augustine, *Letter 140*, 8, 21–22.

that saw me have laughed me to scorn: *I have become a laughingstock all the day* (Jer. 20:7) to the people and the princes; and this distribution, ***all***, for all the people, should be understood to signify specifically the evil ones.

He shows that the mockery was manifold because it was registered in words, so he says, ***They have spoken with the lips***. *Those who passed by derided him* (Matt. 27:39). *Upon whom are you making sport? Against whom do you open your mouth wide and put out your tongue?* (Isa. 57:4). *If he be the true son of God, he will defend him* (Wis. 2:18 DRB). But it was also registered in deeds: ***and wagged the head***. *Wagging their heads* (in derision) . . . *saying, "He saved others"* (Matt. 27:39, 42).

181 ***He hoped in the Lord***: He shows what those words might be that were spoken to mock him, for they *first* taunted him for the hope he had in God. Thus, it says, ***He hoped in the Lord; let him deliver him***. *He trusts in God; let God deliver him now if he desires* (Matt. 27:43)—as if to say, 'If he had hoped in the Lord, he would have delivered him,' because it was said immediately above, ***In thee have our fathers hoped . . . and thou hast delivered them***. But they are deceived since it was not understood about salvation but temporal deliverance.

Second, they taunted Christ, suggesting that he was not acceptable to God, so it says, ***Let him save him, seeing he delighteth in him***. *He . . . calls himself the child of the Lord* (Wis. 2:13).

182 ***For thou art he that hast drawn me out of the womb***: Hereafter, the cause of their mocking is described, and he does two things regarding this mocking. *First*, he describes its cause. *Second*, he breaks out into prayer: ***Depart not from me***.

The cause of derision is usually foolishness. So, the temporal-minded consider good people foolish because the latter do not trust in the world: ***You have confounded the counsel of the poor man, but the Lord is his hope*** (Ps. 13:6). He makes two points about this cause. *First*, he describes the divine favor motivating his hope; *second*, that hope itself, ***my hope***, as if to say, 'They deride me because my hope is in you.' And so, he says, ***Thou art he that hast drawn me out of the womb***.

Here he first discusses what pertains to the head. All those who are born are naturally and universally drawn from their mother's womb by divine power, and all human persons have this same cause: *He . . . separated me from my mother's womb and called me by his grace* (Gal. 1:15 DRB). But of Christ, it is said in a singular sense that he was drawn from his mother's womb since he was conceived miraculously and begotten without semen, preserving his mother's innocence. This is a blessing, and hope follows from it, and he describes three aspects of this hope: *first*, the hope itself; *second*, its perfection; and *third*, its reason. Therefore, he says, ***my hope from the breasts of my mother***—that is,

'You have been my hope from the point at which I became human and sucked my mother's breasts,' since it was not fitting for him to hope when he was the Word with God (John 1:1).[41] ***My hope, O Lord, from my youth*** (Ps. 70:5).

But, on the contrary, Christ had the use of free will from the moment of his conception, and he thus hoped from that moment.[42] I respond by saying that the breasts—that is, breast milk—began to be prepared from the time of his conception, so ***from the breasts*** can be applied to the time of his conception.

I was cast upon thee from the womb: A contrary view holds that if Christ was ***cast upon*** God after he came out of the womb, he was not cast upon God before he exited the womb. To this, I respond by saying that one is 'cast upon' another who is supported by him and not by himself alone: *Cast all your anxieties on him* (1 Pet. 5:7). So, '***I was cast upon thee from the womb*** since I lean upon you alone.' This describes the perfection of hope.

183 ***From my mother's womb***: Here, he gives a reason for hope, as if to say, 'I have hoped in you since I have always had you as God.' ***In him hath my heart confided, and I have been helped*** (Ps. 27:7). And so he says, ***From my mother's womb thou art my God***—that is, 'From when I was made human, since previously there was no human Son of God.' But if it is applied to the members of Christ, being cast or drawn out is to be moved from one state to another according to the flesh. Now, Christ always tended toward God. But it is said of the members who lived according to the flesh that they were habitually in the fleshly womb of worldly desires but were drawn forth by God from this sort of desire and cast upon God so that they might hope in and seek nothing but God.

Afterward, he concludes the prayer when he says, ***Depart not from me***—that is, 'Spiritually defend me and my members,' as if to say, 'You have forsaken me by exposing me to my bodily suffering. ***Depart not from me*** but cherish me with spiritual help.'

184 ***For tribulation is very near***: According to Jerome, this is the beginning of the following verse, and it can be read, as he says, either in connection with

41. Thomas's view is that, in his superlative fullness of being, the divine Word cannot be said to have had hope, the theological virtue by which one looks forward to a blessedness not yet attained. Nevertheless, in his self-emptied incarnate existence he lacked the immortality and glorified body that he would obtain after the Resurrection, and these were things for which Christ could be said to hope even if the theological virtue of hope could not be ascribed to him in the fullest sense. See Thomas Aquinas, *Summa theologiae* 3.7.4.

42. Thomas's point here and below is that the passage "my hope from the breasts of my mother" does not indicate that the virtue of hope was not ascribable to Christ *in utero* before he began to breastfeed. The free choice involved in hope is not usually ascribable to infants in the womb, given that the former involves a mature exercise of intelligence and volition. In Thomas's view, however, Christ was fully developed in this regard from the instant of his miraculous conception, and thus, Christ was capable of hope even in the womb. See *Summa theologiae* 3.34.2; 3.33.2.

the preceding line or with the subsequent.[43] Jerome says that it is read more fittingly in connection with what comes afterward, for the Psalmist, explaining the passion in the person of the Lord, first presents a prayer and, then, includes the progression of the passion, at ***calves have surrounded me.***

He does two things regarding the prayer. *First,* he presents it. *Second,* he shows its necessity: ***For tribulation is very near.*** Therefore, he says, ***From my mother's womb thou art my God,*** 'and so I pray that you ***depart not from me.***' It should be understood that Christ asks in the person of his members that he may remain with them in tribulation. *God is faithful, and he will not let you be tempted beyond your strength* (1 Cor. 10:13). ***Do not thou forsake me. For my enemies have spoken against me, and they that watched my soul have consulted together*** (Ps. 70:9–10). And again, he does not say this on his own behalf.

The need to pray has a twofold occasion: the presence of tribulation and a deficiency of help. So he says, ***Tribulation is very near*** in time: *Behold the hour is at hand, and the Son of man is betrayed* (Matt. 26:45). However, an objection could be raised: If these were the words of Christ when he was already on the cross, why does he say, ***Tribulation is very near***?

We can say that David changes the time.

Augustine solved it in another way: Tribulation is sometimes near, sometimes remote. The sensation of sorrow is in the soul; the body is near the soul; exterior goods are remote. Therefore, when an affliction affects exterior goods, tribulation is not near, but when it is in one's own body, it is near and close, and it is impossible for a person not to experience it.[44] Now, Christ was afflicted in his body. ***I met with trouble and sorrow*** (Ps. 114:3). Likewise, help failed: ***there is none to help me.*** And so, he is hard-pressed in praying: *I looked, but there was no one to help* (Isa. 63:5) since the apostles fled, leaving him.

185 ***Many calves have surrounded me***: Above, the Psalmist, in the person of Christ, showed his questioning or grievance to be reasonable, both in relation to God and to ancient custom or experience. Now here, he follows the progression of the passion regarding the affliction of the flesh. *First,* he describes his persecutors; *second,* the effects of their persecution, at ***I am poured out like water***; and *third,* their manner of persecution, at ***dogs have encompassed me.*** Therefore, the persecutors attacking with their actions are first introduced.

Some of these are lesser, such as the common people and ministers, and regarding those, he says, ***Many calves have surrounded me.*** *The number of fools is infinite* (Eccles. 1:15 DRB). They ***have surrounded me*** since they have invaded on all sides. ***They surrounded me like bees*** (Ps. 117:12). Some are great, so he

43. Jerome, *Divina biblioteca, Liber Psalmos,* Ps. 21 (PL 29:153).

44. Augustine, *Letter 140,* 13, 33.

says, ***fat bulls have besieged me.*** *Extol not thyself in the thoughts of thy soul like a bull* (Sir. 6:2 DRB), who, because of his fatness and strength, is not put into a yoke but begets many and is proud. The bull is said to be a melancholic animal that stays angry for a long time for this reason. And as the lesser have the daring that comes from numbers, so the great have that which belongs to riches. And so he says they are ***fat***. *He . . . is armed with a fat neck* (Job 15:26 DRB).

Have besieged me: They *have besieged my tabernacle round about* (Job 19:12 DRB). Afterward, he describes the persecutors rushing against him with their mouths, saying, ***They have opened their mouths against me.*** And indeed, they did this by tempting him multiple times: *Why do you tempt me, ye hypocrites?* (Matt. 22:18 DRB). They did it by accusing, arousing envy, seeking his death, saying, *Crucify him* (Mark 15:13). *Our enemies have opened their mouths against us* (Lam. 3:46 DRB).

Hereafter he employs an image: ***as a lion ravening and roaring.*** They are compared to a lion because of their cruelty: *My heritage has become to me like a lion in the forest, she has lifted up her voice against me* (Jer. 12:8). For a lion that has caught its prey roars: *Does a lion roar in the forest when he has no prey?* (Amos 3:4). And he says, ***ravening***: lying in ambush; and ***roaring***: in seeking death blatantly. *Like a roaring lion tearing the prey, they have devoured human lives* (Ezek. 22:25).

186 ***I am poured out like water***: Here, he describes the effect of their persecution. *First,* he mentions this effect; *second,* he explains it, at ***my bones are scattered.***

Thus, he says, ***They . . . persecute me and afflict me*** (Ps. 118:157), since they completely prevailed against him as regards his bodily well-being, and so he says, ***I am poured out like water.*** If oil is poured out, some remains in the vessel; if wine is poured out, at least a smell remains in the vessel; but of water, nothing remains. This is to say, 'I am utterly poured out in their opinion.' *We are like water spilled on the ground, which cannot be gathered up again* (2 Sam. 14:14). 'Water is poured out lightly and thrown away; thus am I poured out,' for so the Jews not only tried to remove him from the face of the earth but also wanted to destroy his reputation.

Or, Christ is made like water, since as water cleanses, so the passion of Christ washes away all filth and all sins: *Christ . . . hath loved us and washed us from our sins in his own blood* (Rev. 1:5 DRB). Likewise, as water rains down and makes fruitful, so does the passion of Christ: *I said, "I will water my orchard"* (Sir. 24:31). And it bears the fruit of eternal life: *My blossoms* (that is, my passion) *became glorious and abundant fruit* (Sir. 24:17). Likewise, as water makes the road slippery, so the passion of Christ disposed the Jews to fall: *We preach Christ crucified, a stumbling block to Jews and folly to gentiles, but to those who are called, both Jews and Greeks, Christ the power of God and the wisdom of God* (1 Cor. 1:23–24).

Hereafter, he explains this effect, and so he says, ***all my bones are scattered***—as if to say, 'Whatever in me seemed to be strong is dissolved; whatever seemed to be beautiful is dried up.' And so he says, ***scattered.***

Human strength is twofold. One is the strength of the body, which resides in the bones and nerves, and regarding this, he says, ***all my bones are scattered***—as if to say, 'all the strength of my body has failed.' Nevertheless, it is also said according to the spiritual sense about Christ, for the apostles, who are the bones of Christ, were scattered: *I will strike the shepherd, and the sheep of the flock will be scattered* (Matt. 26:31).

The other strength is that of the soul, and it abides in the heart, so he says, ***My heart is become like wax melting.*** Augustine asks how this is true of Christ the head since this seems to happen through an excess of fear, which should not be ascribed to Christ since even if there was natural fear in him, it would not have been so great as to melt his heart.[45]

And so, it should be understood about Christ not in himself but in reference to his members since indeed they are the heart of Christ whom he loves most: *I hold you in my heart* (Phil. 1:7). And it follows: *God is my witness, how I yearn for you all with the affection of Christ* (Phil. 1:8). The apostles were the bones given to sustain the weak in the Church just as the bones hold up the flesh: *We who are strong ought to bear with the failings of the weak* (Rom. 15:1). And it was their hearts that melted like wax.

This occurs *first* in an evil melting away through fear as happened in the disciples' flight—*All the disciples deserted him and fled* (Matt. 26:56)—and Peter's denial: *He denied it, saying, "Woman, I do not know him"* (Luke 22:57). *Second*, it occurs in a good melting away as in the conversion of the disciples. Such is apparent in the conversion of Peter and Andrew (Matt. 4:18–20).

Or it can be said, also, that this is a liquefaction of love: *My soul melted* (Song of Sol. 5:6 DRB). Before a thing melts, it is hard and holds together tightly; but when it melts, it is diffused and extends from itself to another. Fear sometimes hardens when it is not great, but the same thing is true of love [as is true of liquefaction] because when love is overwhelming, a person extends into something else that was formerly self-contained. And this melting can be applied to Christ as the head, for one is melted in this way by the Holy Spirit and ***in the midst of*** the ***bowels***—that is, in the affections.

Or, by the ***heart*** of Christ, the Sacred Scriptures can be understood, which manifest Christ's heart. These were closed before the passion, since they were

45. Augustine, *Letter 140*, 14, 36.

obscure, but open after the passion, since those with understanding study and discern how the prophets should be explained.

187 ***My strength is dried up***: Here, he shows that whatever beauty was in Christ has vanished. Three things were seen to flourish in Christ before the passion: the working of miracles, eloquence in teaching, and reputation and glory in the eyes of the people.

About the *first*: *A multitude followed him because they saw . . .* (John 6:2). And this power ***dried up*** in the passion as far as their opinion of him was concerned, so they cried, *He saved others; he cannot save himself* (Matt. 27:42). ***My strength is dried up***—that is, it has become worthless ***like a potsherd***. Or it is ***like a potsherd***, which hardens when it dries up. Similarly, in the passion, Christ's strength was hardened to endure: *The furnace trieth the potter's vessels, and the trial of affliction, just men* (Sir. 27:6 DRB).

About the *second*: *He taught them as one who had authority* (Matt. 7:29), but in the passion, ***my tongue hath cleaved to my jaws*** because of his silence. *I will make your tongue cleave to the roof of your mouth so that you shall be mute* (Ezek. 3:26). And this took place in the passion since he did not respond to Herod: *He questioned him at some length, but he made no answer* (Luke 23:9).

About the *third*: *Many spread their garments on the road, and others spread leafy branches* (Matt. 21:8). Then was fulfilled what David prophesied about Christ, saying, ***O Lord, save me: O Lord, give good success. Blessed be he that cometh in the name of the Lord. . . . The Lord is God, and he hath shone upon us*** (Ps. 117:25–27). But in the passion, he was reviled, so he says, ***thou hast brought me down into the dust of death***—that is, you have made me endure a vile death: *Let us condemn him to a shameful death* (Wis. 2:20). Or, if it is taken to refer to the members: ***thou hast brought me down into the dust of death***—that is, 'my members who were burned but not those of Christ.' Or: ***into the dust of death***—that is, 'You have given me into the power of the Jews who are like dust.'[46]

188 ***For many dogs have encompassed me***: Here, the manner of the passion is described. *First*, he describes the things that took place before the crucifixion; *second*, the things that took place during the crucifixion itself; *third*, those that took place after the crucifixion.

Two things happened before the crucifixion. *First*, he was captured, and regarding this, he says, ***many dogs have encompassed me***: *Look out for the dogs, look out for the evil-workers* (Phil. 3:2). *The dogs have a mighty appetite* (Isa.

46. This appears to be an allusion to Genesis 22:17, in which God promises to make Abraham's offspring as numerous as "the sand which is on the seashore." The Jews are thus "like dust," for Thomas, in the sense that they are innumerably many.

56:11). *Second* is how he was mocked, so he says, ***the council of the malignant hath besieged me.***

Afterward, he describes the things that took place in the crucifixion. And first in affixing him: ***They have dug my hands and feet***, affixing him to the cross with large nails. *What are these wounds in the midst of thy hands?* (Zech. 13:6 DRB). Likewise, about his stretching, he says, ***They have numbered all my bones***—that is, 'I was stretched out so they could be numbered.'

189 ***And they have looked***: Here are described those things that took place after the passion, so he says, ***they have looked***—they gathered at the spectacle for mockery. *The soldiers also mocked him, coming up and offering him vinegar, and saying, "If you are the King of the Jews, save yourself!"* (Luke 23:36–37). 'And they ***stared*** at what happened to me.'

They parted my garments, which were many and divisible, ***amongst them, and upon my vesture***, which was sewn as one piece, ***they cast lots***. And they did this either out of greed or for their amusement. These garments signify the Church, but the undivided vesture signifies the unity of the Church, which is possessed by only one—however many believe themselves to have it—since the unity of the Church is singular: *My dove, my perfect one, is only one* (Song of Sol. 6:9).

190 ***But thou, O Lord, remove not thy help***: Having narrated the passion, he proceeds to prayer and prays in two ways: *first*, he asks for divine help; *second*, he asks for the fruit of the assistance supplied, at ***I will declare thy name***.

He asks for divine help in two ways: *first*, he asks for divine assistance in general; *second*, he asks for help of an inherently specific kind: ***Deliver, O God, my soul from the sword***.

Regarding his petition for help in general, he does two things. *First*, he asks for the aid to come quickly. *Second*, he explains its necessity. Therefore, concerning the *first*, he says that they have done this: ***They have dug my hands and feet. . . . But thou, O Lord, remove not thy help to a distance from me***—in other words, 'Do not delay supplying to me, the man Christ, the help of divinity.' This is as if to say, 'It has been done since he was delivered from death through the glory of the Resurrection, which was not removed to a distance since he rose after three days.' And Christ was raised: *Christ has been raised from the dead, the first fruits of those who have fallen asleep* (1 Cor. 15:20).

Look toward my defense, as if to say, 'Your help is necessary to me, for my defense.' ***Protect me under the shadow of thy wings*** (Ps. 16:8). Defend me against those persecuting me to death and against the demons so that they may not detain me in limbo. Therefore, he asked in this way that his body not be dissolved to dust nor his soul be detained in hell. *Having loosed the pangs* *of death, because it was not possible for him to be held by it* (Acts 2:24). ***Forsake me not*** (Ps. 37:22).

191 ***Deliver, O God, my soul***: Here, he presents the specific things against which he prays to be defended. The *first* is death; the *second* is the trial of death, at ***from the hand of the dog***. Therefore, he says, ***look toward my defense*** and ***deliver, O God, my soul***, which they seek, ***from the sword***—that is, from the sword clamoring in action. But on the contrary, Christ was not killed by a sword but by a spear, and he was pierced with a spear after his death.

But it should be said that his sword divides acutely, *sharper than any two-edged sword, piercing to the division of soul and spirit* (Heb. 4:12). And, in the same way, since death divides the soul from the body and the father from the son (and vice versa) and brother from brother, it is called a sword: *Awake, O sword*—that is, death—*against my shepherd* (Zech. 13:7). And he was rescued from death in the Resurrection.

Or ***the sword*** is the tongue of his adversaries, ***whose teeth are weapons and arrows and their tongue a sharp sword*** (Ps. 56:5). Or Christ says this on account of his members, of whom many would be killed with a sword: *He killed James the brother of John with the sword* (Acts 12:2).

And my only one from the hand of the dog: Here he prays against trials, and he describes them as irrational. And he does this under the image of a dog. Due to its sudden anger, a dog barks before knowing at whom he ought to bark. In this way, the Jews raised a clamor before they knew why they were barking at Christ: *Look out for the dogs, look out for the evil-workers* (Phil. 3:2). And above: ***many dogs have encompassed me***. This especially pertains to the Jews who cried out, barking at Christ, *Crucify, crucify* (Luke 23:21).

192 ***Save me from the lion's mouth***: Here, he describes those cruel persons under the likeness of a lion, a cruel animal, and this refers to Pilate, who exercised the power of a lion—that is, of a ruler whom the Apostle calls a lion: *I was rescued from the lion's mouth* (2 Tim. 4:17). Or it refers to the devil, who *prowls around like a roaring lion, seeking someone to devour* (1 Pet. 5:8).

And my lowness from the horns of the unicorns: Here, he describes the proud and refers to the leading priests and the scribes, who are compared to unicorns in their pride. This phrase indicates what has one horn on its head and is so proud that it will not endure any subjugation but dies immediately when captured.[47] *Shall the rhinoceros*—that is, the unicorn—*be willing to serve*

47. Thomas appears to follow what, at his time, were widely accepted reports in medieval bestiaries of a horse-like animal with a single horn whose capture was exceedingly difficult (and usually required a maiden). Although he seems to identify or conflate the unicorn with the rhinoceros here, it is unlikely that the animal he has in mind is a single-horned (Indian) rhinoceros, given the descriptions he gives here and elsewhere (e.g., in his commentary on Isaiah 34, where he calls it "a fierce animal the size of a cat"), which plainly correspond with standard medieval unicorn lore.

thee, or will he stay? (Job 39:9 DRB). By this are signified the princes of the Jews, who prided themselves on their singular knowledge of God. And whoever praises himself singularly is like the Pharisee: *I am not like other men* (Luke 18:11). ***Lift not up your horn on high*** (Ps. 74:6).

193 ***I will declare thy name***: Next, he shows the fruit of divine help. *First*, he shows this fruit in Christ himself; *second*, in others, at ***The poor shall eat***. He considers two things about Christ's fruit. *First*, he describes a twofold fruit: preaching and praise. *Second*, he explains both, at ***Ye that fear the Lord***. So, he describes the double fruit of Christ's liberation.

The *first* of Christ's fruit was preaching throughout the whole world. Therefore, he says, ***Save me from the lion's mouth***, since he was saved and delivered from their jaws. ***I will declare thy name to my brethren***—that is, to the apostles—and this he did after the Resurrection. Now, the apostles are his brothers both through the nature he assumed and through the grace of their calling to the apostolate: *Those whom he foreknew he also predestined to be conformed to the image of his Son. . . . Those whom he predestined he also called* (Rom. 8:29–30).

But did he not declare the name of God before the passion? He even says himself, *Father . . . I have manifested your name* (John 17:5–6). It should be said that he did proclaim the name of God before his passion but that he did so more fully after the passion and Resurrection. *First*, he declared it to his disciples with his own mouth when *he opened their minds to understand the Scriptures* (Luke 24:45). *Second*, he gave them the Spirit, the Paraclete: *When the Spirit of truth comes, he will guide you into all the truth* (John 16:13); *the Counselor, the Holy Spirit, whom the Father will send in my name, he will teach you all things* (John 14:26).

Nevertheless, Christ will declare the name of God most fully when he manifests his divinity in judgment: *I will . . . manifest myself to him* (John 14:21); *then they will see the Son of man coming in a cloud with power and great glory* (Luke 21:27). For then they will know the Father in the Son: *In that day you will know that I am in my Father, and you in me, and I in you* (John 14:20). And this befits the Son alone, as he says: *No one knows the Father except the Son* (Matt. 11:27).

The *second* fruit of Christ's deliverance was divine praise. Thus, he says, ***in the midst of the church, I will praise thee*** and *sing . . . his praise from the end of the earth* (Isa. 42:10). He says, ***in the midst of the church***, which phrase Augustine explains in this first way: *What is manifest we say is "in the midst." In the Old Testament, God was praised in secret—that is, in mysteries—but in* *the New, he is praised in public since he is there in the naked truth.*[48] The Second Epistle to the Corinthians says, *We all, with unveiled face, beholding the glory of the Lord, are being changed into his likeness* (3:18) by the removal of the veil.

In another way, we sometimes say that something is 'in the midst' that is innermost. Innermost to the Church are the perfect ones who praise God in a special way in their hearts. ***In the midst of the church, I will praise thee***—that is, in the doctors and the perfect ones.

194 ***Ye that fear the Lord, praise him***: He discusses both fruits: the *first* first and *second* second: ***With thee is my praise.*** In the *first*, he presents the entire preaching of the New Covenant by which the name of the Lord is proclaimed. *First*, he shows what brings people into the New Covenant. *Second*, what is declared to them, at ***because he hath not slighted.*** People are brought into the New Covenant by three things: confessing God by mouth, seeking to glorify him, and fearing him.

Regarding the confession of the mouth, he says, praise him, ***ye that fear the Lord.*** Now, there are two fears: *one* is filial fear, by which one fears offending God and fears being separated from him and shows reverence toward him, and this comes from charity; *another* is servile fear, by which one fears punishment alone, and this does not come from charity. *Perfect love casts out fear* (1 John 4:18). The Old Law was a law of fear, but the New Law is a law of love. Therefore, ***ye that fear the Lord***—that is, who fulfill his law out of fear—***praise him***, since no one praises him who does not love him. As if to say, 'Confess him out of love.' ***Praise the Lord*** (Ps. 116:1).

About seeking the glory of God, he says, ***all ye seed of Jacob, glorify him***: *Whether you eat or drink, or whatever you do, do all to the glory of God* (1 Cor. 10:31). And he says, ***all ye seed of Jacob***, since the sons of Jacob—that is, the Jews—were given the law of the Old Covenant, in which human glory was promised, but in the New Testament, the glory of God is promised. And he says, ***all***, to include *the children of the promise* who *are reckoned as descendants* (Rom. 9:8), as Galatians 3:7 says—namely, the gentiles.

Now, regarding the fear of the Lord, he says, ***Let all the seed of Israel fear him***, with the reverential fear that exists along with love: *Israel, what does the Lord your God require of you but to fear the Lord your God, to walk in all his ways?* (Deut. 10:12). Israel is the same as Jacob.

195 ***Because he hath not slighted***: Here he shows what is announced to them: the power of Christ, according to what is spoken in the person of Christ praying. Sometimes, a person does not want to grant prayers, either because he does not want to pay attention to the one for whom they are made or because

48. Augustine, *Letter 140*, 17, 44.

he does not want to pay attention to the one who makes them. In some cases, even if he is willing to pay attention to the petitioner, he may remain unwilling to grant his petition, nevertheless.

He excludes this *first* case where he says, ***he hath not slighted*** by ignoring ***nor despised the supplication of the poor man***—that is, the humility of one who does hope for temporal things, namely, the humility of Christ. Against the *second*, he shows ***neither hath he turned away his face from me*** by not accepting me. ***Turn not away thy face from thy servant*** (Ps. 68:18). *Third*, he says, ***when I cried to him he heard me***, 'since the judge has granted what I asked for myself and my own': *If you ask anything of the Father, he will give it to you in my name* (John 16:23). *I called to the Lord . . . and you heard my voice* (Jon. 2:2).

Before the passion, he had spoken of three ways in which he suffered. He said he was cast down: ***I am a worm***; forsaken: ***Why hast thou forsaken me?***; and ignored: ***I shall cry by day, and thou wilt not hear***. Why did he speak this way? Because he was speaking ***the words of my sins***—words belonging to the weakness of the flesh, which seeks temporal things above all. And yet, now he says the opposite because he has led human nature to seek spiritual things through his resurrection to this spiritual kind of life. Thus, whereas above he said, ***I am a worm***, here he says, ***He hath not slighted***. Above, he said, ***Why hast thou forsaken me?*** and here he says, ***Neither hath he turned his face away from me***. Above, he said, ***I shall cry by day***; here he says, ***When I cried to him, he heard me***.

196 ***With thee is my praise***: Above, the Psalmist, in the person of Christ, promised to speak two things: namely, the divine name and the praise of God. Of the *first*, he has already spoken. Here, he treats the *second*, divine praise, and does two things. *First*, he shows what kind of praise of God it is. *Second*, he shows how he joins praise with a deed, at ***my vows***.

To show what kind of praise he gives God, he says, ***With thee is my praise***. And this can be understood in two ways. In one way, it reads like this: ***My praise***—'the praise I receive'—is ***with thee***—'not with human beings, from whom I receive no praise, but from you': *It is not the man who commends himself that is accepted but the man whom the Lord commends* (2 Cor. 10:18). In another way, it goes like this: ***My praise***—'the praise I give you'—is ***with thee*** not in human eyes: *He sang praise with all his heart, and he loved his Maker* (Sir. 47:8).

This praise is given ***in a great church*** gathered together by me and in my name. It is ***great*** in extension: *Enlarge the place of your tent and let the curtains of your habitations be stretched out* (Isa. 54:2). It is ***great*** in power: *On this rock I will build my Church, and the gates of Hades shall not prevail against it. I will give you the keys of the kingdom of heaven, and whatever you bind on earth shall* *be bound in heaven* (Matt. 16:18–19). It is ***great*** in dignity: *The kings of the earth shall bring their glory into it* (Rev. 21:24).

Here he shows how praise is connected to a deed. Christ's vow was to give himself for the salvation of the faithful. Moreover, he made this vow as a human being: ***I should do thy will: O my God, I have desired it*** (Ps. 39:9). And this *will of God* [*is*] *your sanctification* (1 Thess. 4:3). *I have come down from heaven, not to do my own will, but the will of him who sent me* (John 6:38). Christ fulfilled this vow by giving himself over to the passion and again when he gave his body as food for the faithful, so he says, ***I will pay***—on the altar of the cross and in the sacrifice of the faithful—***my vows***—that is, sacrifices—and I will do this ***in the sight of them that fear him***. *He that feareth the Lord honoreth his parents* (Sir. 3:8 DRB).

197 ***The poor shall eat***: Here, he describes the effect of the passion on others. *First*, he describes the various effects of the passion. *Second*, he presents those relating to the future, at ***There shall be declared***. He considers two aspects of these effects. *First*, he describes the effects belonging to the apostles; *second*, he describes those effects poured out to others through the apostles, at ***All the ends of the earth shall remember***.

The ministry of the Lord's sacrament belongs to the apostles. He signifies this ministry when he says, ***The poor shall eat***—that is, the humble and those who despise the things of the world: *Blessed are the poor in spirit, for theirs is the kingdom of heaven* (Matt. 5:3). These eat the sacrifice—namely, the sacrament of the body and blood—sacramentally and spiritually. A threefold effect follows from their eating of the sacrament: spiritual satisfaction, praise, and life.

Regarding the *first*, spiritual satisfaction, he says, ***shall be filled***, because their desire will be appeased by the plenitude of graces they receive through this sacrament: ***Let my soul be filled as with marrow and fatness*** (Ps. 62:6).

Regarding praise, the *second* effect of eating the sacrament, he says, ***they shall praise the Lord that seek him***. This is no wonder since praise follows from joy: *The ransomed of the Lord shall return and come to Zion with singing; everlasting joy shall be upon their heads* (Isa. 51:11). Moreover, fulfillment of desire causes delight: *Delight yourselves in rich food* (Isa. 55:2)—that is, in spiritual richness—***with the voice of joy and praise, the noise of one feasting*** (Ps. 41:5). But not just anyone praises God but ***they . . . that seek him***—that is, those who seek nothing except Christ or God. *Seek the Lord while he may be found; call upon him while he is near* (Isa. 55:6).

Regarding life, the *third* effect of eating the sacrament, he says, ***their hearts shall live***: *He who eats this bread will live forever* (John 6:58). And so, he says, ***shall live***, as if to say, 'Although their bodies die in imitation of the passion of the Lord, they shall live in heart': ***Seek ye God, and your soul shall live*** (Ps. 68:33).

198 ***All the ends of the earth shall remember***: Here he describes the effects of the passion that are directed to others: *first*, to all generally; *second*, to carnal people, at ***All the fat ones of the earth have eaten***; and *third*, to spiritual people, at ***my soul***. Moreover, this effect is threefold, encompassing *first*, the divine knowledge that came to the nations through the apostles; *second*, conversion to Christ; and *third*, the effect manifested in perfect works.

Regarding divine knowledge, the *first* effect of the passion on others, he says, ***shall remember***. A certain knowledge of God is naturally implanted in human persons, but they forget the Lord through sin: *You forgot the God who gave you birth* (Deut. 32:18). Now, the gentiles had some knowledge of God, but they had forgotten it through sin; but through the apostles, they were led back to remember this natural knowledge: *Remember the Lord from afar* (Jer. 51:50). Regarding the *second* effect, conversion, he says, ***shall be converted to the Lord***—namely, through love. Not only Jews but ***all the ends of the earth*** have made this conversion: *If you will inquire, inquire; come back again* (Isa. 21:12).[49] These two effects pertain to the sacrament of the altar, which is a kind of memorial of the Lord's passion, as 1 Corinthians 11 says.[50] Thus, he says, ***shall remember***, since the soul's conversion to the Lord is the effect of the sacrament of the altar. ***He hath brought me up on the water of refreshment*** (Ps. 22:2).[51] They will be worshiping him not in ceremonies but ***in his sight***—namely, with spiritual worship: *God is spirit, and those who worship him must worship in spirit and truth* (John 4:24).

199 ***All the kindreds of the gentiles***: *To him shall bow down, each in its place, all the lands of the nations* (Zeph. 2:11)—as conveying that the gentiles worshiped the God of Israel and left their own place behind to go and dwell with the Jews as proselytes.

The kingdom is the Lord's: Spiritual power over the whole world belongs to Christ. *To him was given dominion and glory and kingdom, that all peoples, nations, and languages should serve him* (Dan. 7:14). Not only over the Jews as

49. The relevance of Isaiah 21:12 is clearer in Thomas's Latin edition, which can be rendered, "If you are seeking, seek; convert and come."

50. In 1 Corinthians 11:24, Christ enjoins the apostles to celebrate the Eucharist in remembrance of him. What is unique about Thomas's understanding of the memorial character of the Eucharist is the scope of what it serves to commemorate. Beyond the narrative of Christ's sacrificial suffering and death, Thomas explains, the Eucharist brings back from the oblivion of sin our memory of things we once knew naturally about God.

51. The relevance of Psalm 22:2 (DRB) to Thomas's point here is clearer in his Latin psalter. The phrase *educavit me*, rendered "brought me up" in the Douay-Rheims translation, also has the force of 'educate me,' which corresponds better to Thomas's point, here, that the sacramental "water of refreshment" (which evidently, for Thomas, refers to Baptism) conveys conversion of the soul.

from *upon the throne of David* (Isa. 9:7), but furthermore, ***he shall have dominion over the nations.*** Psalm 2:8: ***Ask of me, and I will give thee the gentiles for thy inheritance.***

200 ***All the fat ones of the earth have eaten***: Here, he presents two effects of the passion upon carnal persons. *First*, he explains what good they achieve; *second*, what they lack, where he says that the carnal ***shall fall before him.***

The carnal have obtained a twofold good: participation in the sacrament and veneration of God in worship. To this *first* point about the good that the carnal have achieved, he says that ***they have eaten***—unworthily so, of course, since they are carnal: *Flesh and blood cannot inherit the kingdom of God* (1 Cor. 15:50). Of the good (i.e., ***the poor***), he said above that they ***shall be filled, praise the Lord***, and ***live*** because they venerated the sacrament through the faith they possess. But these carnal ones ***shall fall before him***, God, because they are ***the fat ones of the earth***—that is, attached to earthly things, not elevated to spiritual ones. *I will fill the soul of the priests with fatness, and my people shall be filled with my good things* (Jer. 31:14 DRB). Fat cows signify these in Amos 4:1 (DRB). *The beloved grew fat and kicked* (Deut. 32:15 DRB), for *he that eateth and drinketh unworthily eateth and drinketh judgment to himself* (1 Cor. 11:29 DRB). And he says rightly, ***all they that go down***—that is, those who are thrust down to the earth in their affections, since, although, in the eyes of human beings, they might appear to be standing, they will fall in God's eyes (cf. 1 Cor 10:12): *Many shall stumble thereon; they shall fall* (Isa. 8:15). Or they ***shall fall before him*** in the sense that they will be subjected to him, even his enemies: ***all they that go down to the earth***—to the corruption of sin, that is: *At the name of Jesus, every knee should bow* (Phil. 2:10).

201 ***To him my soul shall live***: Here, he describes the effects of Christ's passion on spiritual persons. The ***soul*** of Christ represents those in whom the Holy Spirit rests—namely, the spiritual, who are ordered to God in a twofold way: *first*, in heart, since they live for God or Christ: *It is no longer I who live but Christ who lives in me* (Gal. 2:20). *He died for all, that those who live might live no longer for themselves but for him who for their sake died* (2 Cor. 5:15).

Second, they are ordered to God in their work: ***my seed.*** The good seed is the children of the kingdom—as if to say, 'The children of the kingdom whom I have sown have served God alone, for all the works they have done have been directed to his glory.'

202 ***There shall be declared to the Lord***: Here, he explains when this would be since it was to occur not in his own time but in epochs to come. He predicts three things: *first*, the proclamation of the faith; *second*, those who must proclaim it; and *third*, those to whom it will be proclaimed. Regarding the *first*,

he says, ***There shall be declared to the Lord a generation to come.*** This can be explained in two ways.

In one approach, with Jerome, we can read it as saying, ***There shall be declared***—that is, evangelized—***a generation to come*** so they may be converted to the Lord. For ***shall be declared*** is passive, as if to say, 'This generation will be brought to the Lord by the preaching of the apostles': *The poor have good news preached to them* (Matt. 11:5).

Or it can be understood thus: The good of the generation will be announced to God by the angels, not because he is ignorant or lacking, but to maintain an order, as Dionysius says, and as is said in Tobit: *I am Raphael, one of the seven holy angels who present the prayers of the saints* (12:15).

And the heavens—that is, the heavenly apostles: *Our commonwealth is in heaven* (Phil. 3:20)—***shall show forth his justice***, not human but of God, which the Jews rejected, *being ignorant of the righteousness that comes from God and seeking to establish their own* (Rom. 10:3).

He tells to whom it shall be announced: ***to a people that shall be born***, by spiritual generation: *Unless one is born anew* (John 3:3). Now, this people is not reborn by human work but by divine. They *were born, not of blood nor of the will of the flesh nor of the will of man, but of God* (John 1:13). And so, he says, ***which the Lord hath made.*** As Psalm 99:3 says, ***the Lord . . . made us.***

Psalm 47[52]

The Magnificence of the Church

On Psalms 47 (474–479)

47:1 *A psalm of a canticle, for the sons of Korah, on the second day of the week.*

47:2 *Great is the Lord and exceedingly to be praised, in the city of our God, in his holy mountain.*

47:3 *With the joy of the whole earth is Mount Zion founded; on the sides of the north, the city of the great king.*

47:4 *In her houses shall God be known, when he shall protect her.*

47:5 *For behold the kings of the earth assembled themselves; they gathered together.*

47:6 *So they saw, and they wondered; they were troubled; they were moved.*

47:7 *Trembling took hold of them; there were pains as of a woman in labor.*

47:8 *With a vehement wind, thou shalt break in pieces the ships of Tarshish.*

47:9 *As we have heard, so have we seen, in the city of the Lord of hosts, in the city of our God: God has founded it for ever.*

47:10 *We have received thy mercy, O God, in the midst of thy temple.*

47:11 *According to thy name, O God, so also is thy praise unto the ends of the earth: thy right hand is full of justice.*

52. Psalm 47, so numbered in the Douay-Rheims translation used here, corresponds to Psalm 48 in most modern editions, which follow the Masoretic numbering system.

47:12 ***Let Mount Zion rejoice, and the daughters of Judah be glad because of thy judgments, O Lord.***

47:13 ***Surround Zion and encompass her: tell ye in her towers.***

47:14 ***Set your hearts on her strength and distribute her houses that ye may relate it in another generation.***

47:15 ***For this is God, our God unto eternity, and forever and ever; he shall rule us for evermore.***

474 Above, the Psalmist invited the nations to sing to God about God's favors.[53] Here, he describes the great joy of the people or the city. The title is ***A psalm of a canticle, for the sons of Korah, on the second day of the week.***

Among the Jews, the Sabbath was kept very solemnly, and they named all the days of the week from the Sabbath. Thus, the Lord's day was called the first day of the Sabbath, Monday the second day of the Sabbath, and so on with all the other days.[54]

Therefore, the Psalmist says, ***on the second day of the week***, since on the first day, God said, *Let there be light* (Gen. 1:3). On the second day, he said, *Let there be a firmament* (Gen. 1:6). The light signifies Christ; the firmament, the Church. Therefore, since he treats the magnificence of the Church here, it is appropriate that it be ***on the second day of the week***. Nevertheless, neither in Hebrew nor in Jerome is it said to be for the second day of the week.

Thus, this psalm is divided into two parts. *First*, it describes the magnificence of the city. *Second*, it adds thanksgiving, at ***We have received . . . O God.***

Regarding the *first*, it does two things. *First*, it describes the magnificence of the city. *Second*, it brings forward his testimony, at ***behold***.

The dignity of a city depends on its Lord, so *first*, the psalm commends the Lord; *second*, the city, at ***With joy, it is founded***. It describes the Lord's inherent dignity and that of his works. Of his dignity, it says, ***Great is the Lord***. Again: ***Who is the great God?*** (Ps. 76:14). And his greatness is the immensity of his goodness. Augustine says, *In those things in which greatness does not consist in size, to be great is to be good*.[55]

The psalm describes the Lord's works since they are ***exceedingly to be praised***. Praise properly regards works, and it says ***exceedingly*** since however

53. See Thomas Aquinas, *On Psalms* 46 (not included in this collection).

54. Cf. Thomas Aquinas, *On Psalms* 23.206 (at page 33 above).

55. Augustine, *The Trinity* 6.8, 9.

much you praise him, you nevertheless fall short of the praise he deserves: *When you exalt him, put forth all your strength, and do not grow weary, for you cannot praise him enough* (Sir. 43:30).

The greatness of his works is evident in all of his creations, but it is especially apparent in the gifts of grace by which the Church has been established. And so it says, ***in the city of our God***—namely, the Church: *I saw the holy city, new Jerusalem* (Rev. 21:2). And this city, the Church, is situated ***in his holy mountain***. This mountain is Christ: *The mountain of the house of the Lord* (Isa. 2:2). Of this city, it is said, *A city set on a hill cannot be hidden* (Matt. 5:14).

475 ***With the joy of the whole earth is Mount Zion founded***: Here, the Psalmist commends the city on three counts: *first*, for its breadth or delightfulness; *second*, for its disposition; and *third*, for the wisdom of the citizens.

Therefore, he says, ***With the joy of the whole earth, it is founded***—as if to say, 'It is founded on a mountain—that is, Christ.' But surely this foundation does not belong to one land only? No, it overflows into the joy of the whole earth since all receive the joy of this foundation: ***Shout with joy to God, all the earth. Sing ye a psalm to his name*** (Ps. 65:1–2). They shall *come to Zion with singing* (Isa. 51:11). *Is this the city which was called the perfection of beauty?* (Lam. 2:15). Another text has ***the founder***—as if to say, 'The Lord is great. And I, the Lord, the founder of this city, am speaking.'

With joy . . . is Mount Zion founded; on the sides of the north—that is, placed on the side of Mount Zion toward the north. Zion signifies the Jews, but the north represents the idolatrous nations. Therefore, this city is composed of Jews and gentiles.

Jerome has it otherwise, and his way accords with the mystery of the bride: ***Let the joy of Mount Zion sprout forth for all the earth on the north sides of the little city of the great king.***[56] In the mystical sense, this means that the city is praised for the civilization it cultivates and the humanity of Christ, which he assumed.

I say that the Church is great, and this greatness is from the splendid sprout itself—that is, Christ—and this sprout is the joy of all the world. In the Hebrew, it says, ***beautiful exceedingly great joy***—that is, Christ—and this is on Mount Zion.

In her houses shall God be known: Here, he praises the city for the wisdom of the citizens, for true wisdom consists in the knowledge of God. *Let him who glories glory in this, that he understands and knows me* (Jer. 9:24). Thus, he commends Jerusalem because God is known in it, and he says, ***In her houses shall God be known.***

56. Here, as often, "Jerome" is a reference to the Hebrew Psalter.

Now, the knowledge of God is threefold since it can refer to the state of the city of Jerusalem, to the Church, and to future glory.

Therefore, one form of the knowledge of God is figural and obscure. And this form existed in the Old Testament and in Jerusalem among the Jewish people.[57] ***In Judea, God is known*** (Ps. 75:2), and so it says, ***In her houses shall God be known.***

Jerome has, ***God is recognized***—not in one place but in all houses and cities. And he says, ***in the houses***, for God was known among the Athenians. *In him we live and move and have our being* (Acts 17:28). *Ever since the creation of the world his invisible nature, namely, his eternal power and deity, have been clearly perceived in the things that have been made* (Rom. 1:20). But he was not known in their houses but rather in the schools among some people, whereas in the former nation [Jerusalem], all knew God.

Another kind of knowledge of God is real but obscure and imperfect, and this is the knowledge we have of God through faith: *For now, we see in a mirror dimly* (1 Cor. 13:12). God is known in this way ***in her houses*** with a knowledge that is real but a knowledge of faith. *We all, with unveiled face, beholding the glory of the Lord* (2 Cor. 3:18). And he says, ***in her houses***, since the entire universal Church contains many churches and many schools, of which each house is said to know God. *For they shall all know me, from the least of them to the greatest* (Jer. 31:34).

Next is the real knowledge that is perfect and clear: *Then I shall understand fully, even as I have been fully understood* (1 Cor. 13:12) in the houses of the heavenly Jerusalem. And the various orders of saints—namely, the apostles, martyrs, confessors, virgins, and so on—are said to be many houses. *In my Father's house are many rooms* (John 14:2). The Roman Psalter refers to this when it says, *God will be known in his gradations* since all will not know him to the same degree.[58] There will be distinct degrees of knowledge among those who know God: *Star differs from star in glory* (1 Cor. 15:41). But this will be so because ***he shall protect her*** to help her since he is our protector and helper. Moreover, another of Jerome's texts says, ***while helping her.***

476 ***For behold the kings of the earth assembled themselves***: Here, he proves the city's dignity through testimony. *First*, he presents witnesses; *second*, their goodness; *third*, their testimony.

Three things are needed to make a testimony credible: witnesses with the dignity to have authority as witnesses, for their testimony should not be accepted if they have no authority. Again, there is the factor of the witnesses'

57. Cf. Thomas Aquinas, *Summa theologiae* 2-2.107.2.

58. On the Roman Psalter, see page 4n9 above.

plurality, and lastly, their concord. These three characteristics are present in the witnesses described here.

They have great dignity since they are ***the kings of the earth.*** Among these, one was Constantine, another was Justinian, and then Charlemagne, who confirmed the privileges of the Church. Furthermore, there were many of them since they ***assembled themselves*** from various nations and times. For by ***kings,*** we may understand the wise and just who give testimony to the Church when they converted to the faith: ***The princes of the people*** (Ps. 46:10). Again, they agree: ***they gathered together into one***—one testimony and opinion: ***When the people assemble together, and kings*** (Ps. 101:23).

This passage can be explained differently. Nevertheless, this first explanation is the literal one since Jerome has, ***they bore witness.*** In Greek, it says, ***they shall receive her***—namely, to defend her. And this is necessary: ***behold the kings of the earth assembled themselves; they gathered together*** against the Church. And these, who at last bore witness to the Church, were once opponents and persecuted her. They strengthened her afterward.

So they saw: Here, he describes the goodness of the witnesses, which involves seven things.

The *first* is vision—that is, the knowledge of faith. Hence, he says, ***they saw***—that is, they recognized through faith the miracles that Christ and the apostles did: *The gentiles shall see thy just one, and all kings thy glorious one* (Isa. 62:2 DRB).

The *second* is wonder at what they see, since these are above human sense and reason. *Then shalt thou see and abound, and thy heart shall wonder and be enlarged* (Isa. 60:5 DRB). ***Wonderful are thy works*** (Ps. 138:14).

The *third* is distress about sin.

About the second, he says, ***they wondered.*** About the third, he says, ***they were troubled.*** As Psalm 59:4 says, ***Thou hast moved the earth and hast troubled it.***

The *fourth* is that they are moved. Sometimes, someone is troubled by sin and falls into despair or persists in evil, but these witnesses are moved to repentance: *With trembling shall the earth be moved* (Isa. 24:19 DRB).

The *fifth* is that fear of God should accompany this movement so that one attributes, not to himself, but to God the fact that he is moved intrinsically toward the good, and he says, ***Serve ye the Lord with fear and rejoice unto him with trembling*** (Ps. 2:11).

This state of pain and trembling is fruitful, so he says, ***there were pains as of a woman in labor*** that are transformed into joy because of the hope of offspring and fruit. From fear of you, O Lord, *we have conceived and brought forth the wind of salvation* (Isa. 26:18).[59] And this is the *sixth*.

Seventh: ***With a vehement wind, thou***—that is, the sea, universally—***shalt break in pieces the ships of Tarshish***; thus, 'You, the sea, shall break the ships.'

Or it should be said that there is one province called Cilicia, and Tarshish is its metropolis, where Paul was born. From this city, the whole region is called Tarshish, and there are many ships there. Or, as those who first sailed the Mediterranean Sea built Carthage, so they fought against Tyre and prevailed. And thus, the whole sea throughout the world was called Tarshish.[60]

The ships that go forth to trade signify desire, and this desire is for an abundance of worldly things. And as ships fluctuate in the sea, so the rich fluctuate in the things of this world. But when a person is turned to repentance, the ships—that is, the desires of this world—are broken in pieces. But they are broken ***with a vehement wind***—that is, by the Holy Spirit: *The day of the Lord is near upon all the nations* (Obad. 1:15). *Wail, O ships of Tarshish* (Isa. 23:1).

But according to Cassiodorus, this designates the whole time of the Incarnation of Christ: ***In her houses shall God be known, when he shall protect*** [***suscipiet***: lit. 'take up'] ***her***—that is, human nature in the unity of person.[61] *Therefore, my people shall know my name* (Isa. 52:6). And on what account? ***For behold the kings of the earth assembled themselves; they gathered together. The kings***—namely, the leaders of the Jews and the scribes of the people—***assembled themselves*** when Herod inquired of them where Christ was to be born. ***They gathered together*** as one because he had been born in Bethlehem.

And seeing this, as the prophets said, ***they wondered; they were troubled***, since Herod *was troubled and all Jerusalem with him* (Matt. 2:3). And his fear was so great that his body trembled: ***Trembling took hold of them***, and ***there were pains as of a woman in labor*** because of the murder of the infants killed by Herod. And ***with a vehement wind***, since he gave the order in his fury and killed all boys two years old or younger. And in his wrath, he caused all the ships of Tarshish to be burnt—that is, the Cilician Tarshish—which he

59. Thomas's edition of Isaiah 26:18 appears to be missing a negation that produces a meaning quite opposite to his interpretation here. Whereas Thomas's edition has the "woman with child" bringing forth the "wind of salvation," modern editions say, "We have conceived . . . and have brought forth wind: we have not wrought salvation on the earth" (DRB).

60. Despite references in various places in the Old Testament and other ancient Near Eastern texts, the exact location of Tarshish has remained a mystery since antiquity. Thomas here floats two different interpretations. In the first, Tarshish references a metropolis and, by extension, its surrounding region (Cilicia) in the northeastern Turkish Mediterranean coast. In the second, it refers to the Phoenicians, who founded Carthage and so dominated the Mediterranean from about 1,200 to 800 BC that the sea itself became identified with them, as Thomas indicates here.

61. Cf. Peter Lombard, *Magna glossatura*.

believed the Magi would have taken back to their homeland, returning by another way. And so he says, ***With a vehement wind.***

477 ***As we have heard***: Here, he presents the praise and testimony of the witnesses. And first, they praise his truth, which they have heard. ***As we have heard*** through the preaching of the apostles, ***so have we seen***—that is, 'we have perceived it to be true.' They said this when they converted to Christ. Or it can be understood as indicating the conversion of Jews: 'We heard through the prophets, and behold, now we see.'

But sometimes it happens that someone hears something great but does not believe it to be so until he has experienced it. And Jacob spoke of this: *The place is holy* (Ezek. 42:13; Gen. 28:17). *I [the Queen of Sheba] did not believe the reports until I came, and my own eyes had seen it* (1 Kings 10:7). She saw more incredible things there than those that she had heard about. And so some see more than they hear before coming to faith.

And where do we see? ***In the city of the Lord of hosts***—that is, of the heavenly hosts. He shows that he can bring you there. And lest you believe that, because he is high, you cannot go to him, he says, ***in the city of our God***—as if to say, 'Such is the God of hosts, who is also our God.' And he ***founded it***—namely, this city—not for a time, but for eternity: *As everlasting foundations upon a solid rock* (Sir. 26:24 DRB).

478 ***We have received thy mercy***: Above, the Psalmist described the city's greatness; now here, he gives thanks. And he does two things: *first*, he performs an act of thanksgiving; *second*, people are invited to consider this city's greatness, at ***Surround.***

As was said elsewhere: ***All the ways of the Lord are mercy and truth*** (Ps. 24:10). So the act of thanksgiving pertains, *first*, to the effects of divine mercy and, *second*, to the effects of justice: ***thy right hand is full of justice.***

About the *first*, he does two things: *first*, he asserts the perfection of divine mercy; *second*, the effects of its perfection, at ***According to thy name.***

By a surface reading of the literal sense, this [description of divine mercy] is not from the perspective of the Jews but of those who marvel and say, ***As we have heard, so have we seen.***

We have received thy mercy, O God: This can also be read as said from the perspective of the Jews. But he says, ***We have received thy mercy.*** The mercy of God can be taken in three ways:

First, as the effect of grace, which is conferred in the sacraments of Christ: *He saved us . . . in virtue of his own mercy, by the washing of regeneration* (Titus 3:5). In the Church, all received mercy together, but the good receive mercy when they receive the sacraments—that is, they receive the grace and effect of the sacrament; but the evil receive only the sacrament. Therefore, the good say,

We have received thy mercy—that is, your grace—***in the midst of thy temple.*** Sinners are at the temple's periphery, but the virtuous and just are at its center.

Second, the mercy of God is Christ himself, who was given to us from God's mercy: ***It is time to have mercy . . . for the time is come*** (Ps. 101:14). And, taken this way, the passage can be explained in terms of a twofold temple and a twofold reception.

One way is corporeal, and in this reading, these are the words of Simeon the Just: 'O God, we have received your mercy—that is, Christ—into our arms ***in the midst of thy temple***—that is, the material one.'[62]

It can also be read as concerning the reception of faith, and thus the sense is, 'O God, we have received Christ, mercifully given through faith.' *Receive with meekness the implanted word* (James 1:21). ***In the midst of thy temple***—that is, in consent to the Church—since those who do not accept the common teaching of the Church do not receive this mercy. *In the midst of the Church, she shall open his mouth* (Sir. 15:5 DRB).

According to thy name, O God: The effect of this receiving is given here—as if to say, 'By this fact that we have received your name, your praise has been spread in all the earth.' And this spread has occurred ***according to thy name, O God***, which is good in its essence.

And whoever knows God according to this measure praises him as he knows him, and so he says, ***according to thy name, O God***—that is, 'according to the knowledge I have of you, ***so also is thy praise***.' And since he is known everywhere, he says, ***unto the ends of the earth***: *From the rising of the sun to its setting, my name is great among the nations* (Mal. 1:11).

Or ***unto the ends of the earth*** can mean 'in the whole Church,' which is spread everywhere. Or it can mean, 'There is no true praise of you except in the saints who praise you truly because they truly know you.' *I know him* (John 7:29).

Thy right hand is full of justice: Here, he commends justice. *First*, he presents a commendation of justice; *second*, its effect.

Therefore, I say, ***We have received thy mercy*** but not without justice. On the contrary, ***thy right hand is full of justice.*** God's 'hand' signifies his operative power.[63] And God has two hands: his right, whereby he rewards the good, and his left, whereby he punishes the wicked: *He will place the sheep at his right hand* (Matt. 25:33). Justice is in both hands, but full justice is not in the left hand since he punishes less than is deserved. Yet complete justice is in his right hand since he rewards abundantly: *Good measure, pressed down, shaken together,*

62. For the story of Simeon, see Luke 2:25–35.

63. Cf. Thomas Aquinas, *Summa theologiae* 1.3.1 ad 3.

running over (Luke 6:38). *I consider that the sufferings of this present time are not worth comparing with the glory that is to be revealed to us* (Rom. 8:18). ***Thy right hand***—that is, future glory—***is full of justice*** since none but the just are there: *Your people shall all be righteous* (Isa. 60:21).

Let Mount Zion rejoice: Here, he describes the effect of the justice his left hand has brought about, and this effect is lamentation. But joy is the effect of the justice wrought by his right hand: ***The justices of the Lord are right, rejoicing hearts*** (Ps. 18:9).

Above, he said that mercy's effect reaches the ends of the earth. Here, however, he attributes the effect of justice to Mount Zion and the children of Judah. The Apostle says this too: *I tell you that Christ became a servant to the circumcised to show God's truthfulness* (Rom. 15:8). Therefore, it was promised to the daughter of Zion: *Shout aloud, O daughter of Jerusalem!* (Zech. 9:9).

Let Mount Zion rejoice because it is a matter of justice that the promise to her will be kept. But since the promise was not made to the gentiles, the fact that they received anything was an instance of mercy, not of justice. Moreover, it can be said that Mount Zion means the whole of Jerusalem. ***And let the daughters of Judah***—that is, of the confession—***be glad.*** In other words, 'let the whole Jewish people ***be glad.***' Let them be glad, moreover, ***because of thy judgments, O Lord***, since they are righteous.

479 ***Surround Zion***: Here, he introduces a more thorough consideration to make clear that kings had already seen wonders at times, but David nevertheless invites all to take further consideration. *First,* he makes this invitation. *Second,* he adds the reason for the invitation.

Therefore, he says, ***Surround Zion***—that is, the Church militant or triumphant—with the eye of contemplation: *I will rise now and go about* (Song of Sol. 3:2). With a hostile eye, some surround the Church to assail her, but we surround her in love, and so he says, ***encompass her***—namely, in love: ***I have loved, O Lord, the beauty of thy house*** (Ps. 25:8). Jerome has, ***Go around***—as though to say, 'Go outside, and go around through the neighborhoods.'

Tell in her towers: Here, he leads us to consider the spiritual sense. In a city, there are three magnificent things: towers, walls, and wide streets.

Regarding the *first*, he says, ***tell in her towers.*** Jerome has, ***marvel at her towers.*** Towers are seen from far away. Therefore, the towers of the Church are the prelates and the apostles, as if to say, 'Wonder at the apostles and prelates.' Or ***tell in her towers***—that is, the doctors—according to the doctrine of the apostles and doctors.

Regarding the *second,* he says, ***Set your hearts on her strength.*** Jerome has, ***Put your heart in her hands.*** And this is the power of the Holy Spirit, who protects this city: *Stay in the city, until you are clothed with power* (Luke 24:49). This power is love. *Love is strong as death* (Song of Sol. 8:6).

Regarding the *third*, he says, ***distribute her houses.*** Jerome has, ***separate her houses, distinguish her palaces.*** 'Distinguish them,' in other words, through right judgment. Some want to condemn the whole Church because of some evil persons. Therefore, he says, ***distribute***—that is, 'You should not condemn the good because of the evil': *Far be it from you to do such a thing, to slay the righteous with the wicked* (Gen. 18:25).

Or ***distribute her houses***—that is, by managing the various churches with different ministries, so there may be no confusion in the Church, as Paul was the apostle to the gentiles, and Peter was a minister of the circumcision: the apostle to the Jews. Another text has, ***her grades***—that is, her diverse orders: some are subdeacons, some deacons, and some priests. *His gifts were that some should be apostles, some prophets, some evangelists, some pastors and teachers* (Eph. 4:11).

The aim of this discussion is the praise of God. *First*, he lays out to whom God's praise should be announced; *second*, why it should be announced.

Therefore, he says, ***that ye may relate it***—namely, what you heard. *What I have heard from the Lord of hosts, the God of Israel, I announce to you* (Isa. 21:10), since what someone receives he should communicate to another: ***in another generation***—namely, to sinners. Or ***another generation*** may be taken for a future generation. And what should you relate? Two things, because all preaching should be ordered to two things: showing the magnificence of God, as when someone preaches the faith, or announcing the blessings of God so that love may be kindled in their hearts.

Regarding the *first*, he says, ***For this is God, our God.*** Afterward, *she* [knowledge] *appeared upon earth* (Bar. 3:37). *Jesus Christ is the same yesterday and today and for ever* (Heb. 13:8).

Regarding the *second*, he says, ***He shall rule us for evermore.*** *Behold, I am with you always* (Matt. 28:20). ***The Lord ruleth me; and I shall want nothing*** (Ps. 22:1).

Chapter 5

LAST THINGS

Job 14:5–6

Death and Resurrection

On Job 14.2 (238–239)

14:5 ***The days of man are short, and the number of his months is with thee: thou hast appointed his bounds which cannot be passed.***

14:6 ***Depart a little from him, that he may rest, until his wished for day come, as that of the hireling.***

238 ***The days of man are short***: Job was amazed at God's concern for human beings, even when their condition is so fragile and unfortunate in the state of the present life.[1] Nevertheless, this amazement ceases if one considers that after this life, there is another reserved for human beings in which they remain eternally. Thus, he attempts to demonstrate this thesis from this point on. As though presupposing what he intends to show, he asserts the brevity of the present life as a premise when he says, ***The days of man are short.***

Again, [another premise is] that this same measure of human life is determined by God, when he says, ***the number of his months is with thee***, as we say the number of those things is 'with' us when we have established it.

Furthermore, [he asserts] the immutability of the divine plan [as a premise] when he says, ***Thou hast appointed his bounds which cannot be passed.*** God is not deceived in his decisions, and so it is impossible to live either more or less than the divine plan has established, although, as considered in itself, it may be a contingent matter whether a given person is to die now or at an earlier time. There are boundaries established for human life from certain corporeal causes, for example, from temperament or something of the sort. A human life cannot extend beyond this, although it can be shortened because of some incidental cause. However, a human life cannot deviate, either by surpassing or falling short, from the limits preestablished for it by divine providence, within which all events occur.

1. See Thomas Aquinas, *On Job* 14.1 (not included in this collection).

239 He also asserts as a premise the expectation of another life when he says, ***Depart a little from him, that he may rest, until his wished for day come, as that of the hireling.*** Here, it is necessary to observe that as the sun causes the day, so God is the author of life. When the sun leaves, the day is finished, and night comes. God's withdrawal represents God's termination of the present life of human beings. The present life, moreover, is filled with many disturbances; indeed, he had spoken about this when he described the human being as ***filled with many miseries*** (Job 14:1). Since rest seems to be the end of toil, he calls death rest. So he says, ***Depart a little from him, that he may rest***—that is, take away the strength by which you give a person life so that he may die.

Nevertheless, a person's death is not permanent, for he will be restored to eternal life. Thus, the state of human death, until whatever time resurrection is deferred, is brief in comparison to the state of future immortality, and so he clearly says, ***a little.*** From other beings that perish permanently, God withdraws not for a little while but forever. Nevertheless, from human beings, who perish in such a way that they rise again, he departs for only a short time. He said above that human life on earth is like the day of the hireling (Job 7:1), waiting for his payday. But the time of the repayment is not in this life, as was the opinion of Job's friends, but in that life to which a person is restored by rising. He thus says, ***that he may rest***—meaning, 'that he may die, though not permanently but only' ***until his wished for day come*** just like the hireling's payday, when he receives his pay. Here, for the first time, Job discloses his intention: He does not deny that the present adversities are punishments, as though God did not reward or punish human actions, but [he argues] that the time of retribution is in the other life.

Job 14:7–12

Death and the End of the World Order

On Job 14.3 (240–241)

14:7 ***A tree hath hope: if it be cut, it groweth green again, and the boughs thereof sprout.***

14:8 ***If its root be old in the earth, and its stock be dead in the dust:***

14:9 ***At the scent of water, it shall spring and bring forth leaves as when it was first planted.***

14:10 ***But man, when he shall be dead and stripped and consumed, I pray you, where is he?***

14:11 ***As if the waters should depart out of the sea, and an emptied river should be dried up:***

14:12 ***So a man, when he is fallen asleep, shall not rise again; till the heavens be broken, he shall not awake, nor rise up out of his sleep.***

240 ***A tree hath hope: if it be cut, it groweth green again***: After asserting his view, Job here proceeds to make it clear.[2] *First*, he shows that human beings, given what they experience in this life, are in a worse situation than even certain of the lowest creatures that are restored after being destroyed. This phenomenon is especially observable in trees. The life of a tree, like that of a human, fails in two ways: by violence or naturally. About the loss of a tree through violence, he says, ***a tree hath hope: if it be cut***. About its natural aptitude to renew its existence again, he says, ***it groweth green again*** if it is replanted, ***and boughs thereof sprout***. With this, he demonstrates that it recovers the perfect life it formerly had.

He describes the natural death of a tree where he adds, ***If its roots be old in the earth***, at which point, it cannot take in food due to a loss of its natural vigor. Consequently, he says, ***its stock be dead in the dust***—that is, it turned back into dust by rot in some part of it. ***At the scent of water, it shall spring***—when the

2. See Thomas Aquinas, *On Job* 14.2.239 (included above at page 156).

rain comes because the wood possesses a seminal potency—***and bring forth leaves***—that, is foliage—***as when it was first planted.***

This phenomenon, however, is not found in human beings throughout the course of the present life. Thus, he then says, ***But man, when he shall be dead and stripped and consumed, I pray you, where is he?*** There are three things that a human being loses in sequence. *First,* the soul is separated from the body, and he expresses this, saying, ***when he shall be dead.*** *Second*, he loses the clothing and adornments of the body that sometimes remain with a person after his death. Later, he is stripped even of these, so he says, ***and stripped.*** *Finally,* even the union of the elements in his body is dissolved, and he expresses this, saying, ***consumed.*** After all these things have happened, no sensible appearance of the person remains. Hence, those who believe only in the sensible and corporeal appearances of the human person believe he is entirely reduced to nothing. To express the doubt of these people, Job then says, ***I pray you, where is he?***

241 Note here that what does not perish entirely can be restored, as he has already said about wood that is cut down or old (Job 14:7–9). Nevertheless, it seems impossible to restore something when nothing of it remains, as when the water of a sea or river completely dries up. Likewise, the human being appears to be so consumed by death that nothing remains of him, as the text has already explained. Hence, according to this argument, it seems impossible that he could be restored to life again, and this is what he expresses when he adds, ***As if the waters should depart out of the sea, and an emptied river should be dried up: So a man, when he is fallen asleep*** in death, ***shall not rise again*** from the dead. Just as it seems impossible for incorruptible things to be corrupted, so it seems impossible for what is totally corrupted to be restored. Heaven is incorruptible, and so he says, ***till the heavens be broken, he shall not awake***—that is, come to life again—***nor rise up out of his sleep*** to do the works of the living once again. He is saying, in effect, that it is as impossible for heaven to pass away in corruption as it is for a human being to rise from the dead.

This is expressed, as I have already observed, in the supposition that nothing remains of a person after death, in view of which he asked, ***I pray you, where is he?*** One can also relate this question to the opinion of those who posited that the whole corporeal universe should be corrupted and restored again. They used to assert that, in this restoration, the very same people will return, the implication being that, for the duration of this world, human beings do not rise from the dead.

The catholic faith, however, does not posit that the substance of the world will perish but only the state of this world as it now exists. Paul expresses this in Corinthians: *The form of this world is passing away* (1 Cor. 7:31). Therefore, this change in the figure of the world can be understood here to refer to the breaking open of heaven. For we await the common resurrection of the dead at the last day, as John says: *I know that he will rise again in the resurrection at the last day* (John 11:24).

Job 14:13–17

Hope for the Resurrection

On Job 14.4 (242–245)

14:13 ***Who will grant me this, that thou mayst protect me in hell and hide me till thy wrath pass and appoint me a time when thou wilt remember me?***

14:14 ***Shall man that is dead, thinkest thou, live again? All the days in which I am now in warfare, I expect until my change come.***

14:15 ***Thou shalt call me, and I will answer thee: to the work of thy hands thou shalt reach out thy right hand.***

14:16 ***Thou hast indeed numbered my steps but spare my sins.***

14:17 ***Thou hast sealed my offenses as it were in a bag but hast cured my iniquity.***

242 ***Who will grant me this, that thou mayst protect me in hell and hide me?*** Above, Job showed what one could conclude about the resurrection of the dead based on what is evident to the senses.[3] Here, he asserts his view about the resurrection. Every creature naturally wants to exist, and thus, it would be horrible and sad if human beings should so disappear after death that they can never be brought back to life again. Therefore, Job shows his wish for a future resurrection, saying, ***Who will grant***, even after death, ***that thou mayst protect me in hell***, 'for you will preserve me with the special care with which you protect human beings,' ***till thy wrath pass*** at the hour of death. The death of a person is caused by the removal of the divine action that conserves life, and so, before, he said, ***Depart a little from him*** (Job 14:6). It seems that God is angry with someone when he takes his gift of life away, especially because we believe that death arose from the sin of the first human. He explains how he wishes to be protected even in Sheol when he says, ***appoint me a time when thou wilt remember me***, for it seems that God has forgotten someone when he takes the gift of life away from him. Then he remembers him when he leads him back to life. Therefore, appointing the time when he remembers the dead

3. See Thomas Aquinas, *On Job* 14.3 (included above at page 157).

person is equivalent to determining the time of his resurrection. It is fittingly termed 'protection' (Job 14:13). For when an artist does not want to repair his damaged work with the same material, like a house or something of the sort, he seems to have no care for the material of the house, which is falling into ruin. But when he intends to repair the building from this material, he guards it diligently so it does not perish. He calls this care 'protection.'

243 After he expresses his desire to rise again, he asks if his desire could ever be realized because it is possible for someone to desire what is impossible. He then says, ***Shall man that is dead, thinkest thou, live again?*** He shows what he means by this, saying, ***all the days in which I am now in warfare, I expect until my change come.*** We should note here that he had compared the life of a person on earth to that of a soldier (Job 7:1) and to the days of a hireling in another place (Job 7:2) because both soldiers and hirelings await something after their present state at the end of their service.[4] Therefore, similar to how he described the state of the resurrection above in terms of a hireling's payday, here, he shows the same concept using the image of the soldier. Note that he does not await the desired end at any time in the present life because he likens all the days of this life to the military life, saying, ***all the days in which I am now in warfare.*** One should also note that he does not await another life like this one because then that one, too, would be like warfare. He awaits a life in which he will not struggle like a soldier but will triumph and reign. Thus, he says, ***I expect until my change come.*** He means here, 'For my whole life, I have been struggling like a soldier, changeable and subject to labors and anguish, but I wait to be transformed in the state of the other life, which is free of them.' The Apostle Paul expresses the same theme of transformation in Corinthians when he says, *We shall not all sleep, but we shall all be changed* (1 Cor. 15:51).

244 Lest anyone should believe that a person might be transformed into the state of another life by any natural power, he excludes this possibility by saying, ***Thou shalt call me, and I will answer thee,*** because the future transformation proceeds from the power of your voice or your command, as John says: *The dead will hear the voice of the Son of God, and those who hear it will live* (John 5:28). Calling is characteristic of commanding, but answering is the obedience by which the creature obeys his Creator. Since, at God's command, not only will the dead rise to life but they will also be transformed to some other state by divine power. Thus, he says, ***to the work of thy hands thou shalt reach out thy right hand,*** 'for the risen human will not be the work of nature but of your power, and you will offer the assistance of your right hand to this work when he is elevated to the glory of the new state by the help of your grace.' Or his

4. See Thomas Aquinas, *On Job* 7.1–2 (included above at page 59).

statement ***Thou shalt call me, and I will answer thee*** can be referred to the renewal of the body. When he adds, ***to the work of thy hands thou shalt reach out thy right hand***, this can be related to the soul, which naturally desires to be united with the body. God presents his right hand as a helper when a human being attains by divine power what he cannot attain by his own power.

245 Now that he has asserted his opinion about the resurrection, he returns to the subject of his wonder at how much careful attention God gives to human deeds. He expressed this when he said, ***Thou . . . hast observed all my paths and hast considered the steps of my feet*** (Job 13:27). Here, therefore, he says, ***Thou hast indeed numbered my steps***, 'for now it is no wonder you so diligently examine human deeds since you reserve him for another life.'

Note, however, that God, in his providence, tries human deeds in two ways. *First*, in the fact that he examines and discusses them. He clarifies this when he says, ***Thou hast indeed numbered my steps.*** One numbers things one cares about. Someone might object that it is very severe for God to examine the deeds of a frail human being with such great care. Job consequently emphasizes the tendency of God to pardon us when he says, ***spare my sins.*** He means, 'Although you number these things, still I am filled with hope that you will spare me.'

Second, God keeps the good and wicked deeds of human beings in his memory to repay them with good or evil, and so he continues, ***Thou hast sealed up my offenses as it were in a bag***, for what one seals in a bag is carefully kept. To preclude this sealing of God excluding divine mercy, he then says, ***hast cured my iniquity***, since you lay up punishments for sins, but you nevertheless cure my faults by penance.

Job 14:18–22

The Immortality of the Soul

On Job 14.5 (246–248)

14:18 ***A mountain falling cometh to nought, and a rock is removed out of its place.***

14:19 ***Waters wear away the stones, and with inundation, the ground by little and little is washed away: so in like manner thou shalt destroy man.***

14:20 ***Hast thou strengthened him for a little while that he may pass away forever? Shalt thou change his face and send him away?***[5]

14:21 ***Whether his children come to honor or dishonor, he shall not understand.***

14:22 ***But yet his flesh, while he shall live, shall have pain, and his soul shall mourn over him.***

246 ***A mountain falling cometh to nought, and a rock is removed out of its place***: After Job has posited his idea about the future resurrection, he here strengthens it with probable arguments. The first argument is taken from a comparison of human beings to lower creatures, which are totally consumed without hope of renewal. For all things that are generated are subject to corruption, and so the mountains will be dissolved, although they seem very solid. He speaks to this theme, saying, ***A mountain falling cometh to nought.*** Rocks also are dashed to pieces, either by violence or nature, even though they seem very powerful. He next speaks to this, ***and a rock is removed out of its place.*** Even stones are worn away by water, although they seem very hard. He expresses this, saying, ***Waters wear away stones.*** The earth, too, is gradually changed in its disposition, although it seems most stable, and so he says, ***and with inundation the ground by little and little is washed away.*** However, it would not be fitting to apply the same reasoning to human corruption as applies to the corruption of these other things. So, he concludes, as though leading the argument to an

5. This verse, interrogative in Thomas's edition of the Psalter, is in the indicative mood in the Douay-Rheims translation: "Thou hast strengthened him for a little while, that he may pass away forever: thou shalt change his face, and shalt send him away."

unfitting conclusion: ***so in like manner thou shalt destroy man***. He seems to say here, 'It is not fitting that human beings experience corruption like other corporeal creatures. For all the other creatures mentioned are completely corrupted, and therefore, they are not renewed in the same number. However, although a human being is corrupted in body, he still remains incorrupt in soul, which transcends the whole genus of corporeal things, and so the hope of renewal remains.'

247 He then deduces the same things using reasons drawn from the properties of human beings. The human person surpasses all lower creatures in two ways. One of these is his operative power, for he is truly the master of his actions by free will, which capacity belongs to no other corporeal creature. On this account, the human being is more powerful than any other corporeal creature, and he uses these others for his own benefit.

Another way in which the human person excels is intellectual knowledge. Although this power is in the mind, some indication of it is nevertheless apparent in the body and especially in the human face, which is very different from that of other animals. It is apparent on the basis of these two powers that humans are not subject to corruption as other creatures are that therefore do not exist forever.

Thus, regarding the *first* of these powers [free will], he says, ***Hast thou strengthened him for a little while, that he may pass away forever?***—as if to say, 'It would not be fitting for you to grant such strength to the human being for a short time in this way if he were not to exist perpetually thereafter.' It would seem foolish for someone to make a very strong tool to be used only a short time and then thrown away for good. The power of every corporeal creature is determined by finite effects, while the power of free will extends to infinite actions. Moreover, this itself bears witness to the power of the soul to persist infinitely.

As to the *second* power [intellectual knowledge], he says, ***Shalt thou change his face and send him away?***—as if to say, 'It is not fitting that you should change their face, distinguishing it from the other animals, and yet cast them from the state of eternal life, like other animals, never to return.' Intellectual knowledge is commonly perceived from the facial expression because it is proper to the rational creature. Intellectual knowledge can only fittingly belong to an incorruptible substance, as the philosophers have proved.

248 But someone could object that, although a human being does not return after death to life, he does not still pass away perpetually because he still lives on in his sons. The words of Baldath seem to have spoken to this theme when he said, ***For this is the joy of his way, that others may spring again out of the earth*** (Job 8:19). But Job rejects this answer, saying, ***Whether his children come to***

honor or dishonor, he shall not understand. He means here that a human being seizes eternal good by the intellect, and so he naturally desires it. However, the good consisting in a succession of sons cannot satisfy the intellectual appetite if a person is so totally consumed by death that he no longer exists. A person does not comprehend the good in the succession of his sons either while he lives or after he dies if he completely disappears after death. The human intellectual appetite, thus, does not tend to the eternity of this good but to the good or evil that it has in itself, and so he adds, ***But yet his flesh, while he shall live, shall have pain, and his soul shall mourn over him.*** Here, he distinguishes two sorrows. One is of the flesh in the apprehension of sense. The other is of the soul from the apprehension of the intellect or imagination, which is properly called sadness, and here is termed mourning.

Job 19:23–29

Prophecy of the Resurrection

On Job 19.2 (293–297)

19:23 ***Who will grant me that my words may be written? Who will grant me that they may be marked down in a book?***

19:24 ***With an iron pen and in a plate of lead, or else be graven with an instrument in flint stone.***

19:25 ***For I know that my Redeemer liveth, and in the last day, I shall rise out of the earth.***

19:26 ***And I shall be clothed again with my skin, and in my flesh, I will see my God.***

19:27 ***Whom I myself shall see, and my eyes shall behold, and not another: this my hope is laid up in my bosom.***

19:28 ***Why then do you say now: "Let us persecute him," and "let us find occasion of word against him"?***

19:29 ***Flee then from the face of the sword, for the sword is the revenger of iniquities: and know ye that there is judgment.***

293 ***Who will grant me that my words may be written?*** Job had said above that his hope had been taken away, ***as from a tree that is plucked up*** (Job 19:10). He certainly said this referring to the hope of recovering temporal prosperity, a hope to which the friends urged him in many ways. But he showed many times above (Job 19:11–20) that he ought not to have this hope by deducing various unfitting conclusions. Now, he clearly declares his intention to show that he had not said these things in despair of God but because he bore a higher hope about him, which was not related to goods present here but to future goods. Because he was about to speak about great, wondrous, and certain things, he first shows his desire that the thought he is about to express would endure in the faith of his descendants. We transmit our words and their meaning to our descendants by the service of writing. Thus, he says, ***Who will grant me that my words may be written?*** so that what I am about to say about the hope

that I have fixed in God may not be forgotten. What is written in ink usually fades with the long passage of time, and so, when we want some writing to be preserved for a long time, we not only record it in writing, but we record it on skin, on metal, or in stone. Since what he hoped for was not in the immediate future but must be reserved for fulfillment at the end of time, he then says, ***Who will grant me that they may be marked down in a book? With an iron pen*** like an impression made on skin, ***and*** if this is not enough, by a stronger impression made ***in a plate of lead, or***—if this seems not enough—***graven*** with an iron pen ***in flint stone?***

294 He shows what discourses he would like to preserve with such great diligence, saying, ***For I know that my Redeemer liveth.*** He clearly attributed this to the manner of a cause. Things that we are not sure of, we are not anxious to commit to memory, and so he clearly says, ***For I know***—namely, by the certitude of faith. This hope is about the glory of the future resurrection, concerning which he first assigns the cause when he says, ***my Redeemer liveth.*** Here, we must consider that a human being, who has been established as immortal by God, incurred death through sin, according to Romans, since *sin came into the world through one man and death through sin* (Rom. 5:12). Job foresaw through the spirit of faith that the human race must be redeemed from this sin through Christ. Christ redeemed us from sin by death, dying in our place, but he did not so die that he was consumed by death, for although he died according to his humanity, yet he could not die according to his divinity.

From the life of the divinity, the humanity has also been restored by rising up to life again, according to what is said in Corinthians: *He was crucified in weakness but lives by the power of God* (2 Cor. 13:4). The life of the risen Christ is diffused to all in the general resurrection, and so in the same place the Apostle Paul puts, *We are weak in him, but in dealing with you, we shall live with him by the power of God* (2 Cor. 13:4), and so the Lord says according to John, *The dead will hear the voice of the Son of God, and those who hear will live. For as the Father has life in himself, so he has granted the Son also to have life in himself* (John 5:25–26). Thus, the primordial cause of human resurrection is the life of the Son of God, which did not take its beginning from Mary, as the Ebionites said, but always was, according to Hebrews: *Jesus Christ is the same yesterday and today and forever* (Heb. 13:8).[6] Therefore, he clearly does not say, 'my redeemer will live' but, ***liveth.*** From this cause, he foretells the future resurrection, and he determines its time when he then puts, ***in the last***

6. Ebionites are the members of a second-century Jewish-Christian sect that denied the divinity of Jesus Christ. In their view, Christ was the naturally conceived son of Joseph and Mary who was later chosen or 'adopted' by God, on account of his special righteousness, to be a messianic prophet like Moses.

day, I shall rise out of the earth. Here, one must reflect that some posited that the motion of the heavens and this state of the world would endure forever, and they maintained that after the certain revolutions of years, when the stars return to their same places, the dead would be restored to life. Since a day is caused by a motion of the heavens, if this motion of the heavens will endure forever, there will be no very last day. Thus, to eliminate this anticipated error, he then clearly says, ***in the last day***, and this is consonant with the statement of the Lord, who says in John, *I will raise him up at the last day* (John 6:40).

295 There were others who said that human beings would rise by resuming not an earthly body but some kind of heavenly body. To exclude this, he then says, ***And I shall be clothed again with my skin.*** He expressly says this because he had said above (Job 19:20) that only the skin had remained around his bones. In this way of speaking, he assigns the explanation of the resurrection—namely, that the soul does not always remain divested of its very own skin. Again, there were some who said that the soul will resume the same body it had put aside, but according to the same condition, so that it would need food and drink and would exercise the other fleshly operations of this life. But he excludes this, saying then, ***and in my flesh, I will see my God.*** For it is clear that human flesh is corruptible according to the state of the present life.

As Wisdom says, *a perishable body weighs down the soul* (Wis. 9:15), and so, no one can see God while living in this mortal flesh; but the flesh that the soul resumes in the resurrection will certainly be the same in substance, but will be preserved incorruptible by a divine gift, according to what is said by Paul: *This perishable nature must put on the imperishable* (1 Cor. 15:53). Therefore, the former flesh will be of this latter condition because it in no way will impede the soul from being able to see God, but rather will be completely subject to the soul. Porphyry, not knowing this, said, *The soul must completely flee the body to become happy*, as though the soul and not the whole human being will see God.[7] To exclude this, Job declares, ***whom I myself will see***, as though he should say, 'Not only will my soul see God but ***I myself***, who subsist in body and soul.' To indicate that the body will be a participant in that vision in its own proper way, he adds, ***and my eyes shall behold***, not because the eyes of the body will see the divine essence, but because the bodily eyes will see God made human. They will also see the glory of God shining resplendent in created things, as Augustine says at the end of *The City of God*.[8] So that we would believe that a human being must be restored the same in number and not only the same in species in order to see God, he says, ***and not another***—in number, that is.

7. Augustine ascribes this view to Porphyry in *City of God* 22.26. Porphyry himself makes very similar assertions in *Auxiliaries to the Perception of Intelligible Natures* 1.32; 2.34; and 3.41.

8. Augustine, *City of God* 22.29.

This is so that one might not believe that he expected to return to the kind of life that Aristotle describes in *De generatione*, saying that each and every corruptible substance that has been moved will be restored in species, but not in the same number.[9]

296 After these things as premises about the cause, the time, the manner of the resurrection, and the glory and identity of those who will rise, he then adds, ***this my hope is laid up in my bosom***, as if he should say, 'For my hope is not in earthly things, which you promise vainly, but in the future glory of the resurrection.' He says clearly, ***is laid up in my bosom***, to show that he not only held this hope in words, but hidden in his heart; not doubtfully, but most firmly; not like something of little consequence, but as something most precious. For what is hidden in the heart is possessed in a secret way, is firmly held, and is considered dear.

297 Thus, after he has shown the high character of the hope that he had in God, he rejects their false accusations, which they sought to make against him as if he had rejected the hope and fear of God by not putting his hope in temporal things. So, he then says, ***Why then do you say now: "Let us persecute him"***—namely, as one who despairs of God or does not fear God—***and "let us find occasion of word against him"***—'by condemning my speech as though I would have denied the providence of God?' 'I do not deny but assert this providence, saying that rewards and punishments are prepared by God for a person also after this life.' So, he then says, ***Flee then from the face of the sword***, of divine revenge, reserved in the future life for you, even if you flourish in temporal prosperity; ***for the sword is the revenger of iniquities***—that is, in the vengeance that he properly takes after death. ***And know ye that there is judgment***, not only in this life but also after this life, in the resurrection of the good and the wicked.

9. Aristotle, *De generatione et corruptione* 2.11 (338b).

BIBLIOGRAPHIES

RECOMMENDED ENGLISH TRANSLATIONS OF ANCIENT WORKS CITED IN THIS COLLECTION

Anselm. *Anselm: Monologion and Proslogion.* Translated with Introduction and Notes by Thomas Williams. Indianapolis, IN: Hackett, 1996.

Aristotle. *Aristotle's De Generatione et Corruptione.* Translated with notes by C.J.F. Williams. Oxford: Clarendon, 1982.

———. *Metaphysics.* Translated by Richard Hope. Ann Arbor, MI: Ann Arbor, 2009.

———. *The Nicomachean Ethics.* Translated by Robert C. Bartlett and Susan D. Collins. Chicago: University of Chicago Press, 2011.

———. *Politics.* 2nd ed. Translated by Carnes Lord. Chicago: Chicago University Press, 2013.

Augustine. *Answer to Maximinus the Arian.* In The Works of Saint Augustine, vol. 18/1, *Arianism and Other Heresies,* translated by Roland J. Teske, 246–336. Hyde Park, NY: New City, 1995.

———. *The City of God.* Edited by Boniface Ramsey. Translated by William Babcock. The Works of Saint Augustine 6–7. Hyde Park, NY: New City, 2012–13.

———. *Eighty-Three Different Questions.* Translated by David L. Mosher. The Fathers of the Church 70. Washington, DC: The Catholic University of America Press, 1982.

———. *Expositions on the Psalms.* Edited by John E. Rotelle. Translated by Maria Boulding. The Works of Saint Augustine 15–20. Hyde Park, NY: New City, 2000–2004.

———. *Letter 140 to Honoratus: A Book on the Grace of the New Testament.* In The Works of Saint Augustine, vol. 2/2, *Letters 100–155.* Edited by Boniface Ramsey, translated by Roland J. Teske, 242–89. Hyde Park, NY: New City, 2003.

———. *Letter 147 to Paulina: A Book on Seeing God.* In The Works of Saint Augustine, vol. 2/2, *Letters 100–155.* Edited by Boniface Ramsey, translated by Roland J. Teske, 317–49. Hyde Park, NY: New City, 2003.

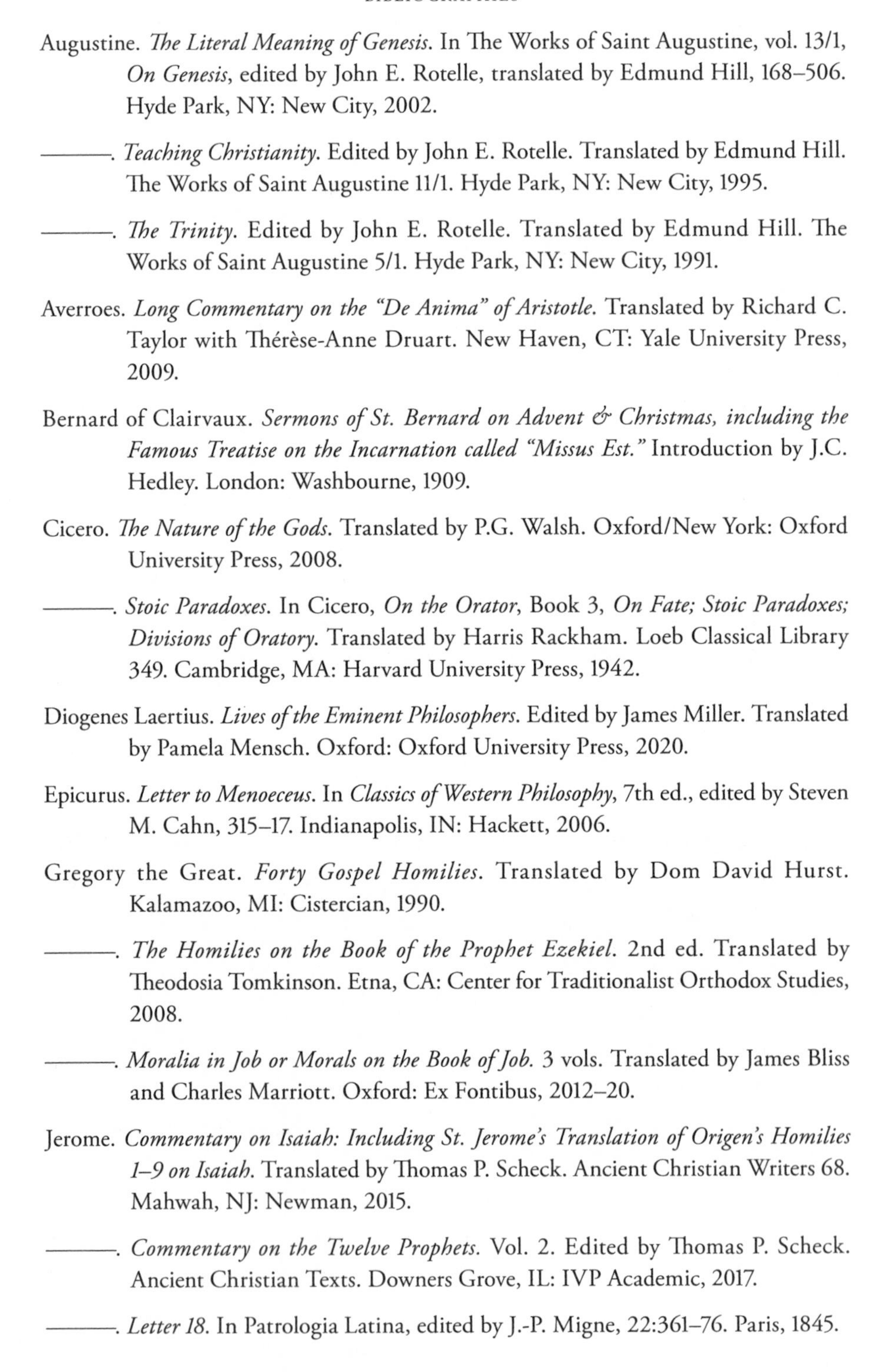

Augustine. *The Literal Meaning of Genesis*. In The Works of Saint Augustine, vol. 13/1, *On Genesis*, edited by John E. Rotelle, translated by Edmund Hill, 168–506. Hyde Park, NY: New City, 2002.

———. *Teaching Christianity*. Edited by John E. Rotelle. Translated by Edmund Hill. The Works of Saint Augustine 11/1. Hyde Park, NY: New City, 1995.

———. *The Trinity*. Edited by John E. Rotelle. Translated by Edmund Hill. The Works of Saint Augustine 5/1. Hyde Park, NY: New City, 1991.

Averroes. *Long Commentary on the "De Anima" of Aristotle*. Translated by Richard C. Taylor with Thérèse-Anne Druart. New Haven, CT: Yale University Press, 2009.

Bernard of Clairvaux. *Sermons of St. Bernard on Advent & Christmas, including the Famous Treatise on the Incarnation called "Missus Est."* Introduction by J.C. Hedley. London: Washbourne, 1909.

Cicero. *The Nature of the Gods*. Translated by P.G. Walsh. Oxford/New York: Oxford University Press, 2008.

———. *Stoic Paradoxes*. In Cicero, *On the Orator*, Book 3, *On Fate; Stoic Paradoxes; Divisions of Oratory*. Translated by Harris Rackham. Loeb Classical Library 349. Cambridge, MA: Harvard University Press, 1942.

Diogenes Laertius. *Lives of the Eminent Philosophers*. Edited by James Miller. Translated by Pamela Mensch. Oxford: Oxford University Press, 2020.

Epicurus. *Letter to Menoeceus*. In *Classics of Western Philosophy*, 7th ed., edited by Steven M. Cahn, 315–17. Indianapolis, IN: Hackett, 2006.

Gregory the Great. *Forty Gospel Homilies*. Translated by Dom David Hurst. Kalamazoo, MI: Cistercian, 1990.

———. *The Homilies on the Book of the Prophet Ezekiel*. 2nd ed. Translated by Theodosia Tomkinson. Etna, CA: Center for Traditionalist Orthodox Studies, 2008.

———. *Moralia in Job or Morals on the Book of Job*. 3 vols. Translated by James Bliss and Charles Marriott. Oxford: Ex Fontibus, 2012–20.

Jerome. *Commentary on Isaiah: Including St. Jerome's Translation of Origen's Homilies 1–9 on Isaiah*. Translated by Thomas P. Scheck. Ancient Christian Writers 68. Mahwah, NJ: Newman, 2015.

———. *Commentary on the Twelve Prophets*. Vol. 2. Edited by Thomas P. Scheck. Ancient Christian Texts. Downers Grove, IL: IVP Academic, 2017.

———. *Letter 18*. In Patrologia Latina, edited by J.-P. Migne, 22:361–76. Paris, 1845.

Jerome. *Letter 53*. In Patrologia Latina, edited by J.-P. Migne, 22:540–49. Paris, 1845.

———. "Preface of St. Jerome to Isaiah." In Thomas Aquinas, *Commentary on Isaiah* 2, trans. Louis St. Hilaire, Latin/English Edition of the Works of St. Thomas Aquinas 30. Lander, WY: Aquinas Institute, 2021.

John Chrysostom. *Commentary on Saint John the Apostle and Evangelist*. 2 vols. Translated by Sister Thomas Aquinas Goggin. The Fathers of the Church 33, 41. Washington, DC: The Catholic University of America Press, 1957–59.

John of Damascus. *An Exact Exposition of the Orthodox Faith*. In *St. John of Damascus: Writings*, translated by Frederic H. Chase Jr., The Fathers of the Church 37:165–406. Washington, DC: The Catholic University of America Press, 1958.

Origen. *Origen: On First Principles*. 2 vols. Edited and translated by John Behr. Oxford: Oxford University Press, 2017.

Porphyry. *Auxiliaries to the Perception of Intelligible Natures*. In *Select Works of Porphyry: Containing His Four Books on "Abstinence from Animal Food"; His "Treatise on the Homeric Cave of the Nymphs"; and His "Auxiliaries to the Perception of Intelligible Natures,"* translated by Thomas Taylor, 201–38. London: Thomas Rodd, 1823.

Pseudo-Dionysius. *The Celestial Hierarchy*. In *Pseudo-Dionysius: The Complete Works*, translated by Colm Luibheid, 143–91. Mahwah, NJ: Paulist, 1987.

———. *The Divine Names*. In *Pseudo-Dionysius: The Complete Works*, translated by Colm Luibheid, 47–131. Mahwah, NJ: Paulist, 1987.

———. *The Ecclesiastical Hierarchy*. In *Pseudo-Dionysius: The Complete Works*, translated by Colm Luibheid, 193–259. Mahwah, NJ: Paulist, 1987.

———. *Letter 9 to Titus the Hierarch*. In *Pseudo-Dionysius: The Complete Works*, translated by Colm Luibheid, 280–88. Mahwah, NJ: Paulist, 1987.

Quintilian. *The Orator's Education*. 5 vols. Edited and translated by Donald A. Russell. Loeb Classical Library 124–27, 494. Cambridge, MA: Harvard University Press, 2002.

Second Council of Constantinople. *Acts of the Council of Constantinople of 553 with Related Texts on the Three Chapters Controversy*. Vol. 1. Translated by Richard Price. Liverpool, UK: Liverpool University Press, 2009.

Sextus Empiricus. *Against the Musicians*. Translated by Denise Davidson Greaves. Lincoln, NE: University of Nebraska Press, 1986.

Theodore of Mopsuestia. *Commentary on Psalms 1–81*. Translated by Robert C. Hill. Atlanta, GA: Society of Biblical Literature, 2006.

Tyconius. *The Book of Rules*. Translated by William S. Babcock. Society of Biblical Literature 31. Atlanta, GA: Scholars, 1989.

UNTRANSLATED ANCIENT WORKS CITED IN THIS COLLECTION

Alain de Lille. *Elucidatio in Cantica canticorum*. In Patrologia Latina, edited by J.-P. Migne, 210:51–108. Paris, 1855.

Glossa Ordinaria. In Patrologia Latina 113–14, edited by J.-P. Migne. Paris, 1852.

Lombard, Peter. *Magna Glossatura*. In Patrologia Latina 191, edited by J.-P. Migne. Paris, 1854.

RECENTLY PUBLISHED OR REPUBLISHED TRANSLATIONS OF THE WORKS OF THOMAS AQUINAS CITED IN THIS COLLECTION

Commentary on Isaiah. Translated by Louis St. Hilaire. Introduction by Joseph Wawrykow. Steubenville, OH: Emmaus Academic, 2021.

Commentary on the Gospel of John. Translated by Fabian R. Larcher. Latin/English Edition of the Works of St. Thomas Aquinas 35–36. Lander, WY: Aquinas Institute, 2013. This translation is published also in an English-only edition, revised by James A. Weisheipl with an introduction and notes by Daniel Keating and Matthew Levering. Washington, DC: The Catholic University of America Press, 2010.

Commentary on Psalms; Rigans Montes; Hic Est Liber. Latin/English Edition of the Works of St. Thomas Aquinas 29. Lander, WY: Aquinas Institute, 2022.

Commentary on the Sentences. 8 vols. Translated by Beth Mortensen and Dylan Schrader. Latin/English Edition of the Works of St. Thomas Aquinas. Lander, WY: Aquinas Institute, 2017–. A complete translation is available at http://aquinas.cc.

Exposition of Aristotle's Treatise "On the Heavens." Translated by Pierre Conway and R.F. Larcher. Columbus, OH: College of St. Mary of the Springs, 1964.

Literal Commentary on Job. Translated by Brian Mullady. Latin/English Edition of the Works of St. Thomas Aquinas 38. Lander, WY: Aquinas Institute, 2012.

Summa theologiae. Translated by Laurence Shapcote. Latin/English Edition of the Works of St. Thomas Aquinas 13–20. Lander, WY: Aquinas Institute, 2012–17.

RECOMMENDED BIOGRAPHIES AND GENERAL INTRODUCTIONS

Barron, Robert. *Thomas Aquinas: Spiritual Master*. Park Ridge, IL: Word on Fire Academic, 2022.

Chenu, Marie-Dominique. *Toward Understanding Saint Thomas*. Translated by Albert M. Landry and Dominic Hughes. Chicago: Henry Regnery, 1964.

Chesterton, G.K. *St. Thomas Aquinas: "The Dumb Ox."* New York: Sheed & Ward, 1933.

Copleston, F.C. *Aquinas: An Introduction to the Life and Work of the Great Medieval Thinker*. Baltimore, MD: Penguin Books, 1955.

Dauphinais, Michael, and Matthew Levering. *Knowing the Love of Christ: An Introduction to the Theology of St. Thomas Aquinas*. Notre Dame, IN: University of Notre Dame Press, 2002.

Foster, Kenelm, ed. and trans. *The Life of St. Thomas Aquinas: Biographical Documents*. Baltimore, MD: Helicon, 1959.

Hütter, Reinhard. *Dust Bound for Heaven: Explorations in the Theology of Thomas Aquinas*. Grand Rapids, MI: Eerdmans, 2012.

Murray, Paul. *Aquinas at Prayer: The Bible, Mysticism and Poetry*. London: Bloomsbury, 2013.

Nieuwenhove, Rik Van, and Joseph Wawrykow, eds. *The Theology of Thomas Aquinas*. Notre Dame, IN: University of Notre Dame Press, 2005.

Sertillanges, A.G. *St. Thomas Aquinas and His Work*. Translated by Godfrey Anstruther. London: Burns, Oates, and Washbourne, 1933.

Torrell, Jean-Pierre. *Saint Thomas Aquinas*. Vol. 1, *The Person and His Work*. Rev. ed. Translated by Robert Royal. Washington, DC: The Catholic University of America Press, 1996.

———. *Saint Thomas Aquinas*. Vol. 2, *Spiritual Master*, translated by Robert Royal. Washington, DC: The Catholic University of America Press, 2003.

Weisheipl, James A. *Friar Thomas D'Aquino: His Life, Thought, and Works*. Garden City, NY: Doubleday, 1974.

BOOKS AND ESSAYS ON THOMAS AQUINAS'S USE OF SCRIPTURE

Baglow, Christopher. *"Modus et Forma": A New Approach to the Exegesis of Saint Thomas Aquinas with an Application to the "Lectura Super Epistolam Ad Ephesios."* Rome: Gregorian University Press, 2002.

Bonino, Serge-Thomas. *Reading the Song of Songs with St. Thomas Aquinas.* Translated by Andrew Levering. Washington, DC: The Catholic University of America Press, 2023.

Boyle, John F. *Aquinas on Scripture: A Primer.* Steubenville, OH: Emmaus Academic, 2023.

———. *The Order and Division of Divine Truth: St. Thomas Aquinas as Scholastic Master of the Sacred Page.* Steubenville, OH: Emmaus Academic, 2021.

———. "St. Thomas, Job, and the University Master." in *Reading Job with St. Thomas Aquinas*, ed. Matthew Levering, Piotr Roszak, and Jörgen Vijgen, 21–41.

Dahan, Gilbert. "The Commentary of Thomas Aquinas in the History of Medieval Exegesison Job: *Intentio et materia.*" *Nova et Vetera* 17, no. 4 (Fall 2019): 1053–75.

Elders, Leo J. "Aquinas on Holy Scripture as the Medium of Divine Revelation." In *La doctrine de la revelation divine de saint Thomas d'Aquin*, ed. Leo J. Elders, 132–52. Vatican City: Libreria Editrice Vaticana, 1990.

Ginther, James R. "The Scholastic Psalms' Commentary as a Textbook for Theology: The Case of Thomas Aquinas." In *Omnia disce: Medieval Studies in Memory of Leonard Boyle*, edited by A.J. Duggan, J. Greatrex, and B. Bolton, 211–29. Aldershot, UK: Ashgate, 2005.

Hankey, Wayne John. "Aquinas, Pseudo-Denys, Proclus and Isaiah VI.6." Archives d'histoire doctrinale et littéraire du Moyen Âge 65 (1997): 59–93.

Harkins, Franklin T. "Christ and the Eternal Extent of Divine Providence in the *Expositio super Iob ad Litteram* of Thomas Aquinas." In *A Companion to Job in the Middle Ages*, edited by Franklin T. Harkins and Aaron Canty, 161–200. Leiden, BE: Brill, 2015.

Healy, Mary. "Aquinas's Use of the Old Testament in His Commentary on Romans." In *Reading Romans with St. Thomas Aquinas*, edited by Matthew Levering and Michael Dauphinais, 183–95. Washington, DC: The Catholic University of America Press, 2012.

Levering, Matthew. "Mystagogy and Aquinas's *Commentary on Isaiah*: Initiating God's People into Christ." In *Initiation and Mystagogy in Thomas Aquinas: Scriptural, Systematic, Sacramental and Moral, and Pastoral Perspectives*, edited by Henk Schoot, Jacco Verburgt, and Jörgen Vijgen, 17–40. Leuven, BE: Peeters, 2019.

Levering, Matthew, Piotr Roszak, and Jörgen Vijgen, eds. *Reading Job with St. Thomas Aquinas.* Washington, DC: The Catholic University of America Press, 2020.

Mandonnet, Pierre. "Chronologie des écrits scripturaires de saint Thomas d'Aquin." *Revue Thomiste* 34, no. 55 (1929): 489–519.

Manzanedo, M.F. "La antropología filosófica en el comentario tomista al libro de Job." *Angelicum* 62 (1985): 419–71.

McNair, Bruce. "Thomas Aquinas, Albert the Great and Hugh of St. Cher on the Vision of God in Isaiah Chapter Six." *Downside Review* 124, no. 435 (2006): 79–88.

Meyer, Ruth. "A Passionate Dispute over Divine Providence: Albert the Great's Commentary on the Book of Job." In *A Companion to Job in the Middle Ages*, edited by Franklin T. Harkins and Aaron Canty, 201–24. Leiden, BE: Brill, 2015.

Narváez, Mauricio. "Intention, *probabiles rationes*, and Truth: The Exegetical Practice in Thomas Aquinas. The case of *Expositio super Iob ad literram*." In *Reading Sacred Scripture with Thomas Aquinas: Hermeneutical Tools, Theological Questions and New Perspectives*, edited by Piotr Roszak and Jörgen Vijgen. Turnhout, BE: Brepols, 2015.

Nutt, Roger, and Michael Dauphinais, eds. *Thomas Aquinas: Biblical Theologian*. Steubenville, OH: Emmaus Academic, 2021.

Pandolfi, Carmelo. *San Tommaso filosofo nel "Commento ai Salmi": Interpretazione dell'essere nel modo 'esistenziale' dell'invocazione*. Rome: Edizioni Studio Domenicano, 1993.

Paone, Jason C. Introduction to *Thomas Aquinas: Selected Commentaries on the New Testament*, edited by Jason C. Paone, xi–xxiv. Park Ridge, IL: Word on Fire Academic, 2022.

Prügl, Thomas. "Thomas Aquinas as Interpreter of Scripture." In *The Theology of Thomas Aquinas*, edited by Rik Van Nieuwenhove and Joseph Wawrykow, 386–415. Notre Dame, IN: University of Notre Dame Press, 2005.

Roszak, Piotr. "*Depravatio Scripturae.* Tomás de Aquino ante los errores hermenéuticos en la exegesis bíblica." *Scripta Teologica* 49 (2017): 3158.

———. "Exegesis and Contemplation: The Literal and Spiritual Sense of Scripture in Aquinas' Biblical Commentaries." *Espiritu* 65 (2016): 481–504.

———. *Reading the Church Fathers with St. Thomas Aquinas: Historical and Systematical Perspectives*. Turnhout, BE: Brepols, 2021.

———, ed. *El Comentario de Santo Tomás de Aquino al Salmo 50(51)*. Pamplona, ES: Universidad de Navarra, 2011.

Roszak, Piotr and Jörgen Vijgen, eds. *Reading Sacred Scripture with Thomas Aquinas: Hermeneutical Tools, Theological Questions and New Perspectives*. Turnhout, BE: Brepols, 2015.

———. *Towards a Biblical Thomism: Thomas Aquinas and the Renewal of Biblical Theology*. Pamplona, ES: Ediciones Universidad de Navarra, 2018.

Ryan, Thomas F. *Thomas Aquinas as Reader of the Psalms*. Notre Dame, IN: University of Notre Dame Press, 2000.

Sirilla, Michael G. "*Lectio Scripturae* at the Heart of Aquinas's Theology and Preaching." In *Thomas Aquinas: Biblical Theologian*, edited by Roger Nutt and Michael Dauphinais, 61–77.

Smith, Randall B. *Aquinas, Bonaventure, and the Scholastic Culture of Medieval Paris: Preaching, Prologues, and Biblical Commentary*. Cambridge: Cambridge University Press, 2021.

Spezzano, Daria. "'Its Lamps Are Lamps of Fire and Flames': Thomas Aquinas on the Song of Songs." In *Thomas Aquinas: Biblical Theologian*, edited by Roger Nutt and Michael Dauphinais, 107–32. Steubenville, OH: Emmaus Academic, 2021.

Valkenberg, Wilhelmus. *Words of the Living God: Place and Function of Holy Scripture in the Theology of St. Thomas Aquinas*. Leuven, BE: Peeters, 2000.

Wawrykow, Joseph. Introduction to *Thomas Aquinas: Commentary on Isaiah*, translated by Louis St. Hilaire, 1–18. Steubenville, OH: Emmaus Academic, 2021.

Weinandy, Thomas G., Daniel A. Keating, and John P. Yocum, eds. *Aquinas on Scripture: An Introduction to His Biblical Commentaries*. New York: T&T Clark, 2005.

Yaffe, Martin D. "Interpretive Essay." In *Thomas Aquinas: The Literal Exposition on Job*, translated by Anthony Damico, 1–65. Atlanta, GA: Scholars, 1989.

Yocum, John P. "Aquinas' Literal Exposition on Job." In *Aquinas on Scripture*, edited by Thomas G. Weinandy, Daniel A. Keating, and John P. Yocum.

OTHER STUDY RESOURCES

Deferrari, Roy J. *A Lexicon of Saint Thomas Aquinas*. Fitzwilliam, NH: Loreto, 2004.

Wawrykow, Joseph P. *The Westminster Handbook to Thomas Aquinas*. Lexington, KY: John Knox, 2005.

GENERAL INDEX

INDEX OF ANCIENT SOURCES

Job (*continued*)

Psalms

Psalms (*continued*)

Psalms (*continued*)

Psalms (*continued*)

Proverbs

Ecclesiastes

Song of Solomon

Song of Solomon (*continued*)

Wisdom

Sirach

Sirach (*continued*)

Isaiah